Risk Management at the Top

For other titles in the Wiley Finance series
please see www.wiley.com/finance

Risk Management at the Top

A Guide to Risk and its Governance
in Financial Institutions

Mark Laycock

Library of Congress Cataloging-in-Publication Data

Laycock, Mark
    Risk management at the top : a guide to risk and its governance in financial institutions /
Mark Laycock.
        pages cm
    Includes index.
    ISBN 978-1-118-49742-5 (cloth)
    1. Financial institutions—Management.   2. Banks and banking—Risk management.
3. Corporate governance.   4. Risk management.   I. Title.
    HG173.L376 2014
    332.1068′1—dc23   2013039722

A catalogue record for this book is available from the British Library.

ISBN 978-1-118-49742-5 (hardback) ISBN 978-1-118-49743-2 (ebk)
ISBN 978-1-118-49745-6 (ebk)

Cover image: Shutterstock.com

Set in 11/13pt Times by Aptara Inc., New Delhi, India
Printed in Great Britain by TJ International Ltd, Padstow, Cornwall, UK

This book is dedicated to all those individuals who generously gave their time, knowledge, experience and guidance. In particular, I would like to thank my good friend Prof Dean Paxson, of Manchester Business School, who has encouraged my inquisitiveness over many years.

Contents

About the Author

Mark Laycock has experience across the risk disciplines that attract regulatory capital. He is highly regarded within the Operational Risk discipline. He began working on Operational Risk in 1998 whilst at Deutsche Bank, which he joined in 1996. Until this change he was assessing potential future exposures of customised Over-the-Counter derivatives for Deutsche Bank's Credit Risk management team.

In 1999 banking regulators wanted an explicit capital requirement for operational risk. As a result, he worked with several industry groups developing practices and liaising with the regulators. It was during this time that Mark helped to establish the Operational Risk Data eXchange (ORX) in 2002.

His involvement in Market Risk spans a decade from the mid-1980s. During this time he developed Market Risk reports (pre-VAR) for Fixed Income portfolios. He was also a trader of Fixed Income and Equity strategies, such as equity index arbitrage. Some of the products, involved in these strategies, were traded on exchange and others off-exchange. This early stage of Over-the-Counter Equity products raised Operational Risk issues, especially Legal Risk due to poor documentation prevailing at the time.

The later part of the Market Risk decade was spent at the Bank of England, Banking Supervision Division. The task was to support the implementation of the first Capital Adequacy Directive by the regulators and the industry.

Since 2008 Mark has worked for ORX on topics such as the scope of Operational Risk, Scenarios and Operational Risk Appetite. He also has a consulting company Alder Partners.

Mark has an MBA, from Manchester Business School, where his dissertation was on Maturity and Interest Rate Mis-Matching of Banks.

1
Introduction

In the years since the 2007–2009 financial crisis, a number of expectations and requirements for financial institutions have changed and been published. Alongside technical issues, such as changes to capital requirements, stakeholders have outlined their expectations for revitalised oversight of risk issues by the Board.

This book is intended to support Non-Executive Directors (NEDs) in their oversight of risks to which the firm is exposed. While some NEDs will specialise in particular topics, such as risk, the Board has overall responsibility for risk oversight. This oversight of risk is part of the Board's responsibility for supervising the activities of the Executive and establishing boundaries within which they act. To promote an effective dialogue there needs to be shared terminology and concepts, which in turn lead to improved communication and appreciation between the NEDs, the Executive and the risk managers.

1.1 INTRODUCTION

The topic of risk oversight at the Board level and the materialisation of risk issues have a higher profile since the financial crisis. In response to expectations of NEDs and risk, some firms have established a Board-level Risk Committee, while others may nominate one or more NEDs to be the risk specialist representing the Board on the Enterprise or Group Risk Committee. Risk is an aspect of many, if not all, discussions at Board meetings. For example, risk is expected to feature in the discussions on compensation, business tactics and strategy.

Over the past 30 years the discussion of risk has become increasingly technical. This evolution has been stimulated by initiatives of regulators of the financial sector. Basel I, II and III, European Directives and Dodd–Frank are examples of these initiatives. Very often, these initiatives are transposed into national requirements, each with their own variations that correspond to national priorities or perspectives. For firms that operate in many countries, the complexity generated by national differences can substantially expand the details that affect the Executive and influence Board decisions.

In the post-financial crisis landscape some firms are winners. The winners were either lucky or had something that provided competitive advantage. Unfortunately, luck is not reproducible. A perceived aspect of the competitive advantage through the financial crisis is risk management. There are tales of firms reducing their exposure to particular activities or changing their long/short positions before others and weathering the crisis better than others. Whilst some firms got through the financial crisis, the winners were able to grasp opportunities.

This competitive advantage through risk management did not arise by accident; it developed over time and is an integral part of how these firms operate. Not all firms are the same, not all firms face the same risks to the same extent and so a single template is not appropriate. Nevertheless, there will be common themes such as the risk appetite, monitoring compliance with the risk appetite, risk and return, and the variety of risks with different emphases. Pro-active oversight of risk by the Board is now an expectation of many powerful stakeholders to prevent crises and reinforce the competitiveness of the firm. To meet this objective the Board needs to have a meaningful dialogue on risk with the Executive. With the technical evolution of risk, this is not a simple objective.

Some risk management queries are universal, but will only take the risk oversight and challenge dialogue so far:

(a) What can go wrong?
(b) How likely is it to go wrong?
(c) How badly wrong can it go?
(d) What is the relative upside versus downside?
(e) What can be done to manage the downside and change the ratio to the upside?

The Board, and their designated risk specialists, need sufficient knowledge to enable a productive dialogue with the Chief Risk Officer (CRO) or their risk specialists, such as the Chief Credit Risk Officer (CCRO), but without replicating the full extent of their knowledge. Risk is also expected to be an integral part of the Board's dialogue on strategy with heads of businesses and countries or regions. Without going into extensive detailed technicalities, this book supports that productive dialogue.

The rest of this chapter looks at:

1.2 Boards
1.3 Why Now?
1.4 Rest of the Book

1.2 BOARDS

Irrespective of the jurisdiction in which it operates, one of the Board's responsibilities is the oversight of risk.

In non-legal terms, the Board has a number of responsibilities:

- strategy formulation,
- policy making,
- oversight of Executives, and
- accountability to the owners of the company.

Risk is a subtext to all of these responsibilities.

The expectation is that the NEDs on the Board will be able to provide "constructive challenge to the decisions and effective oversight" of the Executive.[1] The European Banking Authority (EBA) expectation is that NEDs "should be able to demonstrate that they have, or will be able to acquire, the technical knowledge necessary to enable them to understand the business of the credit institution and the risks that it faces sufficiently well".

One approach to meeting this objective is to have a NED who has the role of being more expert than others on risk issues. Nevertheless, the Board has shared responsibility, even in the presence of specialists. The optimal attributes required of a risk specialist NED have been grouped into the following categories:[2]

- risk management acumen
- personal attributes
- business acumen
- education.

Each of these categories is supported by subcategories such as "an understanding of how incentive and compensation design influence risk taking". Alongside these headings is the necessary experience, for example having been a CRO and experienced a complete business cycle. These attributes, when considered as a set, are challenging. As not all firms are the same, so the importance of meeting certain attributes will vary by firm. Depending upon the exact role, the variety of experience may be more important than its duration, for example 20 years' practical knowledge of a narrow aspect of banking may be of limited value. The suitability of experience needs to be proportional to the firm's activities in terms of scope, scale and complexity.

---

[1] European Banking Authority (November 2012), paragraph 14.6.

[2] The Directors and Chief Risk Officers Group, "Attributes of a qualified risk director" – these are intended to be broadly applicable.

1.3   WHY NOW?

Following the 2007–2009 financial crisis there were many initiatives by:

- governments,
- trans-government bodies (such as the G20),
- financial regulators (national and international), and
- industry bodies.

These initiatives are intended to prevent reoccurrence of an equally grave crisis and fall into two broad categories – governance and technical. The initial rush of initiatives appears to be over and the focus is upon migrating from concept to rules and requirements. Firms are implementing various processes in response to these rules and requirements and are being "encouraged" by regulators, regulatory groups (such as the Basel Committee) and politicians with deadlines.

1.3.1   Governance Expectations

Stakeholder expectations on governance have been published, including:

- the Walker Report,[3]
- documents from the Financial Reporting Council[4] and the International Corporate Governance Network,[5] and
- the UK Report of the Parliamentary Commission on Banking Standards.

In some instances the expectations and requirements apply to the entire corporate sector, in others they relate specifically to banks and other financial institutions.

The EBA has produced a set of guidelines to focus on the experience of individuals on the Board and key Executive functions.[6] These guidelines apply to unitary as well as two-tier Boards. These functions can also be known as significant influencing functions (SIFs). Several national regulators had SIF regimes established before the publication of the EBA guidelines. These regulators were able to raise their expectations

---

[3] HM Treasury (November 2009).

[4] http://www.frc.org.uk/Our-Work/Codes-Standards/Corporate-governance/UK-Corporate-Governance-Code.aspx

[5] https://www.icgn.org/

[6] European Banking Authority (November 2012).

and implement the new standards almost immediately. In some cases, this has been accompanied by greater assertiveness by the regulators about SIFs meeting these expectations. These guidelines were adopted by EU banking regulators in May 2013.

For regulators that already had a SIF regime, the interviews may, originally, only have been conducted pre-appointment. A satisfactory outcome influenced whether the appointment could proceed. With the changed environment, it is expected that these interviews with regulators will occur on a regular basis when the individual has been in position for a period of time.

Some regimes are expected to go beyond the SIF interview prior to appointment and these "in-position" inverviews.[7] The UK regime has a proposal that SIFs, "in a case of failure, should demonstrate that they took all reasonable steps to prevent or mitigate the effects of a specified failing".[8] This obligation is reinforced by the suggestion that a criminal offence should be created for SIFs "carrying out their professional responsibilities in a reckless manner". It is not clear if other jurisdictions will adopt similar expectations and sanctions.

1.3.2 Technical Changes

In addition to changes in expectations on governance, the post-financial crisis technical changes are adding complications and complexity for the firms. Some of these technical changes are expected to amend the business models as they have implications for return on capital. Other changes will affect the organisational structure of firms. These changes have consequences for Board-level oversight of risk and effective challenge of the Executive.

Amongst the complicating factors is the characterisation of some financial firms as systemically important financial institutions (SIFIs) by the Financial Stability Board (FSB).[9] The designation of SIFI means that the firm is important to the smooth operation of domestic and global financial systems.[10] The implication of being a SIFI means that the firm

---

[7] UK Report of the Parliamentary Commission on Banking Standards, p. 10.

[8] The Parliamentary Commission on Banking Standards refers to "Senior Persons".

[9] Financial Stability Board (2011, 2012).

[10] The FSB plans to review the list of SIFIs on an annual basis, possibly moving firms between categories of SIFIs, adding or deleting firms from the list. The FSB is also considering whether some insurance companies, and other parts of the financial sector, should be given a SIFI designation.

needs a sophisticated approach to risk management and its oversight, as well as holding additional capital.

In some regimes the technical changes are likely to result in different business models for banks. The changes that fall into this category include:

- the Volker proposals, in the Dodd–Frank Act in the USA,
- the Vickers Report in the UK,
- "Living Wills" – resolution and recovery plans, and
- liquidity risk requirements.

These initiatives will affect proprietary trading, the separation of retail from wholesale banking, the distribution of capital within a group, guarantees provided to subsidiaries and sources of funding, as well as internal transfer pricing for funding. While the scope of some initiatives will be national, their consequences may be international. For example, a reduction in proprietary trading may affect the liquidity of individual securities with consequences for their use as collateral to mitigate credit risk.

These technical changes add complexity to the Board's oversight of existing risks. In addition, responding to these regulatory initiatives is expected to alter the risk profile of the firm. While some risks may diminish – the underlying purpose of these technical changes – other risks can be expected to raise their profile, and potentially new risks may be added.

1.4 REST OF THE BOOK

The rest of the book is in three parts (see Figure 1.1): Risk Oversight, Specific Risks and Regulatory Environment.

Part I describes the main elements of the risk management and oversight apparatus. A challenge is to arrive at a conceptual description of the various elements and practical implications.

Most of the chapters in this part contain sections on terminology. This terminology, when combined with the description of the risk oversight apparatus, will support a dialogue, including challenge, as opposed to engaging in a monologue with the potential to be confused and frustrated. The organisational and human aspects, for example risk culture and biases, which can affect decision making are also covered in this section.

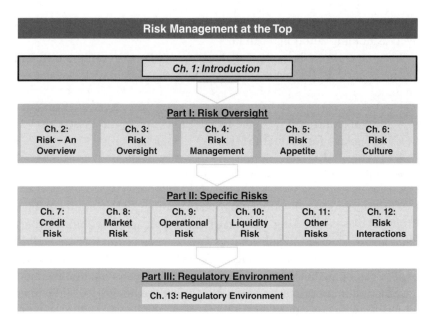

Figure 1.1 Book overview

Risk management, appetite and culture are all part of the risk consciousness of the organisation. For a portion of these topics the Board needs to perform a comparison between where the firm is and where the Board wants it to be, communicating any changes to the Executive for implementation.

Part II covers risk types that are common to financial firms. Other risk types, such as underwriting risk or investment risk, may be specific to subsections of finance such as insurance. Some second-order effects are described, where one risk source can influence the severity of another risk source. This interaction presents a challenge for risk oversight and management.

Part III looks at the regulatory environment. The regulatory framework is influential on the firm's risk management through the creation of technical requirements and governance expectations, for example "principles for enhancing corporate governance". The technical requirements have consequences for the amount and composition of capital of the firm. In turn, this has consequences for various stakeholders, for example the impact on dividends.

FURTHER READING

Basel Committee on Banking Supervision (October 2010) Principles for Enhancing Corporate Governance. http://www.bis.org/publ/bcbs176.pdf

European Banking Authority (November 2012) Guidelines on the Assessment of the Suitability of Members of the Management Body and Key Function Holders.   http://eba.europa.eu/cebs/media/Publications/Standards%20and %20Guidelines/2012/EBA-GL-2012-06–Guidelines-on-the-assessment-of-the-suitability-of-persons-.pdf

Financial Stability Board (4 November 2011) Policy Measures to Address Systemically Important Financial Institutions. http://www.financialstability board.org/publications/r_111104bb.pdf

Financial Stability Board (1 November 2012) Update of Global Systemically Important Banks. http://www.financialstabilityboard.org/publications/ r_121031ac.pdf

HM Treasury (November 2009) A Review of Corporate Governance in UK Banks and Other Financial Industry Entities – Final Recommendations [the Walker Report]. http://www.hm-treasury.gov.uk/d/walker_review_ 261109.pdf

The Directors and Chief Risk Officers Group (5 June 2013) Qualified Risk Director Guidelines.   http://www.thegoverenancefund.com/DCRO/PDF/ Qualified_Risk_Director_Guidelines.pdf

UK Report of the Parliamentary Commission on Banking Standards (June 2013) Changing Banking for Good. http://www.parliament.uk/documents/ banking-commission/Banking-final-report-volume-i.pdf

Part I
Risk Oversight

Risk Management at the Top

Ch. 1: Introduction

Part I: Risk Oversight

Ch. 2: Risk – An Overview	Ch. 3: Risk Oversight	Ch. 4: Risk Management	Ch. 5: Risk Appetite	Ch. 6: Risk Culture

Part II: Specific Risks

Ch. 7: Credit Risk	Ch. 8: Market Risk	Ch. 9: Operational Risk	Ch. 10: Liquidity Risk	Ch. 11: Other Risks	Ch. 12: Risk Interactions

Part III: Regulatory Environment

Ch. 13: Regulatory Environment

Part I – Risk Oversight describes the main elements of the risk management and oversight apparatus. One challenge is to arrive at a conceptual description of the various elements. An equal, or possibly larger, challenge is the transition from concept to reality.

Most of the chapters in this part contain sections on terminology. This terminology, when combined with the description of the risk oversight apparatus, will support a dialogue, including challenge, as opposed to engaging in a monologue.

Chapter 2 begins with the terminology of risk and uncertainty and their relationship. Also mentioned is the precautionary principle which often underlies comments by third parties on events, not just in the financial sector. The relationship between banks, or other financial intermediaries, and the risks that they choose to take has evolved. This evolution has influenced the wider discussion about capital, its various forms – book, economic and regulatory – and their related purposes.

Chapter 3 starts with the different perspectives of risk oversight – the top, bottom and middle. Each has its challenges. The bottom needs the detail for day-to-day risk management activities. The top needs aggregated data, which reduces the amount of variety. This reduction in variety is achieved by the application of models of various types. (Models are described in more detail in Part II.) The "three lines of defence" – a phrase related to risk management – is described in addition to other key roles. Biases are mentioned as they influence people when discussing topics and making decisions about risk.

As with other chapters, Chapter 4 on risk management begins with terminology. The terminology includes cause, effect, exposure, events, effects and consequences. Data about these topics form the foundation of risk management and monitoring. Risk management has a series of process steps that identify, analyse, evaluate, manage and monitor risks. While the description of these steps tends to focus on where the risks manifest themselves, a similar sequence is applied as the risks are escalated upwards, ultimately to Board level. A key element is when to escalate, and that is connected to risk appetite.

Risk appetite is the subject of Chapter 5. All firms and individuals have a risk appetite, but most of the time it is informal. Risk appetite is connected to limits and thresholds. Risk appetite needs to be expressed throughout the organisation using terminology that is appropriate for that level. To be effective these various risk appetite statements, cascading down from the Board, need to be consistent. The risk appetite statements should also have connections with stakeholders. A source of complexity, for the Board, is that some stakeholders may have conflicting risk appetite preferences.

The last chapter in Part I (Chapter 6) focuses on risk culture. All firms have a risk culture. The current challenges include finding a concept to describe risk culture, appreciate the influences and feedback loops, and then amend the prevailing risk culture. Culture is not just an issue in the financial sector, but has also been reported in the media in connection with politicians, health services, police, journalists and others. The risk culture influences behaviour and decisions related to risk. As not every aspect of risk management can be written in a policy or procedure, risk culture is a complement to formal activities such as risk appetite.

2

Risk – An Overview

Risk Management at the Top					

Ch. 1: Introduction					

Part I: Risk Oversight

Ch. 2: Risk – An Overview	Ch. 3: Risk Oversight	Ch. 4: Risk Management	Ch. 5: Risk Appetite	Ch. 6: Risk Culture

Part II: Specific Risks

Ch. 7: Credit Risk	Ch. 8: Market Risk	Ch. 9: Operational Risk	Ch. 10: Liquidity Risk	Ch. 11: Other Risks	Ch. 12: Risk Interactions

Part III: Regulatory Environment

Ch. 13: Regulatory Environment

Risk is half of the subject of this book, the other half being its measurement. Therefore, a chapter devoted to the concept of risk will assist the reader.

Although risk is a four-letter word, its meaning can change depending on the context and related interpretation. Very often these differences are subtle, but can have significant implications for the dialogue. Many of the parties involved in the conversation are not aware of these subtle differences, so the dialogue is not as effective as it might be. When discussing risk it becomes necessary to consider the role of banks in relation to risk, the various sources of risk and the impact on the organisation.

The rest of this chapter looks at the:

2.1 Terminology
2.2 Role of Banks and Risk
2.3 Sources of Risk and Uncertainty
2.4 Capital
2.5 Issues to Consider

Part II goes into more detail on major risk types and some of the issues around their measurement and management.

2.1   TERMINOLOGY

The Board is responsible for risk oversight. For banks, this requires a statement of risk appetite and is a significant influence on strategy; for example, the composition of the bank's assets and liabilities, on- and off-balance sheet items, the range of products and services and where to offer them.

2.1.1   Definition of Risk

The *Oxford English Dictionary* defines risk as:

- A situation involving exposure to danger;
- The possibility that something unpleasant or unwelcome will happen;
- A person or thing regarded as a threat or likely source of danger; and
- The possibility of financial loss.

Related terms include:

- hazard, peril, threat, jeopardy and "challenge";
- probability, likelihood or frequency of event; and
- severity of event or loss, or consequences.

The International Standardisation Organisation (ISO)[1] defines risk as the:

- Effect of uncertainty on objectives.

In the ISO definition, the "effect" includes a positive or negative deviation from the expected. The "objectives" could be financial, environmental or something else, and could be applied at the strategic, tactical or operational level. "Uncertainty" refers to the deficiency of information or knowledge of an event in terms of the likelihood of its materialisation or its consequences.

On occasions, risk is referred to as the cause of volatility in the profit and loss (P&L).

All of these statements about risk are accurate, but the subtleties of interpretation and the management of risk depend on the context. For example, risk as the source of volatility in the P&L is a general concept, but does not take the dialogue much further forward.

2.1.2   Risk

The essential components around risk appear to be:

1. The materialisation of the event is not guaranteed.
2. The event will have some sort of effect on the value of the firm.
3. The consequences of the event could be positive or negative.

Some interpretations may go further, such as distinguishing between risk and uncertainty. For example, a risk will have a range of possible outcomes, what is unknown is the likelihood of materialisation and which outcome. Uncertainty has a role in that not all of the possible outcomes may be known ex ante. This links into the concept of uncertainty associated with the ISO definition of risk.

Figure 2.1 shows the difference between risk and uncertainty. In Figure 2.1(a) and (b) the possible outcomes are known, but not which one so

---

[1] ISO Guide 73 (2009) Risk Management – Vocabulary.

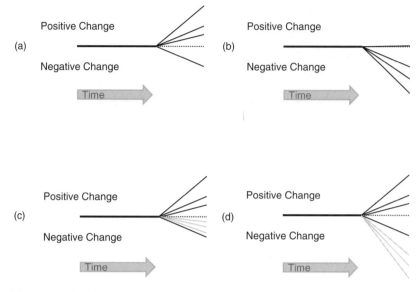

Figure 2.1   Risk and uncertainty

there is risk but no uncertainty. In Figure 2.1(c) the grey lines represent uncertainty, but in this case the uncertainty is bounded by the possible range of risk outcomes. In Figure 2.1(d) the uncertainty is outside the range of possible risk outcomes and on the negative side. By definition, whether the uncertainty is in the form of Figure 2.1(c) or (d) is not known at the time of the discussion, just that there is some uncertainty about the range of outcomes.

2.1.3   Uncertainty

> There are known knowns; there are things we know that we know. There are known unknowns; that is to say there are things that, we now know we don't know. But there are also unknown unknowns – there are things we do not know we don't know.[2]

This quotation summarises the situation with regard to uncertainty – the unknowns. A known unknown is the degree to which the mathematical or mental model describing the situation is accurate. For example, how robust are some of the choices around statistical distributions used in measuring risks such as credit risk or market risk?

---

[2] D. Rumsfeld (21 February 2002).

Table 2.1   Terminology for uncertainty

Terminology		Degree of confidence	
Virtually certain	=>	>99% probability	
Very likely	=>	>90%	
Likely	=>	>66%	Increasing Uncertainty
About as likely as not	=>	33%–66%	
Unlikely	=>	<33%	
Very unlikely	=>	<10%	
Exceptionally unlikely	=>	<1%	

Source: Spiegelhalter, D.J. and Riesch, H. (2011) Don't know, can't know: embracing deeper uncertainties when analysing risks. *Philosophical Transactions of the Royal Society* **369**, 4730–4750, Table 5. Reproduced by permission of the Royal Society.

Similar issues have arisen in discussions over climate change. This has led to the development of categories and terminology around uncertainty (see Table 2.1).

These terms relate to expert opinion. As a result, using terms such as "virtually certain" may add more meaning to the discussion than something more technical such as "in excess of 99% confidence".

On occasions, having high degrees of precision for risk estimate values can be misleading when the confidence is only "likely". Under these conditions the most meaningful description might be orders of magnitude or ranking as opposed to an estimate with many significant figures. For example, the risk is about $10 million may be more useful to the discussion than $9,876,540, which may convey a spurious degree of precision.

The sources of uncertainty around risk decisions can be subdivided:

1. Inputs to the statistical/mathematical/mental model
2. Construction and complexity of the statistical/mathematical/mental model
3. Internal environment
4. External environment.

The first two items can be very technical and should be left to technicians. Ideally they will be "virtually certain" or at least "likely" about the results in relation to reality. Where there are perceived deficiencies then they will use supplementary techniques, such as stress tests and scenarios.

The last two items contain more uncertainty. The internal environment includes many types of resources, as well as governance and risk culture.

The external environment includes the economy, competitors – direct and indirect – as well as various stakeholders, including regulators.

Frameworks for exploring some of these issues and conceivable impacts include real options and game theory. While these techniques may, in some cases, resolve to numerical answers, their frameworks and approaches can be valuable when dealing with uncertainty. For example, a major branch of real options relates to the application of resources to expand, contract or defer and the timing of the actions. Some firms have begun using real options in preference to net present value (NPV) for certain decisions.[3] Real options could be applied to decisions around investing in risk management information systems associated with a new product. For example, the decision to scale up to automated data capture can be linked to the volume of business in the product. Other decisions may relate to the adaptability of the planned system in relation to regulatory requirements that are expected to emerge or evolve over the next couple of years.

While the most popular game is probably the Prisoner's Dilemma, senior management and Boards face many parties or actors as represented by stakeholders (see Chapter 5, Section 5.3) and competitors. The importance of various stakeholders may vary between scenarios. For example, increasing return by taking more risk will be of interest to shareholders and regulators due to the impact on return on equity and the consequences if it goes wrong.

These frameworks can assist in identifying specific sources of uncertainty (known unknowns) and potentially converting ignorance (unknown unknowns) into uncertainty. Having identified sources of uncertainty, the decision can be made to apply resources and when they should be applied to reduce uncertainty, for example moving from an "unlikely" to a "likely" degree of confidence on potential outcomes.

Alternatively, the uncertainty can be accepted. Accepting the uncertainty at one point in time does not mean that it is accepted forever. The unknown unknowns may migrate to becoming known unknowns or even known knowns. This migration may have implications for risk appetite as more information becomes available.

An example is the robustness of netting in the event of liquidation of a credit risk counterparty. Netting has an impact on determining the extent of credit exposure and subsequently credit risk. Ultimately, the decision to permit or over-rule a netting agreement will be made

---

[3] Chevalier-Roignant, B. and Trigeogis, L. (2011) *Competitive Strategy: Options and Games.* MIT Press, Boston, MA.

by a judge. However, it is not feasible to get judges to opine upon these legal agreements prior to the liquidation of a firm. To reduce the degree of uncertainty around netting agreements, the industry took legal opinions in the relevant jurisdictions. Taking one legal opinion would have reduced the level of uncertainty, for instance to "likely", but taking several legal opinions enabled the uncertainty to be reduced to "very likely" or even "virtually certain". In liquidations, netting agreements have proved to be robust and continue to evolve in reaction to additional information.

2.1.4 Precautionary Principle

The "precautionary principle" can often be found as part of the background to discussions on risk. Although devised for environmental risks, it is often implicit in dialogue on risks and financial institutions.

The precautionary principle[4] is:

> When an activity raises threats of harm to human health or the environment, precautionary measures should be taken even if some cause and effect relationships are not fully established scientifically.

When adapted for financial firms, the principle is in reference to the wellbeing or wealth of one or more stakeholders.

The essential features of the principle are that cause and effect do not have to be proved scientifically, but only a suspicion of harm is needed for action to be required. The responsibility for mitigating the risk belongs to the instigator of the risk. This perspective is implicit in a number of the post-mortems on the financial crisis and regulatory response.

Over recent decades the precautionary principle has been combined with understanding by the counterparty of the possible range of outcomes (risk). This has led the judiciary to categorise counterparties into knowledgeable or unknowledgeable. The assumption is that the knowledgeable counterparties can be considered to be experts or have the capacity to be aware of the possible outcomes. For unknowledgeable counterparties the firm is assumed or even required to apply a higher standard of care. The presence of knowledge, or not, is not limited to the purely economic or logical outcomes, but increasingly needs to take into account behavioural aspects of decision making. So what may be behaviourally desirable may not always be economically desirable.

---

[4] The Wingspread Statement on the Precautionary Principle (January 1998) http://www.sehn.org/state.html#w (accessed April 2012).

The precautionary principle, together with the concept of unknow-ledgeable counterparties, has stimulated a number of consumer pro-tection initiatives in the UK, the USA and elsewhere, for example the Financial Conduct Authority in the UK.

These interpretations, on what is meant by "risk", provide the context for the Board exercising risk oversight and its related dialogue with the Executive. This dialogue may take place as part of Board-level discus-sions on strategy and various developments, in addition to statements of risk appetite and defining the risk culture of the firm.

2.2   ROLE OF BANKS AND RISK

Banks, and the financial sector more generally, perform a crucial role in the management of financial risks for the broader society. This role can involve the acceptance of risk and in some cases its intermediation. For helping others manage their risks, for example the provision of trade finance, banks get paid. As a generalisation, without a risk there is seldom an excess return.

The risks taken by financial institutions are shown in Figure 2.2. These risks drive the volatility in the profit and loss statement. The risk types shown on the left of the figure have individual chapters in Part II. The risks shown on the right of the figure are outlined in Chapter 11.

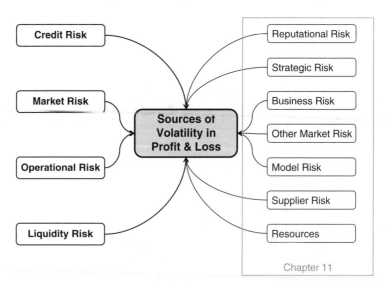

Figure 2.2   Risk types influencing the volatility of profit and loss

Most of these risks are taken voluntarily, as part of the financial institution's business activity. Additionally, the scope of operational risk includes actions performed against the bank, such as natural disasters, external fraud and other external threats.

The items on the left of the figure have regulatory determined metrics for reporting to the regulators. In the case of credit, market and operational risks, the most aggregated metric is capital. These are elements of the regulatory Pillar 1 requirements. For liquidity risk there are two metrics, one focuses on the high-quality reserve assets and the other the longer-term profile of funding.

The risks on the right of the figure fall within the scope of Pillar 2 regulatory requirements. They are also hard to quantify with the same degree of precision and accuracy as credit or market risks. Nevertheless, the regulators require sufficient capital to cover these risks.

2.2.1   In the Beginning

Banks started to become involved with risk when they accepted deposits and made loans. Skills in managing risk have since been extended to other activities.

For many people, accepting deposits and making loans is the archetypal activity of banking. These activities are not risk-free. The bank is acting as a transmission mechanism for the supply of funds between the individual depositor and the borrower – intermediation. In addition, the bank is interposing itself between the depositor and the risk that the borrower will not repay.

For the bank, these initial activities brought two main risks: liquidity risk and credit risk. The bank's liquidity risk arises from the terms of the deposit, often enabling the depositor to repossess their funds at short notice, while lending longer term to the borrower. An extreme example of this maturity transformation is the on-demand or current deposit account and the 30-year mortgage.

If the depositors withdraw their funds then the bank has to replace them in order to keep funding the loan, such as a 30-year mortgage. This is a very simple version of liquidity risk that will be explored in more detail in Chapter 10.

The bank takes the credit risk of the borrower.[5] If the borrower fails to make payments according to the contractual terms then the bank

---

[5] For the depositor there is the credit risk of the bank where it has deposited its funds.

has a shortfall. The shortfall may be temporary, in the case of delayed payment, or permanent if the borrower goes into liquidation. Both the temporary and permanent conditions can be described as the borrower being in default. One role of capital is to enable the bank to continue to operate when there are defaults.

A way in which the bank manages the credit risk is through having a portfolio of counterparties. This will be covered in more detail in Chapter 7.

A risk that the firm faces, by virtue of its existence, is operational risk. In the case of legal risk, a subset of operational risk, this arises from being an intermediary of credit and liquidity. Some external threats, such as robbery, arise because the money is in the banks! As discussed in Chapter 9, operational risk generally reflects the type of business that is undertaken and there are few examples of undertaking more operational risk in order to obtain a higher return, unlike credit or market risks.

2.2.2   Where are We Now?

The experience of managing the liquidity and credit risks associated with the intermediation of deposits and loans has been extended to a wide variety of risk types. Some of these risk types are subsets of market risk, including:

- foreign exchange
- interest rates
- commodities.

In addition to risk intermediation, banks may be exposed to these risks from their own corporate activities. For example, by having items on the balance sheet in different currencies the bank has foreign exchange risk in the form of translation and/or transaction exposure. The difference between translation and transaction exposures is linked to the length of time that the exposure is on the balance sheet.

Further, the bank may be exposed to inflation risk, where inflation is measured as a basket of commodities. The risk of inflation can materialise in the provision of inflation-linked pensions.

This section has shown that banks face a diverse array of risks, some that arise from being corporate organisations and some through their role as risk intermediaries. This variety can be dazzling and make risk management challenging. The next section proposes some simple approaches that align with risk management choices.

2.3 SOURCES OF RISK AND UNCERTAINTY

How banks manage certain risks may be influenced by their source. Particular risk management strategies and tactics may be preferable depending on whether the risk arises internally or externally (see Figure 2.3). The suitability of various risk management tactics can also be influenced by the stakeholders.

2.3.1 External Sources of Risk and Uncertainty

In this context the sources of risk come from outside the bank. Some of these risk sources increased their profile during and since the financial crisis.

One external source of risk is the economic environment. Changes in the economic environment can influence the volume of activity – business or strategic risk – as well as the likelihood of default by borrowers. At the extreme, the economic environment can also affect the provision of services by vendors, especially if the vendor goes bankrupt. As discussed in Chapter 7, some risk management actions can have unintended

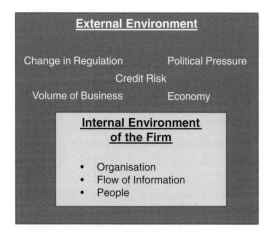

Figure 2.3   Sources of risk and uncertainty

consequences, for example when regulatory frameworks are pro-cyclical and amplify the effects of changes in the economic environment.

Some external risks may be amplified by the economic environment. Examples in this category include criminal activity such as fraud, which may increase with an economic downturn. Other external risks, such as natural disasters, are independent of the state of the economy.

An additional external source of uncertainty is action by governments and their various agents, such as regulators. These actions can be initiated due to the concept that many financial services, including banking, are a "common good" that is necessary for the smooth functioning of society.

A reaction to the financial crisis has been the development and publication of additional regulatory requirements for banks. Some of these additional requirements have been published at the international level, such as by the Basel Committee for Banking Supervision, and some at the national level, for example in the UK. Other regulatory requirements may be published at the national level but have international implications, for example the Dodd–Frank Act with its implications for the liquidity of securities.

The uncertainty due to these initiatives comes in waves. There is the initial wave of the scope and intent of the initiative. The second wave is the detailed implementation requirements and standards, how that is going to be achieved and the timeline. The third wave is achieving and monitoring the ongoing compliance with the requirements and standards.

The uncertainty from these regulatory requirements can be considered to be one consequence of being in the financial sector. Other corporate sectors are not immune from government initiatives, for example environmental or employment requirements. An aspect that is different, for the financial sector, has been the volume of these requirements since the onset of the financial crisis in 2007. Some groups are counting these regulatory changes in the hundreds and thousands.

The discussion about the first wave can involve significant differences in opinion about the detailed scope of banking as a common good. Although banks can influence the second wave of requirements and standards to be implemented, this is limited. The third wave is under the control of banks and their application of resources. How banks comply with these requirements will be reviewed by regulators from prudential or conduct perspectives.

2.3.2   Internal Sources of Risk and Uncertainty

Internal sources of risk are ones over which the Board has more choice regarding the type and amount. These risks tend to be organisational and people-related, in particular staff.

Organisational sources of risk include the flow of information around the firm, the organisational culture, risk culture and the oversight mechanisms. Some of this will be addressed in more detail in Chapter 3.

The people component of risk is not unique to banking. At its simplest, human error is always with us. However, there are steps that can be taken to minimise human error by deploying preventative or detective controls, in addition to mitigating the consequences. For example, we are all grateful for the low level of human error amongst pilots, even if our luggage gets mislaid occasionally.

The people component also includes risks such as the volume and quality of resources and their distribution around the key roles in the firm. Mitigating or offsetting these factors, and their influence on adverse events, is made all the more complicated during an economic downturn and reduction in business activity. Other types of people risk are facets of operational risk, for example internal theft or fraud, rogue trading or some IT security issues.

Although many of these people risks are not unique to banking, they may get a higher level of scrutiny because they happen at firms in the finance sector. The focus on these risks can arise due to the size of the financial impact or other consequences for the stakeholder when it does go wrong.

2.3.3   Systemic Risk

Systemic risk relates to a cascade effect through a system; in the current context this refers to the financial system as part of the external environment. Broadly, a systemic risk event can lead to a dislocation or significant disruption to the financial system, nationally or internationally, with the possibility of adverse effects for the users of the system, for example rendering a key component unable to perform. It is these effects, in the form of recent experience and possible future effects, that have resulted in a significant increase in regulation of the financial sector. A way of thinking about systemic risk is along the same lines as the transmission of a disease, such as flu, through a population.

A common feature of systemic risk is that there is a trigger event. The trigger may relate to an individual firm or a market event affecting several firms. The systemic portion is that there is a cascade and other firms become affected. What may begin as a particular risk event for an individual firm, or the financial system infrastructure (such as a clearing house), can infect other activities at the same firm or other firms, for example credit risk concerns leading to an inability of the industry to fund its assets.

The cascade is influenced by the risk management behaviour of individual firms in the financial system. The more connections that a firm has within the financial system, the more likely it will be classified as a SIFI. For some types of firm the number of connections is related to their size, role in the financial system and/or geographic scope. Size may be in the form of balance sheet size, or market share of a particular segment of the financial system, for example clearing or custody.

The geographic scope of connections raises the level of complexity for regulators trying to mitigate an issue or close down a group. In the ultimate situation, significant national differences in bankruptcy codes contribute to this complexity. One consequence has been that large interconnected firms have to create recovery and resolution plans, also known as "Living Wills". The aim is to explore choices if a subsidiary is affected or if the parent is affected while some subsidiaries are not. The result is intended to be an orderly management of the situation, rather than raising complex questions in the middle of a crisis.

For example, some firms got into difficulties due to their inability to source funds from the wholesale money markets. Within the firm this may have been amplified by their asset/liability profiles, such as funding long-term assets with short-term liabilities and deposits. To contain their own credit risk, counterparties implemented a rapid reduction in their credit lines to the affected firm. This withdrawal of credit facilities, even short-term facilities, exacerbated the situation for the affected firm, but limited contagion and prevented an issue becoming systemic.

2.4   CAPITAL

In the financial sector, discussions of risk are often linked to capital directly or indirectly. As with risk, unless there is a common understanding as to the type of capital, it is possible to have an unproductive dialogue. Amongst the different sorts of capital are book, economic and regulatory. These capital types will be the focus of attention for different stakeholders and have implications for strategic and tactical decisions.

Capital, for financial firms, makes up a small portion of the liability and equity side of the balance sheet. The question of how much capital is needed often starts with the confidence interval and the underlying distribution of possible outcomes.

2.4.1   Confidence Interval

In the context of risk measurement the confidence interval is a quantum of risk. Most of the focus is on the downside, what can go wrong and how wrong it can go. The ratio of the potential upside to the downside may be an input to the decision.

The confidence interval is usually expressed as a percentage, for example 99%. The point being made is that there is a 1% chance that the downside or loss will be equal to or greater than the value at the 99% confidence interval. The 99% confidence interval may represent a possible loss of £5,000,000. As a result, there is a 1% chance that the loss will be larger than £5,000,000, but it does not indicate how high that loss could be.

The choice of confidence interval might be explicit, for example equivalent to an "AAA" credit rating for a risk appetite statement or it might be implicit, for example in regulatory capital ratios. Numerically the confidence interval could be 90%, 95%, 99% or higher.

Some risks, such as market, credit and operational risks, can be modelled and quantified using statistical distributions. The confidence intervals are applied to the statistical distributions and a value is read off the chart. Figure 2.4 shows the normal and lognormal distributions. The figure shows the probability of a loss of a particular size. Some of the actual distributions used in these models are more complex than illustrated here.

This normal distribution is symmetrical around zero, so Figure 2.4 shows the distribution for the downside. The lognormal distribution is not symmetrical as the smallest value that it can take is zero. From a capital perspective the focus is on possible losses. Figure 2.5 is an extract from Figure 2.1, which if turned 90° has some similarity to the lognormal distribution in Figure 2.4.

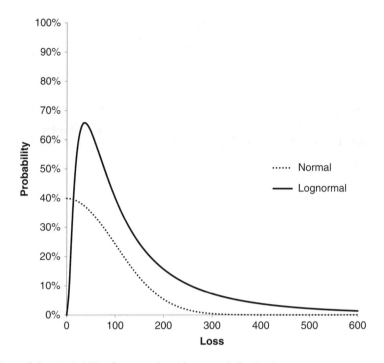

Figure 2.4   Probability for normal and lognormal distributions

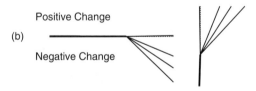

Figure 2.5   Downside range of outcomes

Figure 2.4 shows the probability of any particular downside value being achieved. For the downside risk perspective the data tends to be re-arranged into a cumulative probability view against which the confidence intervals can be imposed. The cumulative probability view is shown in Figure 2.6.

The cumulative probability view shows the probability up to a certain loss, or the loss for a given cumulative probability.

The lognormal distribution is said to be "fat tailed" in comparison to the normal distribution. The loss value at which the 95% confidence interval intersects the distributions is 164 for the normal distribution

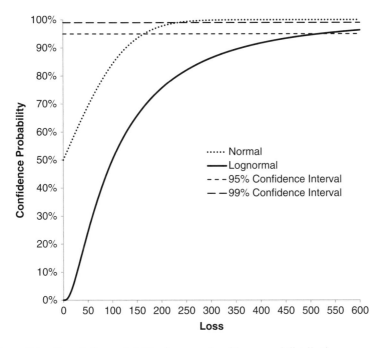

Figure 2.6 Cumulative probability for normal and lognormal distributions

and 518 for the lognormal. Although the confidence intervals are the same, at 95%, the loss implied by the lognormal distribution is about three times larger. For the 99% confidence interval the values are 233 and 1024, respectively, with the lognormal now being about 4.5 times larger. From a risk perspective the lognormal is showing a riskier set of outcomes. While the use of statistical distributions can address some of the uncertainties outlined in Figure 2.1, there are risks/uncertainties in the choice of statistical distribution for the risk type and time horizon; this is an element of model risk.

The distributions will be estimated using data for a particular time horizon. For market risk data the time horizon may be daily, but for credit and operational risk it may be annual. As a result, the possible loss number acquires additional descriptions "there is a 99% probability of losing less than 233 in the next day from market risk".

Around these estimates it may be possible to provide uncertainty bands, as outlined in Table 2.1. As a result, the information may be provided as "very likely" to be 225–240 for the 99% confidence interval.

Although the cumulative distribution chart and confidence interval combine to provide an estimate of the size of loss, they do not specify when it could occur. For example, if the underlying is market risk, with daily valuations, then the loss equivalent to the 95% confidence interval (233) could occur tomorrow.

Statistical distributions and confidence intervals are used in internal reporting, for example economic capital. These concepts are also implied objectives for some regulatory capital calculations and explicit in others.

2.4.2 Book Capital

Book capital refers to the capital on the firm's balance sheet as determined by the related accounting standard. Book capital includes the amounts raised from the issuance of equity. This may be subdivided into the notional value of the equity, for example $2.00 per share, and equity premium – the amount that each share was actually sold for, such as $5.00 per share. Also part of this account is retained earnings. The notional value of the equity, plus equity premium plus retained earnings, may have a value of $12.00 per share. This may compare with the 12-month trading range of $11.90–$14.00 per share.

Minority investments in companies may also be included in this section of the balance sheet. These will be investments which fail to meet the requirements for consolidation. These might include investments where the firm owns less than a specific percentage, such as 50%.

2.4.3 Economic Capital

Economic capital is not capital in the sense of book capital. Economic capital does not appear on the balance sheet. The calculation of economic capital is not bound by industry-wide standards, such as the accounting standards. As a result, it can be difficult to compare economic capital estimates between firms.

Economic capital is an expression of the amount of downside risk being taken by a firm, at a point in time, for a period into the future with a specific confidence interval. Economic capital can be a part of the risk-adjusted performance review, sometimes known as RAROC (risk-adjusted return on capital). For RAROC, the actual or anticipated return is divided by the economic capital, estimating the return per unit of risk taken.

The economic capital figure may be limited to a number of risk types, such as credit and market risk, or may apply to all risks faced by the organisation. Risk calculations may be performed at the level of the individual risk type, and these are then aggregated to obtain a view of the portfolio of risks to which the firm is exposed.

A time horizon will usually be part of the economic capital specification, for example 12 months into the future. If the time horizon for estimating the risk for a particular risk type is shorter, say one week, then this result will need adjusting to be made consistent with the economic capital time horizon.

In addition to the time horizon, the economic capital estimate is also defined by reference to a confidence interval. The confidence interval will usually be quite high, 95% or even 99.95%. How the confidence interval is chosen can be the subject of lengthy discussions related to the overall soundness of the organisation, its credit rating ("AAA" or "A") and its attitude to risk.

In reality, a firm is extremely unlikely to hold the same position for the duration of the economic capital time horizon, for example 12 months. Nevertheless, the economic capital estimate is a useful way of obtaining an overview of the amount of risk, how it changes and linking risk into performance assessment of businesses. Having the 12-month time horizon provides the same perspective as tactical and strategic decisions, such as raising additional capital or the dividend policy.

2.4.4   Regulatory Capital

Regulatory capital is to absorb losses, like book capital. The scope of instruments eligible to be treated as regulatory capital is specified and published. Internationally, the range of instruments eligible for regulatory capital is overseen by the Basel Committee on Banking Supervision.[6] The national requirements may be more or less restrictive than those published by the Basel Committee. The eligible instruments to meet the regulatory capital requirements are broader than book capital and represent some types of liability issued by the firm, such as some bonds, as well as equity.

---

[6] Basel Committee on Banking Supervision (June 2011) Basel III: A global regulatory framework for more resilient banks and banking systems. http://www.bis.org/publ/bcbs189.htm

Regulatory capital is subdivided into Tier 1 (going-concern capital) and Tier 2. Tier 1 is composed of equity and equity-like instruments, and certain reserves after the deduction of goodwill.[7] Tier 2 instruments are various forms of subordinated debt. The subordination means that, in the event of liquidation, the holders of these debt instruments rank lower than other creditors, such as depositors. The dividing line over whether a capital-raising instrument is Tier 1 or Tier 2 can be very fine.

The regulators specify certain ratios, for example Tier 1 cannot be less than 4.5% of Risk Weighted Assets, which are described in more detail in Chapter 13. National regulators will normally require firms to have more than the minimum amount of regulatory capital. The size of the increment may be influenced by the size and complexity of the firm as well as findings from regulatory dialogue and examinations.

The national regulators can have significant influence over composition and amount of Tier 1 and Tier 2 capital. This regulatory influence extends beyond the allocation between the two categories of capital to include payouts such as dividends, interest and even the repayment of principal on subordinated bonds. Five years after the beginning of the financial crisis, some banks still had restrictions on dividend payments and equity buyback programmes.

2.5   ISSUES TO CONSIDER

- Are regulatory and economic capital estimated using similar techniques?
- What is the reconciliation between the regulatory and economic capital estimates? Do they have the same time horizon and confidence interval?
- What is the relationship between book capital and instruments eligible to meet Tier 1 regulatory capital requirements?
- When discussing "return on capital", which form of capital is the point of reference?

---

[7] Examples of regulatory capital calculations can be found: Barclays plc 2011 Annual Report, p. 133; HSBC Holdings plc 2011 Annual Report, p. 214; JP Morgan Chase & Co. 2011 Annual Report, p. 120.

FURTHER READING

Bank of England (2011) Systemic Risk Survey.

Chevalier-Roignant, B. and Trigeogis, L. (2011) *Competitive Strategy: Options and Games*. MIT Press, Boston, MA.

Financial Stability Board (2009) Report to the G-20 Finance Ministers and Central Bank Governors: Guidance to Assess the Systemic Importance of Financial Institutions, Markets and Instruments: Initial Considerations— Background Paper.

Financial Stability Board (2011) Intensity and Effectiveness of SIFI Supervision.

Financial Stability Board (2011) Policy Measures to Address Systemically Important Financial Institutions.

Osterwalder, A. and Pigneur, Y. (2010) *Business Model Generation: A Handbook for Visionaries, Game Changers and Challengers*. John Wiley & Sons, Chichester.

Porter, M.E. (2004) *Competitive Advantage: Creating and Sustaining Superior Performance*. Free Press, New York.

Randall, A. (2011) *Risk and Precaution*. Cambridge University Press, Cambridge.

Rumsfeld, D. (12 February 2002) http://en.wikipedia.org/wiki/There_are_ known_knowns#Donald_Rumsfeld

Schwarz, S.L. (2008) Systemic risk. *Georgetown Law Journal* **97**, 193.

Spiegelhalter, D.J. and Riesch, H. (2011) Don't know, can't know: Embracing deeper uncertainties when analysing risks. *Philosophical Transactions of the Royal Society A* **369**(1956), 4730–4750.

de Weert, F. (2010) *Bank and Insurance Capital Management*. John Wiley & Sons, Chichester.

3
Risk Oversight

Risk Management at the Top

Ch. 1: Introduction

Part I: Risk Oversight

Ch. 2: Risk – An Overview	Ch. 3: Risk Oversight	Ch. 4: Risk Management	Ch. 5: Risk Appetite	Ch. 6: Risk Culture

Part II: Specific Risks

Ch. 7: Credit Risk	Ch. 8: Market Risk	Ch. 9: Operational Risk	Ch. 10: Liquidity Risk	Ch. 11: Other Risks	Ch. 12: Risk Interactions

Part III: Regulatory Environment

Ch. 13: Regulatory Environment

The role of the Board in overseeing risk has come to the fore. Comments from regulators, industry groups and the wider society are making their expectations known. This chapter looks at some of the mechanics and issues in overseeing risk. Chapter 5 will consider issues around setting risk appetite.

Oversight in this chapter refers to supervision of processes; in this case the risk processes. For the Board to have the information they need, it is necessary to have a degree of consistency and appreciate how this oversight is put into practice within the firm.

3.1   INTRODUCTION

Elements of risk oversight include:

- The direction of risk – is it getting larger or smaller?
- The quantum of risk – how much change is there?
- The distribution of risk across the organisation.

If all the employees are involved in risk management, to some degree or other, then the information about risk and its oversight will be influenced by their position in the organisational hierarchy and their perspective. The operator of a step in a process needs different information from that provided to the Board.

As data migrates up the organisation there is a need to reduce the volume of data and reduce its variety. The reduction in variety of information is part of the discipline of cybernetics. This reduction is largely achieved by the use of models. These models also change the data into information. The distributions mentioned in Chapter 2 are part of these models.

The models and their outputs are used as part of a risk management framework. Aspects of the framework are structural, other aspects are human. People bring with them a series of biases, some of which have contributed, directly or indirectly, to the financial crisis.

The Board, as a whole, does not need to know the details of these various components of risk oversight, the details belong to executive management. However, without some knowledge it is difficult for the Board to understand how various risk appetite decisions, made by the Board, are consistently cascaded down the organisation. The publically available description of communications surrounding LIBOR fixings at Barclays shows that this consistency can be difficult to achieve.

The rest of this chapter looks at the:

3.2 PERSPECTIVE

Data and information are basic inputs for risk oversight. To some degree or other, all employees are involved in risk management, including formal and informal processes. The data and information requirements vary with the level of the hierarchy as different formal risk management tasks are performed.

The purpose of risk oversight is to assess the direction of risk, increasing or decreasing, and the extent of any change. The risk management actions are in response to that information, for example is the quantum of risk within appetite?

Broadly, there are three internal perspectives of risk oversight:

1. bottom-up
2. top-down
3. middle outwards

as illustrated in Figure 3.1.

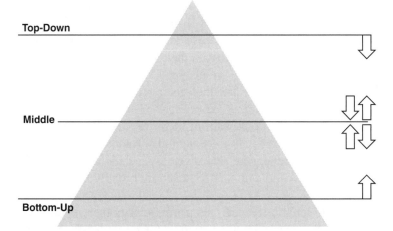

Figure 3.1   Risk oversight perspectives

3.2.1   Bottom

From the middle, the bottom receives the risk appetite statements and amounts. There may be some discussion on turning the risk appetite statements into metrics that are useful and usable at the bottom. This may involve the creation of "zero-tolerance" statements, which should be interpreted as forms of risk for which there is no appetite. Where the risk is "done to the firm", for example natural disasters, zero tolerance is interpreted as the event initiates risk management action.

Periodically, the bottom sends data and information to the middle for aggregation and reporting upwards. The frequency of information aggregation and reporting may be:

(a) intraday
(b) daily
(c) weekly
(d) monthly
(e) quarterly
(f) semi-annually
(g) annually.

The reporting frequency is influenced by issues such as the nature of the risk and the information content. For example, the profit and loss of the trading portfolio will be daily, but an operational risk and control self-assessment might be an annual process.

The bottom of the risk oversight is populated by people who need to know about the specific risk consequences of their tasks. Given the variety of tasks performed in firms, the range of information is diverse. The information may relate to credit risk from incremental mortgage transactions, to data quality, to the time taken to complete certain processing tasks.

For these individuals, the data they get is often related directly to their activities. This data is sometimes described as metrics, for example the number of transactions waiting to be processed, or the value of credit card transactions that are potentially fraudulent. The complete range of these metrics can be very diverse. A select few metrics may be designated key risk indicators (KRI) or more broadly key performance indicators (KPI).

For the individuals receiving and using the data there is often a clear link between the metric and the action that is needed. Whether a metric stimulates action is part of the concept around risk appetite. However, not every risk needs a formal risk appetite statement, sometimes common sense should be sufficient, for example "don't shoot customers". Issues can arise when "common sense" is interpreted differently, for example, due to bias or risk culture.

Other sources of information at the bottom are scenarios. Scenarios can be considered as thought-experiments about a possible sequence of events and the related consequences.[1] Although scenarios can also be performed at the top, for example to explore strategic alternatives or consequences, a significant number are performed at the bottom.

From an organisational perspective, the bottom-up risk oversight is dominated by the volume and variety of KRI data. The aim of the KRI is to be a metric that is related in some way to the potential frequency or severity of loss (i.e., risk). Some KRIs may have a qualitative link to risk, while others may have a quantitative relationship to risk. The KRIs will often be in the form of numbers, especially where the data can be captured from systems. In other cases the KRIs are transformed into information and possibly linked to opinions – such as high, medium and low – as in the case of risk and control assessments.

3.2.2 Top

The top creates the risk appetite for the overall firm. This is often followed by the risk appetites for each of the main risk types, for example credit, liquidity, market and operational risks. This information is then cascaded down to the middle.

Periodically, the top will receive information from the middle. For heads of some corporate risk functions this may mean daily reports, for others it means weekly or monthly regular reports. For the Board Risk Committee the information will correspond to their meeting cycle, for example fortnightly or monthly.

In contrast to the volume and variety of data at the bottom of the firm, the top gets information that summarises the wealth of data. The summaries not only reduce the volume of data, but also the variety of information.

A common example of this reduction in information is the market risk VaR number, a commonly used economic capital measure. The market

---

[1] Scenarios and stress testing are related. For stress testing, the possibility of occurrence is 100%. The organisation's exploration of consequences and any mitigating actions is based on the assumption that the sequence of events will materialise.

risk VaR number represents a loss at a particular confidence interval for the trading activities of the firm. The trading activities may have thousands of positions in hundreds of individual securities, and these are converted into a single VaR number. By comparing this VaR number over time it becomes possible to assess whether risk is increasing and the amount of change, but not the detailed sources of the change.

A factor to be considered at the top is not only the risks covered by the summaries, such as economic capital, but also those that are not addressed. For instance, it is unlikely that succession planning or reputational risk will ever feature in an economic capital model.

The top will determine the risk appetite and allocate a ration of economic capital to the Executive. This ration may already be subdivided between the major risk types, for example credit, market and operational risks. These portions of the ration will need to be subdivided across various businesses, products and locations. This task is often performed by the middle.

3.2.3   Middle

The middle tries to link the information coming upwards from the bottom with the requirements coming downwards from the top. This involves the aggregation of KRIs and other information and its transposition into units of measure comparable with those used for the requirements from the top for risk monitoring purposes. In the other direction, the middle also has to convert the requirements from the top, such as risk appetite, into metrics that are useful for the bottom.

There are two dimensions to this aggregation, the same data from two sources and different scopes of data from the same source. This data is aggregated to form a "picture" or impression of what is going on in a particular process or business or location. Is risk decreasing or increasing and by how much?

An example of aggregating the same scope of data from two sources is staff turnover in a retail banking business, but across two different regions. Assuming that they have the same definition of staff turnover, how should the numbers be combined for reporting purposes, expressed as a percentage of staff or something else? This is the simplest form of model. Assume that the two regions have staff turnover scores of 10% and 50%. When combined, is the result 30% or is the result shown as a range covering the extremes 10%–50%? To add to the complexity of interpretation, the 10% may represent a team of 100 people, while the 50% represents a team of 10.

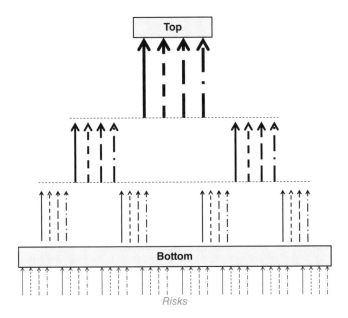

Figure 3.2   Aggregation of metrics showing reduction in volume

A ration of economic capital, or some other requirement from the top, needs to be disaggregated to link to the information coming from the bottom (Figure 3.2). This linkage is assisted if the bottom-up metrics are model inputs for the top-down metric. This linkage may be important depending on the use of risk information in the components determining compensation (Figure 3.3). If the risk information is used in compensation, then it is one feature that supports consistency in the risk culture of the organisation. Difficulties around consistency arise if the bottom-up metrics are not used as inputs to the model for the top-down metric.

3.3   MODELS

The previous section mentioned the need for models to summarise information and in doing so reduce its volume and variety. This section looks at models more closely. Individual models are mentioned in Part II. A model is a simplified description, especially mathematical or mental models, of a system or process to assist calculations and predictions.

Models are widespread. For example, the stock exchange indices are models to represent the price performance of a predetermined portfolio of shares. While mental models assist in understanding complicated situations, this section focuses on mathematical or statistical models.

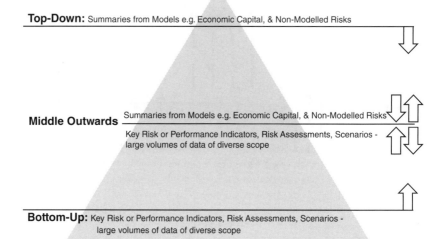

Figure 3.3   Risk perspectives, types of information

For risk management, the most common type of model is the portfolio model. Variants of the portfolio model include actuarial models. Which broad model type is appropriate depends on the purpose of the model.

Portfolio models form the backbone of risk oversight from the top down. The market risk VaR model is a portfolio model. The portfolio model has significant value as it summarises thousands or even hundreds of thousands of positions into a few numbers. As an interim step, various factors may be extracted from the individual positions and modelled within the portfolio model. An example would be having a submodel for the factors representing the risk-free yield curve; another submodel might focus on the incremental yield over the risk-free yield curve.

Other significant portfolio models in risk management include credit risk and operational risk economic and regulatory capital models. The liquidity risk framework can be considered a portfolio model, but it has a structure that differs fundamentally from the others as it does not produce an estimate related to some form of capital.

A key component of these portfolio models is how the individual factors are aggregated to provide the overview of the portfolio. This aggregation usually involves correlation, which is intended to describe the co-movement of two factors. The correlation not only describes the direction (do the two factors move in the same or a different direction?), but also the extent of the co-movement.

The identification of the portfolio factors starts with the individual products and product models that describe the behaviour of their price to changes in factors. These product models may be relatively simple, as in the case of pricing a certificate of deposit, or may be complicated, as for a model used to value a mortgage. Some of the complications are derived from the presence of embedded or explicit options. For example, the choice of the borrower to repay a fixed-rate mortgage early is an embedded option that will be linked to the level of interest rates.

These product models may be used not only for risk management, but also in estimating a fair value for the firm's balance sheet and P&L statements. An error in these models can have implications beyond risk management. These two issues come together in a hedging model. The purpose of the hedging model is to immunise the P&L statements from changes in value of one or more factors, such as changes in the risk-free yield curve.

The significant role played by portfolio risk and product models means that there needs to be some associated governance and oversight. As a result, these models will have to go through a degree of testing before they can be used to generate valuations and risk estimates. This testing will usually be conducted by an individual or team independent from those involved in designing and constructing the model. This testing may be periodic, to confirm that as conditions change the model output is still fit for purpose.

3.4   RISK FRAMEWORK

The risk framework is the structure of risk oversight. It provides the skeleton within which risk management (Chapter 4) operates. The risk framework begins with the risk owners, the various corporate functions and then aspects of the documentation.

The ISO defines the risk (management) framework as:

> A set of components that provide the foundations and organizational arrangements for designing, implementing, monitoring, reviewing and continually improving risk management throughout the organization.[2]

3.4.1   Three Lines of Defence

Risk framework in the financial sector is built around the concept of "three lines of defence". The degree to which the implemented risk

---

[2] ISO Guide 73 (2009) Risk Management – Vocabulary.

framework corresponds to the three lines of defence will be reviewed by the regulators and possibly the external auditors. The three lines of defence are to maintain independence from each other. The participants in the three lines of defence are:

(i) risk owners
(ii) corporate risk functions
(iii) internal audit.

The risk owners, sometimes referred to as the businesses, are that part of the firm that bear the risk and get paid for taking the risk. The businesses have day-to-day, hour-to-hour and minute-to-minute risk management responsibilities. These responsibilities include identification, assessment, risk decision and reporting of risks. Many of these detailed processes will be described in procedure documents originating from the corporate risk functions supported by the risk specialists in the businesses. Key to discharging these responsibilities is access to timely and accurate information on risks. The risk information is then compared with risk appetite figures, for example a ration of economic capital or other limits. The ration or limits are effectively thresholds that should not be crossed, no matter what the level of return.

While the three lines of defense report to the Chief Executive Officer (CEO), some communicate with the Board directly or indirectly via Board-level committees (see Figure 3.4). In particular, the Group Head of Internal Audit and the CRO will participate in Board-level committees, for example the Board-level Audit Committee, Risk Committee and possibly Compensation Committee. This gives members of the Board independent access to information flowing up these reporting lines.

The corporate risk management functions will define many of the day-to-day risk management activities as part of their oversight responsibilities. These information requirements, generated by the corporate risk management functions oversight responsibilities, will in turn drive the regular collection of data and transformation into information. From this oversight function, the corporate risk management functions are also expected to challenge the businesses, for example the amount of risk being taken in comparison with the risk appetite.

Additionally, the corporate risk management functions need to advise or coach the risk owners, while also having the authority to independently escalate issues. This requires a degree of knowledge about the business activities, for example where does the business add value, how does it differentiate itself from its competitors and what risks does it

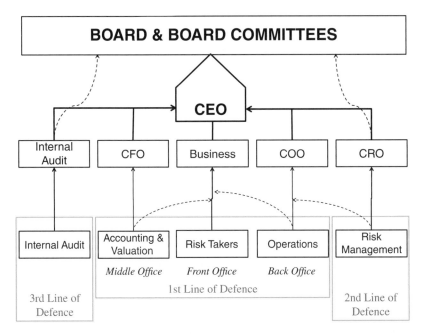

Figure 3.4   Reporting lines for the "three lines of defence"

take as a result? Making this advisory or coaching role more complicated is that under the three lines of defence concept, each of the three
lines is to be independent of the other. If the corporate risk function gets
too close to the business, will it compromise its independence? (This is
sometimes described as business capture of the risk function.)

Ultimately, the corporate risk management functions need to have
policies and standards for the risks that the firm has experienced, is
experiencing or might experience in the future. The risk function needs
to be able to create a firm-wide view of the risks. Creating a firm-
wide view requires consistency of information in terms of scope and
format. In times of turbulence the risk functions may need to create
these views daily for decision making and monitoring against thresholds
and appetites. In turbulent conditions not only may the exposures to risk
change quickly, but also the risk appetite of the Risk Committee and the
Board. Achieving these timely decisions requires investment in systems
and timely updates. Adherence to risk appetite, from top to bottom, is
intended to be continuous, not just at quarter-end.

Internal audit is the third line of defence. One role is to confirm
adherence to policies, standards and procedures by the various units

to which they apply. Another role is to stand back from the detail and assess the overall shape and configuration of the policies, standards and procedures. Are there any material holes in the risk coverage? Is the reporting fit for purpose in the current environment, as opposed to the environment in which they were created?

In being the third line of defence, internal audit provides an independent perspective on the scope of the risk framework of the firm. Internal audit reports to the Audit Committee of the Board and provides an opinion to the Board separate from the communication from the corporate risk functions, the CEO and the businesses.

3.4.2   Risk Owners

To begin, as a generalisation, the risk owners are the businesses. The risks are part of the business activities. In addition, the businesses have allocated part of their budget, directly or indirectly, to risk management activities. The businesses have day-to-day, hour-to-hour and minute-to-minute risk management responsibilities. These responsibilities include identification, assessment, risk decisions and reporting of risks.

The business ownership of risk is an easy response, but is not the entire picture. The businesses can be said to be the owners of risks that the firm deliberately takes in the pursuit of revenue. However, there are risks that the firm as a whole takes in addition to the risks taken by the businesses, for example some operational risks. As described in Chapter 9, it can cover external threats such as crime and terrorism. Some of these risks apply to the firm as a whole or buildings occupied by multiple businesses. Operational risk also includes employment law, and these issues can arise anywhere in the firm, not just the businesses.

As a result, every employee has a role in risk management and oversight.

The scope of risk oversight also extends to those activities that have been outsourced. This might be outsourced to a company outside the group or outsourced to another company within the group, sometimes referred to as offshoring. The banking regulators view the activities carried out by the insourcer, and associated risks, as part of the scope of the business. This view applies whether the insourcer is a third party or a subsidiary within the group. A consequence is that the outsourcer (the business) may need to specify various KRIs or KPIs as well as establishing a process for monitoring them and tolerances. The scope of outsourcing can range from sales agents distributing your products or services, to firms executing parts of the transaction chain.

3.4.3 Corporate Risk Management Functions

Large firms have corporate risk management functions. These functions are often aligned with the risk types, such as credit, liquidity, market and operational risks. Increasingly, these corporate risk functions report to a CRO. Other corporate risk management functions include legal, IT and physical security, business continuity management, building maintenance, human resources, compliance, finance and accounting. These other functions have roles to play as centres of specific risk knowledge, even if they do not report directly to the CRO. As seen in Figure 3.4, some of these functions are part of the middle or back office and have reporting lines to the CEO additional to the dotted lines to the business.

For subsidiaries it may be necessary for an individual to multi-task. For example, the local Head of Compliance may also have a role in overseeing operational risk or vice versa.

An essential aspect of these corporate risk functions is their independence from the businesses. Independence refers to reporting and lines of communication. Following this independence, the Board can rely on these corporate risk functions to provide an independent perspective of the risks across the business as well as monitoring adherence to risk limits and appetites. The outcome may result in the corporate risk functions advising and coaching the businesses on achieving their revenue targets within the risk limits and appetites of the firm.

As part of the "three lines of defence", the corporate risk functions have oversight and challenge roles. It is inevitable that some aspects of the top-level risk appetite statement require interpretation. Part of the role of the corporate risk functions is to challenge the risk owners on their interpretations. Care is needed between the risk owners and corporate risk functions as to which role is being undertaken at any one point in time and ensuring independence.

The Board, businesses and corporate risk functions come together in setting the risk appetite. For example, the businesses will propose a revenue target to the Board, which involves taking a certain amount of risk. The corporate risk functions will aggregate these units of risk for presentation to the Board. The quanta of risk are usually accompanied by recommendations from the various risk functions. The Board will then consider the proposals in comparison with their risk appetites. Possible outcomes include adjustments to the revenue targets and/or adjustments to the risk appetite.

Other occasions when the businesses and corporate risk functions work together will include change programmes. A change programme could be the introduction of a new product, strategic decisions to buy or sell businesses or to outsource an activity. The businesses will sponsor these changes and there needs to be a risk-related review. Some of the decisions around change may require the approval of the CRO at the regional or group level. This approval, or right of veto, may be closely defined and in the event of a dispute may even have an escalation process so that ultimately the Board can decide.

For new products the firm will have a new product approval process. The objective of this process is to ensure that the organisation can process the transactions and there is no material change to the risk profile of the firm. A new product will usually be defined by a related policy, for example the policy will determine whether an existing product sold to a different client type or using a different distribution channel is a new product? Some firms give reviewers the authority to reject a proposal, or ask for certain aspects to be reworked and resubmitted by the business. The corporate risk functions that can be involved in these reviews include, but are not limited to:

- Accounting/Finance
- Corporate Risk Functions – Credit, Liquidity, Market and Operational
- Compliance
- Legal
- Tax
- Operations.

Other sources of change that can require input from the corporate risk functions include system or process changes. System changes can alter the risk profile. For example, a change in a process to reduce high-frequency low-impact human error can result in low-frequency high-impact system failure risk. Until the before and "possible after" comparison has been made, it is not clear whether the change is beneficial, from a risk perspective. Other issues that may be part of the discussion include the impact on business risk, for example going from semi-variable costs to fixed costs, flexibility of capacity and the ability to address issues before they become losses.

These interactions between the corporate risk functions and the business require some common understanding. It requires the corporate risk functions to have an understanding of the businesses and their respective business models. This common understanding is often supported by having risk specialists embedded within the businesses. These business risk specialists will report into the business, so they are not independent. They speak the language of the corporate risk function and so can act as "translators".

3.4.4 Chief Risk Officer

The CRO needs to have a balance of skills, blending an understanding of the businesses with knowledge of technical aspects of risk. This combination is required in the role of being a senior manager at the top of the firm, having a communication line to the Board, being independent from the businesses and yet influencing management and business decisions; dialogue with the Board to promote a dynamic approach to risk appetite, as opposed to limiting discussions to once a year. The management decisions may be about change, for example buying or selling businesses, or obtaining budget for significant investment in risk management information systems.

The CRO is at the top of one of the "three lines of defence". Either directly, or by implication, the remit of the CRO covers all the risks that the firm takes. Part of the CRO's role is to reinforce the message that the business owns the risk and that the role of the corporate risk functions involves oversight and challenge. At the same time, the CRO has to be involved in management decisions due to the risk implications, for example extending the flow of risk data to match the growth of businesses in terms of product range, customer segments served and geographic coverage. The Board-level Risk Committee has a role in reinforcing these requirements and reinforcing the authority of the CRO to execute.

To support the CRO, there will probably be a Risk Committee. Depending on the firm, this Risk Committee may be integrated with the Board-level Risk Committee. Participants on this committee are likely to include:

- Group Head of Credit Risk
- Group Head of Liquidity Risk
- Group Head of Market Risk
- Group Head of Operational Risk
- Group Head of Compliance
- Legal

- Operations
- IT
- Accounting/Finance.

Internal audit may be an observer on the Risk Committee, so they do not compromise their independence within the "three lines of defence".

This committee may meet regularly, on a fortnightly or monthly basis. However, during the financial crisis many of these committees met daily.

The CRO and Risk Committee will be involved in top-level risk appetite statements and their cascade down the organisation (Figure 3.5). Individuals on the Risk Committee will have a significant involvement in drafting the risk appetite statements for the various individual risk types. Owing to the relationship between revenue and risk taking, there must be dialogue with the risk owners, the businesses.

The distribution to the businesses will be in the form of a matrix. Some businesses will need a combination of credit, market and operational risks, whilst others may just need operational risk.

Owing to this process, the CRO or possibly the Risk Committee will be responsible for the mechanism of aggregating the metrics into risk information. This is a consequence of the risk oversight role. At the top of the firm, the mechanism is likely to be the economic capital framework. The group heads of the corporate risk management functions will have responsibility for the credit, market, operational and other risk models.

Figure 3.5   Iterative relationship between risk appetite statements

Their constraint is consistency of concept and interpretation of output. Without these constraints it becomes very difficult, maybe impossible, to arrive at firm-wide quantitative expressions of risk appetite. Even at this level it is necessary to use correlation estimates to integrate the values from the individual risk types to produce a top-level quantitative element of risk appetite. This aggregation enables concepts such as RAROC.

3.4.5   Policies, Standards and Procedures

These documents, published to the employees, describe how the risk oversight process works in practice, and effectively constitute the risk framework. The volume of documentation follows a triangle with principles and policies at the top, followed by standards and procedures at the bottom.

The policies are likely to describe the objectives, roles and responsibilities and information requirements. The standards will define terms, event escalation, systems to be used and expectations such as timeliness and completeness of reporting, etc. The procedures are mostly granular and may be customised for different businesses or various subcategories of risk, for example project finance within commercial lending.

The policies, standards and procedures need to be proportionate. That is to say, for larger and more complex businesses these documents are expected to be more extensive than for simpler/smaller firms. For example, such documents may describe the aggregation of information across corporate subsidiaries to enable a group-wide picture to be obtained. The subsidiary may have additional costs to bear as the group requirements may differ from national regulatory requirements and the subsidiary has to comply with both simultaneously.

The Board is expected to review the risk policies annually. In this task the Board may be supported by a Risk Committee chaired by a Non-Executive Director (NED). The review is to confirm that the policies are still applicable given changes in the internal and external environment, for example changes in regulatory requirements.

The publication of the policies and standards, either in hard or soft copy versions, adds to the risk culture of the organisation. It becomes clearer where the information is going and what is being done with it. This also means that it is clearer who to go to when there is uncertainty over an issue.

3.5 BIASES

All the activities associated with risk are performed by people. People bring various forms of bias to discussions and decision making. The origin of a bias may be intellectual or it may be emotional. Bias is defined as an inclination or prejudice, and a concentration on or interest in one particular area. Bias implies a distortion or deviation from a perfect reference point. This perfect reference point can be based on hindsight, logic, economics or some other framework for rational decisions.

For risk management it is cognitive bias, on perceptions and interpretations, that needs to be recognised and appreciated.

The reason that biases should be recognised is due to the need to use expert opinion. Even the most highly regarded experts should be expected to have some degree of bias. The majority of the time biases are implicit rather than explicit. These biases arise, along with heuristics ("rules of thumb") and other shortcuts, as a means of dealing with a complex world. This can be exacerbated by time pressures. As a result, these biases, heuristics and other shortcuts can feature in our mental models. Biases may be built into mathematical models, as a form of model risk, reflecting the bias of the model designer. Meanwhile, heuristics can be applied to inappropriate situations.

There is no definitive list of biases and their descriptions. The same type of bias may have different names or labels depending on the source.[3] Table 3.1 provides a brief description of some cognitive biases, including many from Bazerman and Moore, that may be present in discussions on risk and influence decisions.

The first step in managing biases and heuristics is to recognise their existence. Some biases can be mitigated by requesting more than one opinion. This is effectively what happens when a model is independently reviewed and validated. Addressing and reducing the impact of biases and heuristics takes time, effort and resources. Part of the issue lies in identifying the decisions on which the biases and heuristics could have a material effect and justifying the application of additional resources.

These biases can be present throughout the risk management framework, from creating a firm-level risk appetite statement to assessing the frequency and severity of an individual risk event. A mitigant to some of these biases is the structure of the "three lines of defence" with

---

[3] For additional comments and discussion see Bazerman and Moore (2013), Celatti (2004) or Koenig (2012) listed in the Further Reading.

Table 3.1   Some biases that influence risk oversight (including Bazerman and Moore)

Bias label	Description
Ease of Recall	Individuals judge events that are more easily recalled from memory, based on vividness or elapsed time, to be more numerous than events of equal frequency whose instances are less easily recalled.
	This reliance upon memory creates a disadvantage when considering "Black Swan" events.
Retrievability	Individuals are biased in their assessments of the frequency of events based on how their memory affects the recall process. Also influenced by the length of memory span and the tendency to give more weight to recent than distant past.
Insensitivity to Base Line	When assessing the likelihood of events, individuals tend to ignore base lines if any other descriptive is provided, even if it is irrelevant.
Insensitivity to Sample Size	When assessing the reliability of sample information individuals frequently fail to appreciate the role of sample size. This can be important when the sample size is small and the risk assessment extrapolates to an entire population.
Misconception of Chance	Individuals expect that a sequence of data generated by a random process will look "random" even when the sequence is too short for the expectations to be statistically valid.
Regression to the Mean	Individuals tend to ignore the fact that extreme events tend to regress to the mean in the long run.
Confirmation Trap	Individuals seek confirmatory information for what they think is true and fail to search for disconfirmatory evidence.
Anchoring	Individuals make estimates for values based upon an initial value (derived from past events, or other information) and typically make insufficient adjustments from that anchor point when establishing a final value.
Conservatism Bias	The tendency to underestimate large losses and high likelihoods. This also includes that two events will occur simultaneously in a connected or disconnected manner.
Conjunctive and Disjunctive Event Bias	Individuals exhibit a bias towards overestimating the probability of conjunctive events and underestimating disjunctive events.
Hindsight	After finding out whether or not an event occurred, individuals tend to overestimate the degree to which they would have predicted the correct outcome. Furthermore, individuals fail to ignore information that they possess that others do not when predicting others' behaviour.
Overconfidence	Individuals tend to be overconfident in the correctness of their judgements, especially in relation to difficult questions.
Framing Effect	Drawing different conclusions from the same information depending on how it is presented.

(continued)

Table 3.1 (*Continued*)

Bias label	Description
Groupthink	The tendency of individuals in a group to submerge their opinions because they do not want to disrupt the group, be seen as a dissenter or query a powerful personality.
Time Horizon	Individuals tend to give greater weight to the near term than the more distant future. This can lead to inconsistencies between decisions and strategy.
Omission	Judging harmful *actions* as being worse than equally harmful *inactions*.
Zero Risk	Preference for reducing a small risk over a larger reduction in a greater risk.

its oversight and challenge roles involving risk owners, corporate risk functions and internal audit. Another antidote to some of these biases is to use data and mathematical models. However, even these can have biases. Although policies, standards and procedures can embed biases, they are also a way to control for biases. For example, when creating a scenario a group may come together to produce an estimate of frequency and severity. The procedure may be to compare these estimates against data (internal or external) and provide the group with the opportunity to revise their estimates.

Biases are not limited to management of financial firms, but are present every day for most people including, but not limited, to:

- customers
- regulators
- politicians.

Some of the deviations from the "perfect rational decision" are part of the developing topic of behavioural finance. For example, it is not clear if all cases of mis-selling arise from actions by the firm or if the biases employed by the customers also have a role to play. This places additional emphasis on the duty of care obligation of the firm when dealing with customers.

3.6   ISSUES TO CONSIDER

- Is there a clear and consistent message on risk from the Board to the bottom?

- When did the Board last discuss the terms of reference of the Board-level Risk Committee?
- What is the basis for escalating risks to the Board for decision?
- When did the Board last discuss emerging risks?
- Does the Board have a proactive or reactive approach to setting the firm's risk appetite?
- Are the three lines of defence working effectively?
- When did the Board-level Audit Committee last discuss the risk framework?
- Is the Board getting the right information from the risk framework?
- Do the corporate risk functions have adequate resources?
- Do internal audit and the CRO participate in the Compensation Committee?
- When did input from the CRO last have an impact on a strategic decision?

FURTHER READING

Ayyub, B. (2001) *Elicitation of Expert Opinions for Uncertainty and Risks.* CRC Press, Boca Raton, FL.

Basel Committee on Banking Supervision (2013) Principles for Effective Risk Data Aggregation and Reporting. http://www.bis.org/publ/bcbs239.pdf

Bazerman, M.H. and Moore, D.A. (2013) *Judgement in Managerial Decision Making*, 8th edn. John Wiley & Sons, Chichester.

Celatti, L. (2004) *The Dark Side of Risk Management: How People Frame Decisions in Financial Markets.* Pearson Educational, Oxford.

Espejo, R. and Reyes, A. (2011) *Organizational Systems: Managing Complexity with the Viable System Model.* Springer-Verlag, Berlin.

European Banking Authority (2011) EBA Guidelines on Internal Governance (GL44).

Hoverstadt, P. (2008) *The Fractal Organization: Creating Sustainable Organisations with the Viable System Model.* John Wiley & Sons, Chichester.

Institute of International Finance (October 2012) Governance for Strengthened Risk Management.

Koenig, D.R. (2012) *Governance Reimagined: Organizational Design, Risk and Value Creation.* John Wiley & Sons, Chichester.

Morini, M. (2011) *Understanding and Managing Model Risk: A Practical Guide for Quants, Traders and Validators.* John Wiley & Sons, Chichester.

Teschner, C., Golder, P. and Liebert, T. (2008) Bringing Back Best Practices in Risk Management: Banks' Three Lines of Defence. Booz & Co. http://www.booz.com/media/uploads/Bringing-Back-Best-Practices-in-Risk-Management.pdf

Wikipedia "Cognitive Biases" http://www.en.wikipedia.org/wiki/List_of_cognitive_biases

4

Risk Management

Risk Management at the Top

Ch. 1: Introduction

Part I: Risk Oversight

Ch. 2: Risk – An Overview	Ch. 3: Risk Oversight	Ch. 4: Risk Management	Ch. 5: Risk Appetite	Ch. 6: Risk Culture

Part II: Specific Risks

Ch. 7: Credit Risk	Ch. 8: Market Risk	Ch. 9: Operational Risk	Ch. 10: Liquidity Risk	Ch. 11: Other Risks	Ch. 12: Risk Interactions

Part III: Regulatory Environment

Ch. 13: Regulatory Environment

With the role of the Board in risk oversight there needs to be a clearly understood and appreciated process for identifying risks, determining whether they are within policy and escalating issues for risk-based decisions where necessary. This chapter describes the formal risk management processes. These processes need to be aligned with the next two chapters on risk appetite and risk culture to reduce the likelihood that the Board and senior management will be adversely surprised by events.

4.1 INTRODUCTION

Chapter 3 provided an overview of risk oversight, including the risk framework. This chapter describes the processes that make the risk framework function and enable oversight. Unless risk management is effective then the risk oversight will be ineffective as the information does not flow up the organisation to decision makers and risk-oriented decisions are not explicitly made.

4.1.1 Definition of Risk Management

The ISO defines risk management as "coordinated activities to direct and control risk".[1]

Risk management as a set of activities has been practiced since before man found fire and realised that you could get burnt. In most instances the activities are performed subconsciously or implicitly by individuals in their daily lives. Relatively recently risk management has become explicit for organisations ranging from the military to charities to financial institutions and other corporates. Amongst the organisations that have focused on risk management is COSO, which started in 1985.[2]

As activities have become more complex so it has been necessary to make risk management a formal explicit activity. This formality brings consistency and transparency. Factors promoting this formality include the precautionary principle, the possibility of affecting a broad group of stakeholders and a range of severities, including the catastrophic for individuals, organisations and wider society.

---

[1] ISO (2009) Risk Management – Vocabulary, Guide 73.

[2] COSO is the Commission of Sponsoring Organisations of the Treadway Commission (www.coso.org) and its objective is to provide thought leadership on enterprise risk management, internal control and fraud deterrence.

Without effective risk management processes risk oversight cannot function. There may be suspicions that individual risks are not being captured or are underreported, or locations or certain types of activities are not being fully represented in the information. As the risk information flows up the organisation then issues about completeness, timeliness and accuracy become exacerbated. In turn this affects decision making, in particular the uncertainty element.

The rest of this chapter looks at the:

4.2 Terminology and Components
4.3 Risk Management Cycle
4.4 Issues to Consider

4.2 TERMINOLOGY AND COMPONENTS

Terminology is important to enable a dialogue between the Board and the Executive. Without clear terminology dialogue can be unsatisfactory and purposes can be frustrated. In the area of risk management firms may have proprietary terminology for various activities. One firm's risk assessment is another firm's risk analysis. This section will refer to the ISO's "Risk Management – Vocabulary" as it is being used more frequently.

4.2.1 Cause and Effect

Causes can be identified, but they can be difficult to formally define, so information flows often refer to effects such as losses; to prevent or influence the effect so the focus falls on the cause. In some instances the discussion will be about increasing the beneficial consequences, for example revenues from actively taking risk. In other instances it will be about reducing the adverse consequences cost effectively.

In the sequence of actions, causes come before effects. So for risk reduction the focus tends to be on identifying the causes and managing them. Causes can be broadly categorised into internal or external. Internal causes may include segregation of duties, clear roles and responsibilities, data quality and many others. Sometimes a cause leads to an effect, other times a cause can be amplified by another cause then lead to the effect. For example, the impact of poor data quality may be amplified by inadequate resources – in terms of numbers or knowledge. To address the effect, changes may be made to the data quality and/or enhancing

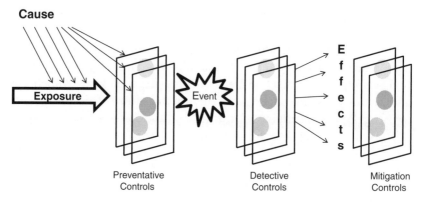

Figure 4.1   Exposure, causes, controls and effects

the resources, for instance via training. In Figure 4.1 monitoring data quality and training programmes are preventative controls.

Several different causes can have the same overall effect; namely, loss in economic value to the organisation and even the form that the loss takes. Some events materialise in response to a single cause, on other occasions it can be multiple causes appearing simultaneously or in sequence or both. Certain industries have adopted root-cause analysis techniques when conducting post-mortems into events, actual or potential. The result of this analysis may be changes to the control environment, for example preventative controls, detective controls or mitigation controls. A possible cause may be a design gap in the control framework, or that a control failed to operate.

Preventative controls are intended to influence causes so that they do not materialise into events. These controls can take a wide variety of forms, for example staff training or new product approval processes. The legal function can be viewed as preventative control over poor contractual documentation or interpreting regulatory requirements, such as health and safety. In reality there are often many layers of control, and this can be described as the "Swiss cheese" model of controls. The name refers to the holes in Swiss cheese, indicating that no individual control is likely to be effective against all causes, so individual controls can be viewed as having "holes". However, if the number of controls is taken too far then the cumulative cost of controls has a significant impact on net income.

Detective controls are intended to identify when there is an abnormal state. An abnormal state can be in the form of incorrect data describing a transaction or the counterparty. Part of the function of the accounting or finance function is to detect certain types of theft or unauthorised activity, such as rogue trading.

Mitigation controls are to manage the consequences of an event. Disaster recovery or business continuity plans are examples of mitigation controls. Another example is public relations when trying to reduce the impact of reputational risk.

The controls may be aligned with steps in the value chain or front-to-back processes. Each process step or element of the business model is likely to have multiple controls, for instance multiple preventative controls, to affect different aspects of the value chain. Controls do not have to be aligned with the value chain, but it may assist when managing the level of risk to the risk appetite.

4.2.2   Exposure and Event

An event arises when there is an occurrence or change of a particular set of circumstances. An event can have multiple individual consequences, for example when there is an error in the amount of interest charged to hundreds of thousands of customer accounts. An event can even be the failure of something that was supposed to happen. An example would be the failure to execute payment instructions or due diligence of a new customer. An event may have no material consequences, in which case it is often described as a "near miss" or a "close call". Events can also be referred to as incidents.

For an event to happen, the cause has to coincide with or meet an exposure. Exposure may be measured in thousands of transactions, the value of property, number of staff, number of clients and many other metrics. For credit risk the exposure might be the notional amount of the loan, for example $10 million representing a $10 million loan. For market risk the exposure could be the notional amount of the position, for example $5 million representing an investment of $5 million US Treasuries. For operational risk the limit to exposure might be the maximum value of transaction that can be processed. For liquidity risk the exposure might be the maximum value of deposits accepted from one individual counterpart.

Exposure represents the simplest metric underlying limits. For credit risk a limit might be expressed as $15 million loan exposure limit to a particular individual borrower. For market risk it might be $20 million US Treasuries. For liquidity risk it might be $50 million deposit. These constraints are related to losses, but are not risk dynamic. If the volatility of US Treasuries increases then to keep the level of risk the same an action is required to reduce the limit. In this context risk is the likelihood of incurring a loss and the severity of the loss. In a more sophisticated environment exposure measures are used as an input to more complex risk estimates. This enables the risk metrics to be dynamic and change the exposure as the level of risk changes.

4.2.3 Effects and Consequences

As mentioned earlier, risk as a concept is neither positive nor negative, but refers to uncertainty of outcomes. Unless banks and other financial industry participants take risk, they generate no revenue. However, most of the material on risk refers to undesirable outcomes, effects or consequences and does not consider the need to take risk to generate revenue.

The undesirable effects affect the profitability and/or the economic value of the firm, directly or indirectly. Some of these undesirable consequences are as follows.

Direct effects

- Compensation payments to stakeholders, e.g. customers.
- Cost to fix.
- Regulatory sanction.

For example:

Cause	product categorisation error
Effect	product mis-selling
Exposure	many customers
Consequence	loss in the form of compensation paid to customers
Cost to fix	internal or external resources
Regulatory sanctions	fines and/or additional work

Indirect effects

- Reputational impact on counterparties and future business activities.
- Opportunity costs – diversion of scarce resources.
- Increased engagement with regulators and other stakeholders, e.g. investors.

Events that can give rise to all of the direct and indirect effects include mis-selling events. The mis-selling of Payment Protection Insurance in the UK has cost a great deal in compensation payments, processing applications for compensation, changing systems and processes, the allocation of management time, increased scrutiny and dialogue with regulators and the loss of reputation, causing customers to change service or product providers.

In some instances undesirable indirect effects can have a larger long-term impact on the firm than direct effects. An undesirable indirect effect might be the active departure of customers or increased difficulties in attracting new customers. This can depress the revenue stream several years into the future.

With all this data and information about risk, the tendency is to report effects and consequences up the organisation. This choice of what to report is a key early step in the cybernetic and "modelling" activity that reduces the variety of information and the richness of the data communicated upwards. There are also difficulties in adding richness back in when cascaded down the organisation, for example with the risk appetite. The difficulties in reporting risk are increased when the topic of concern is an emerging risk and the type or exact consequences are surrounded by uncertainty, making accurate estimates difficult to obtain.

4.3   RISK MANAGEMENT CYCLE

The risk management cycle is a sequence of steps that:

(a) identify the risk
(b) analyse the risk
(c) evaluate the risk
(d) manage the risk
(e) monitor and review the risk.

It may also be referred to as a risk management process or risk assessment. As shown in Figure 4.2, the process is iterative until compliance with the policies and standards is achieved.

In many instances the individual steps in the risk management cycle are implicit in an assessment of the risk. In particular, the steps are implicit when the focus is on generating revenue from taking the risk, as opposed to managing actual or potential undesirable consequences. Also, when risk reporting has matured, the risk management cycle may

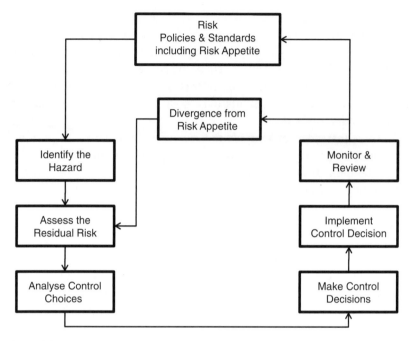

Figure 4.2   Overview of the risk management cycle

only be used explicitly when the risk appetite is about to be breached, or has been breached, or there is an emerging risk.

The individual risk management cycles are linked to provide a flow of information upwards. This is needed to correspond to the cascading down of risk appetite and other policies, standards and requirements (see Figure 4.3).

It is the risk management cycle and related risk reporting requirements that provide the source data that feeds the reporting process and ultimately arrives at the Board. The responsibility for the operation of the risk management cycle is firmly with the Executive, but without its efficient operation the Board will only have a limited view of the sources of risk and individual risks to which the firm is exposed.

For some sources of risk, such as credit risk, the source may not require much identification and various steps may be highly formalised. Other risk sources, such as market risk, may need to go through this process to identify subcategories of risk and ensure that they are reflected in the risk calculations, such as the impact of volatility on the value of options embedded in bonds.

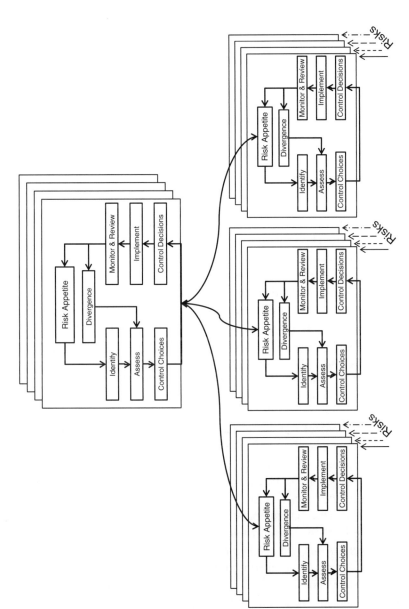

Figure 4.3 Linkage of risk management cycles

The day-to-day operation of the risk management cycle is the responsibility of the risk owners. This is an activity where the corporate risk functions act as advisers and coaches to the risk owners. Once the process has been designed and implemented for a specific risk and business then the role of the corporate risk functions can change. For a functioning risk management process the corporate risk management functions may be involved in oversight, challenge and advising on the control choices and divergence from the risk appetite. Owing to their role, the corporate risk management functions may have seen a variety of control decisions to address similar risks.

4.3.1 Identify the Risk

This step can have two triggers, the self-assessment of an activity or process, or reacting to an event that has materialised with consequences. The process could be signing up new customers or archiving transaction details or physical security or any one of the other many activities that enable a financial institution function.

Under self-assessment the aim is to identify all the possible risks associated with the activity or process before they materialise. This occurs at the bottom of the information pyramid. For undesirable consequences, care is needed to distinguish between inherent risks and residual risks. Inherent risks are risks without any controls applied to the activity or process. Residual risk is the level of risk after controls are applied and assumptions are made about their effectiveness.

The identification of risks should be as comprehensive as possible, including sources of risk, or causes, and whether they are internal or external to the firm. For external causes, the firm may be unable to prevent occurrences but may be able to manage the consequences, for example a mitigating control such as a disaster recovery plan. If a risk is missed during the identification stage then it is unlikely to be recognised further into the risk management cycle.

Given the level of granularity it will be possible to identify the types of consequences that can arise from each of these risks. "Cost to fix" is likely to be a very common consequence for operational risk. For credit risk the consequences tend to be write-downs and provisions, while for market risk they are reduction in value and impact on the P&L.

The resultant list and consequences can be used to create a risk profile. The advantage of creating a risk profile for a single activity in a business, in a location, is that it can be shared with the same business in other locations. This sharing is a form of knowledge transfer, and validation. Review by a separate and knowledgeable team may identify causes, or risks, or consequences that have been missed by the originators. It is also an efficient use of resources in comparison with reinventing the risk profile many times over.

In some firms the risk identification is linked to the internal audit process. The business managers, who own the risk, are looked upon in a better light if they have identified the risks (being pro-active) rather than waiting for internal audit, or the risk to materialise and create a loss (being reactive). A pro-active stance towards risk means that there is more likelihood that it will be an implied feature of budgets and in process changes.

4.3.2   Assess the Risk

The inputs for this step are the risks identified in the prior step. The analysis of the risk is to obtain a better understanding of the causes, effects and consequences. Part of this process will be determining the relationship, based on a mathematical or mental model, between the exposure and the consequences. For example, a parallel adverse move in interest rates will result in $X change in the value of assets. If the assets are marked-to-market then $X will be the P&L consequence.

Having developed some ideas for the relationship between the causes, effects, exposure and consequences, the issue is how often the event is likely to materialise. For some risks, estimating the likelihood of occurrence is more difficult than the severity of the consequences. There will also be a difference in whether this is an inherent or a residual risk that is being analysed. If it is a residual risk then some assumptions are made about the effectiveness of the controls.

In estimating the frequency, or likelihood, and severity there is no alternative but to use expert opinion. This opinion may be supported by internal or external data, such as the number of customers, market turnover or severity of a rogue trading event at a peer. As a result, this is a step in the process where bias can have a significant impact. Even if the firm has experienced similar events in the past, in the same business/location, expert opinion is needed. External data may come with its own biases, for example the population that the data is collected from or the reliance on the media to report the events. Expert opinion may be able to adjust for these biases. However, with the additional data it is hoped that there is less error in the estimates generated by the expert.

4.3.3   Evaluate the Risk

The frequency and severity of the consequences are then used in the evaluation. Is the risk within the risk appetite for the activity? If not then a decision is required. Assuming that the individual risk represents an actual or potential breach of the risk appetite, the issue will be escalated and into the information flow on risk.

At this stage it may be appropriate to bring in specialists, such as the corporate risk functions, legal, tax and others to ensure that the consequences have been fully explored. For example, are there any legal issues? How could the risk affect different categories of stakeholders, such as regulators or customers?

4.3.4   Manage the Risk

There are a limited number of management choices which may be used independently or in combination to get the risk to an acceptable level:

- reduce the severity of the event
- reduce the frequency of the event
- transfer/transform the risk
- avoid the risk
- accept the risk.

The objective is not necessarily zero risk, but to take the risks that the firm wants to take in the amount that it wants to take them. Some risk has to be taken to achieve a return. Other risks have to be maintained within appetite. While the firm's risk appetite statement is created at the top of the firm, to be effective it needs to be cascaded down the organisation. This cascade involves allocating different quanta of risk to different activities, businesses, legal entities and locations.

Reduction is an available choice when the risk being considered has not yet materialised, or has materialised and may do so again.

Reduction in the severity of the risk is likely to require investment in controls or a change in the nature of the business. For example, if the risk is of misdirected payments then the management decision could be to have additional controls for payments over a certain size. A reduction in the severity can also be achieved by reducing the exposure. For example, requests to make large payments could be rearranged into a series of smaller transactions. The severity of fraud may be reduced by improving detecting controls so that the event is identified earlier.

Reduction in the frequency of an event may require changes to the business model or the control environment. The control environment changes would primarily be to preventative controls and in some situations detective controls. The choice to reduce the frequency of an event may be linked to amending processes or parameters in processes. For example, reducing the probability of default may require changes to the credit scoring models and use of the outputs.

Transferring the risk may be done, in part, for many consequences. The most traditional form of risk transfer is insurance, which transfers operational risk. Credit derivatives transfer the risk for credit risk, as do securitisations. The equivalent for market risk might involve exchange-traded future contracts with daily margin calls and possible knock-on effects for liquidity risk. This risk transfer is often described as hedging.

The transfer of operational risk, for example to an insurance company, gives rise to contingent credit risk, so this risk reduction tactic increases other risks. If the event occurs, will the insurance company be able to pay? Likewise, hedging other risks may increase credit or liquidity or market or operational risks.

The transformation of one risk into another may not be perfect or a complete transformation. In addition to considering the residual risk, there is the question of whether the risk being increased is still within appetite. If it breaches the appetite of the other risk then the risk transfer/transform is unlikely to be a viable tactic.

Avoiding the risk may require changing the business model or shutting down this business activity altogether. Assuming that the business has been generating revenues then shutting down the business is not a natural first choice for managing the risk.

The last item on the list is to accept the risk. Risk acceptance effectively requires the risk appetite to be increased. The increased risk appetite will require the firm to provide sufficient capital to match the risk, in particular regulatory capital. Owing to correlation effects in the portfolio models, an increase of X in the risk appetite does not necessarily result in an increase of X in the capital.

Which of the above possible actions is undertaken, individually or in combination, requires a degree of cost/benefit analysis. The initial consideration may be the cost of investment in additional controls or changes to the business model upon the near-term P&L.

When there is an increase in capital, whether from a risk acceptance decision or a transformation decision, a return has to be generated on the additional capital. This may encourage the reconsideration of a reduction decision.

Assuming that a decision is made to reduce the severity and/or frequency of the event and the costs can be met, there is then the question of available knowledge. The firm will have only so many project managers and IT programmers. For some resources it may not be possible to find external substitutes amongst the consulting firms. This means that until the project is completed and the new controls established and operating, the firm effectively has to accept the risk.

4.3.5   Monitor and Review the Risk

Having managed the risk it needs to be monitored (to ensure that it does not breach the risk appetite) and included in the upward reporting of risk. The monitoring may not be of the risk itself, but the controls or changes implemented in the risk management stage.

If the risk management actions are not having the desired effect then the risk management cycle returns to the risk identification stage. For example, the residual risk may still not be below the risk appetite or tolerance, after going through the risk management cycle several times.

Monitoring and reviewing the risk may occur continuously, daily, periodically or on an ad hoc basis. An example of daily monitoring is the market risk calculations performed daily. The individual trader will be monitored on a continuous basis. Another example of continuous monitoring is IT security. In comparison, controls linked to the month-end cycle of accounting and financial reports will be periodic. An ad hoc trigger for a particular risk analysis might be media reports that peer organisations have experienced such an event, for example rogue trading.

4.3.6   Escalation and Reporting

The risk appetite will indicate whether something needs to be escalated, and whether it is escalated for information or for decision. The escalation for decision may also be triggered by the cost of additional controls or the impact on the business. This is an activity where bias can have an impact. This is often addressed by perceptive procedures on when something must be escalated and to whom. This may be a point in the process where the corporate risk management functions execute their oversight and challenge roles.

The risk management cycle can be used in a "lessons learned" process. For this process the risk management cycle is used to structure a post-mortem. For efficiency, the post-mortem should be distributed to other businesses and their supporting risk functions for inclusion in the library of possible risks.

The risk information requirements require the risk to be reported even if it is within appetite. This reporting is required so that a comprehensive overview of risk can be obtained, ultimately by the Board members. Although the individual instance of the risk at the bottom of the pyramid may not breach individual appetites or tolerances, the accumulation of the risk up to the middle may breach appetites. This is explored in more detail in the next chapter.

The risk management cycle approach can be applied to the risks that have not yet materialised as well as to events that have materialised. For events that have not yet materialised the process may be described as a scenario. Scenarios can vary in sophistication with the maturity of the scenario process in the firm and also the purpose of the specific scenario. The outcome of the scenario is to provide an indication of what could go wrong, the frequency and severity if it does go wrong and the opportunity to discuss risk management possibilities. A "reverse" scenario asks the business to envisage a sequence of events that could lead to a loss of a specific size, usually quite large.

Scenarios and stress tests are related. The difference between a scenario and a stress test is that the stress test assumes with 100% certainty that the sequence of events will materialise.

4.4   ISSUES TO CONSIDER

- When risk decisions are escalated for resolution are the causes and effects distinguishable?
- Are the direct and indirect consequences clearly identified?
- Are the control and support functions involved in the decision or description of the issue and related recommendations?
- Are the risk management choices presented with commentary on the various costs and benefits?
- If the decision is to "accept the risk" is the impact on the firm's risk appetite taken into account and possible regulatory and/or economic capital implications?

- If the decision is to "accept the risk" will the issue appear on a future agenda in case circumstances have changed and acceptance is no longer appropriate?

FURTHER READING

Borghesi, A. and Gaudenzi, B. (2013) *Risk Management: How to assess, transfer and communicate critical risks.* Springer-Verlag, Berlin.

Chapman, R.J. (2011) *Simple Tools and Techniques for Enterprise Risk Management.* John Wiley & Sons, Chichester.

International Standards Organization (2009) Risk Management – Principles and Guidelines. ISO 3100.

International Standards Organization (2009) Risk Management – Vocabulary. ISO Guide 73.

5

Risk Appetite

Risk Management at the Top					

Ch. 1: Introduction

Part I: Risk Oversight					
Ch. 2: Risk – An Overview	Ch. 3: Risk Oversight	Ch. 4: Risk Management	Ch. 5: Risk Appetite	Ch. 6: Risk Culture

Part II: Specific Risks					
Ch. 7: Credit Risk	Ch. 8: Market Risk	Ch. 9: Operational Risk	Ch. 10: Liquidity Risk	Ch. 11: Other Risks	Ch. 12: Risk Interactions

Part III: Regulatory Environment
Ch. 13: Regulatory Environment

"Risk appetite" is a phrase that has become more popular in recent years. In particular it has been used in describing one of the Board's responsibilities, setting the risk appetite for the firm. However, the concept of risk appetite is not new, even if the phrase is. It is unlikely that a firm will be able to fully express their risk appetite as a single number. The firm may have a more aggressive attitude towards some risks than others, for example risks that generate revenue. Not all of the risks faced by a firm are currently capable of being quantified, for example key man risk.

5.1   INTRODUCTION

The phrases "risk appetite" and "risk tolerance" are relatively recent additions to the dictionary of risk terms. In fact, firms have been practising these concepts for years. They have gained prominence by being mentioned explicitly in various regulatory documents, at national and international level.

Firms have been implying that there should be a limited risk appetite in their oversight and governance frameworks for many years. A recent development has been the increasing formality of the frameworks and linkage to compensation.

Transparency around risk appetite is an important component of the risk culture of a firm.

The rest of this chapter looks at the:

5.2 Terminology and Concept
5.3 Stakeholders
5.4 Expressions of Risk Appetite
5.5 Framework
5.6 Risk Reporting
5.7 Issues to Consider

One of the issues is what the terms mean. Some documents use the terms interchangeably while others refer only to risk tolerance or risk appetite. The issue of terminology is addressed immediately below.

The chapter then considers stakeholders. Since the financial crisis, a diverse range of stakeholders have made their voices heard on risk issues. Because stakeholders are such a diverse group, there may be times when they have conflicting objectives.

Chapter 3 referred to the flow of information up and down the organisation, the Board being at the top of the pyramid and the risk takers at the bottom. Important elements are the metrics used and related risk model inputs that can serve to express limits and appetite at the bottom.

Risk appetite or risk tolerance does not exist in a vacuum, but needs to be related to business activities and decision making. This becomes part of the risk appetite framework. The detailed nature of this framework will be influenced by the maturity of the framework in the firm, the range of risks that the firm takes and key stakeholders.

5.2   TERMINOLOGY AND CONCEPT

Without a consistent terminology there is opportunity for confusion and frustrated dialogue between the Board, the Executive and key stakeholders.

Risk capacity – the maximum quantum of risk that the organisation can bear.

Risk appetite – the amount and type of risk that the organisation is willing to pursue or retain.

The Basel Committee and others recognise that the distinction between risk appetite and risk tolerance may be blurred in practice and definition, so the Basel Committee, and this book, refer to risk appetite. The Basel Committee description of risk appetite is "the level and type of risk that a firm is able and willing to assume in its exposures and business activities, given its business and obligations to stakeholders. It is generally expressed through both quantitative and qualitative means."[1]

Essentially, risk appetite is the amount and type of risk that the firm wants to take in order to achieve its objectives.[2]

Risk appetite is smaller than or equal to risk capacity. Figure 5.1 shows the relationship between risk universe, risk capacity and risk appetite.

A practical consideration is the role of controls. While it may be overly optimistic to assume that all controls work 100% of the time (residual risk), it is also overly pessimistic to assume that the controls never function (inherent risk).

---

[1] Basel Committee on Banking Supervision (January 2013) Principles for Effective Risk Data Aggregation and Risk Reporting, Annex 1 – Terms used in the Document. http://www.bis.org/publ/bcbs239.pdf

[2] Institute of Risk Management (2011) Risk Appetite and Tolerance – Guidance Paper.

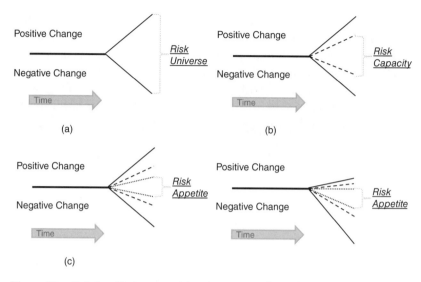

Figure 5.1   Relationship between risk universe, capacity and appetite
Source: Based on Institute of Risk Management (2011) Risk Appetite and Tolerance –
Guidance Paper.

Figure 5.1(a) shows the range of outcomes from the risk universe. In this case the risk universe refers to the extremes of the outcomes from all the possible risk(s) being considered.

Figure 5.1(b) shows that the firm's capacity for risk is within the boundaries determined by the risk universe. This might be from the selection of risk sources or subtypes of the various sources. This can be achieved by avoiding certain risks or reducing the size of the exposure. Additionally, the firm may not have the capability to support larger amounts of risk due to capital or other constraints.

Figure 5.1(c) shows the risk appetite as being smaller than the risk capacity. This difference is usually achieved by further reductions in exposure and combination of the various risks.

The extent to which risk appetite is smaller than risk capacity may be due to a number of factors. One factor may be the need for a buffer in case the controls fail, and/or the need to retain capital for strategic purposes. Other factors include the possibility that the regulators may raise the capital requirement. The buffer can be increased through raising additional capital and retaining earnings. For dividend payments and equity buybacks it may be necessary to obtain approval from regulators, resulting in a reduction in flexibility. There is also the ability to revise the

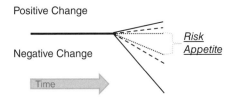

Positive Change

Negative Change

Risk Appetite

Time

Figure 5.2   Risk appetite when outcomes are skewed to the negative

balance sheet assets, for example selling portfolios or disposing of entire businesses globally or in specific locations. For example, some insurance companies have sold portions of pension liabilities to specialist firms.

Figure 5.1(a to c) shows a symmetrical range of outcomes, which is a simplifying assumption. In practice, some risks do not have the possibility of a positive change or it is very small in comparison to a very large negative change, as shown in Figure 5.2. A risk source with this type of distribution of outcomes could be operational risk.

Considerations of risk appetite can be influenced by the duration of a risk source. Some risks may be linked to transactions; however, the transaction can create a position on the firm's balance sheet that may last 30 years, as in the case of a mortgage. Even after the transaction has been completed, and removed from the balance sheet, some risks may persist, for example aspects of taxation.

Firms are likely to have differing degrees of appetite for different sources of risk.

5.3   STAKEHOLDERS

In general, the Board serves as a mechanism to look after the interests of the shareholders as they oversee the activities of the Executive, including risk appetite. The detailed legal responsibilities of the Board, in relation to risk appetite, will vary between jurisdictions. Stakeholders, a diverse group, also have an interest in the risk appetite of the firm (see Table 5.1).

A stakeholder is a person or an organisation that can affect or be affected by or perceive themselves to be affected by a decision or activity of the firm.[3]

---

[3] International Standards Organization (2009) Risk Management – Vocabulary (ISO Guide 73).

Table 5.1 Stakeholders and expectations

Category	Stakeholders	Expectations
Investors	Board	Value growth
	Retail shareholder	Dividends
	Institutional shareholder	Competitiveness
	Bond holder	Business management
	Retail depositor	
	Wholesale depositor	
	Fund manager	
	Equity analyst	
	Bond analyst	
	Rating agency	
	Financial media	
Employees	Executives	Ethical standards
	Current employees	Health & safety
	Potential employees	Employment law &
	Pensioners	regulations
	Contractors	Engagement with unions
	Temporary staff	Pension obligations
	Unions & trade bodies	
Suppliers	Suppliers	Co-operation
	Sales agents & distributors	Prompt payments
	Subcontractors	Adherence to contracts
		Supportive business
		relationships
Customers	Retail customers	Customer satisfaction
	Corporate customers (national)	Quality product/services
	Corporate customers (international)	Perform as expected
	Wholesale market counterparts	
	Product agents & distributors	
	National governments	
	Local governments	
Government & society	National financial industry regulators (home state[a])	Comply with standards Act responsibly
	National financial industry regulators (host state)	Respect stakeholders Good corporate citizenship
	International financial industry regulators	
	Economics/Treasury Ministry	
	NGOs	
	Community/neighbours	
	Media	

[a] The home state is the one regulating the consolidated group. The host state regulates subsidiaries and branches operating in other states. For example, APRA (the Australian regulator) could be a home state regulator whilst the FSA (the UK regulator) could be a host state regulator.

Source: Based on Scandizzo, S. (2011) A framework for the analysis of reputational risk. *Journal of Operational Risk* **6**(3), 41–63 and Chartered Institute of Management Accountants (2007) Corporate Reputation: Perspectives of measuring and managing a principal risk.

There are multiple layers to the stakeholder concept. For example, the Executive are stakeholders as well as making decisions that could affect other stakeholders. This rationale has led to increases in the equity component of the remuneration of the Executive in order to more closely align their interests with those of shareholders and other stakeholders.

Within and between stakeholder categories, the expectations are not always consistent. For example, there may be tension between the shareholders and bond holders over distribution of cash flows generated by the firm. The Economics/Treasury Ministry may want increased lending to small and medium-sized enterprises whilst national regulators want the firm to take less risk or provide more capital to support the same amount of risk.

Since the financial crisis, stakeholders have become more vociferous. This is particularly in relation to risk. Some of this increase in volume arises from various stakeholder groups not appreciating the sources or amount of risk appetite that financial firms were taking, the speed with which things deteriorated and the extent of the deterioration.

Part of the strength of the reaction to the financial crisis can be related to the psychology of risk. For example, individuals are generally more comfortable with risks over which they feel they have a degree of control. This psychological aspect may over-ride data, such as people feeling more comfortable driving a car than sitting in a train, even though fatalities per mile travelled may favour the train. A contributing factor to these preferences is familiarity with the specific risk under consideration.

For the Board, the communication of the risk sources and appetite to stakeholders, and their appreciation, can be challenging. There are disclosures in annual reports, but it is not clear that they are comprehensible to all stakeholders. It may not be clear why the firm is taking risks and their relationships to initial and ultimate objectives, such as dividend payments or customer satisfaction. The stakeholders can be expected to react to this uncertainty, especially if it affects their emotional and economic wellbeing.

A consequence is that the Board has to take into account the expectations of the stakeholders when considering and expressing the risk appetite of the firm. As indicated above, this gets more complicated when there are conflicts between various stakeholders. In turn, this appears to be affecting the basis of corporate governance, possibly moving away from agency theory towards stewardship.

Agency theory, or principal–agency theory, is about the Board representing the shareholders (principals) in their contract with the Executive (agents). The underlying assumption is that the Executive seek to max-imise their own personal benefit to the detriment of the shareholders, so the Board acts as a controlling mechanism.[4] This approach to corporate governance has been established for over 100 years.

Stewardship is a recognition that the Board needs to identify the interests of the wider range of legitimate stakeholders, but that their first obligation is to their shareholders. Any conflicts between stakehold-ers can be addressed via market forces and legislation – employment laws, competition laws, consumer protection laws, etc.[5] The concept of stewardship is still under exploration, alongside other possible concepts underlying corporate governance.

5.4   EXPRESSIONS OF RISK APPETITE

Risk appetite can be expressed using quantitative or qualitative terms. While the firm's risk appetite is set by the Board, there is a need to cascade these concepts down the organisation. Without the cascade it is difficult to ensure that the firm is keeping within the risk appetite set by the Board. As the risk appetite cascades down the organisation it may be necessary for refinement to make the statement relevant to various levels of the organisation. How this cascade and consistency is achieved is a question for the Board to ask the Executive.

5.4.1   Board-level Risk Appetite Considerations

The Board-level risk appetite statement may include some of the fol-lowing references:

- trust
- products/services
- return on equity
- creditworthiness
- resources.

The trust element may refer to all stakeholders or a subset, such as regulators, counterparts and customers. This trust element also implies a

---

[4] Tricker, B. (2012) *Corporate Governance: Principles, Policies & Practices.* Oxford Univer-sity Press, Oxford, p. 60.

[5] Ibid., p. 65.

sustainable business, as without customers or counterparts it is difficult to have an ongoing business.

The reference to products/services links the risk appetite statement to the actual activities of the firm. This may be reinforced by mentioning the volatility of revenues or the pace of new product development. When taken with the trust element, the underlying cross-reference is to mis-selling products to customers.

The return on equity can be mentioned for its meaning within the firm and also for the investor group of stakeholders. Firms using return on equity or return on economic capital as one of their performance metrics now have a link to the risk appetite statement.

The mention of creditworthiness has implications for the amount of capital held by the firm. For example, an "AAA" rated firm has a lower probability of default than an "A" rated firm. This probability of default turns into a confidence interval, such as 99.9% or 99.5%, that is applied to the distribution of risk. For the same risk, the firm with the higher confidence interval will hold more capital. To make the same return on capital, the firm with the higher confidence interval will need to be more efficient to produce higher net profits on the same activity.

The above elements may be expressed in quantitative or qualitative terms. For example, the return on equity might be expressed as "20%" or "commensurate with making a return that is satisfactory to shareholders".

Other aspects of the risk appetite statement can only be expressed qualitatively, for example the relationship with the customer.

5.4.2   Cascading Risk Appetite Down the Firm

For the Board to know that the firm is complying with risk appetite, the language used has to change as the risk appetite is cascaded down the firm (Figure 5.3). The terminology needs to be compatible with the level of the organisation. For example, "treating customers fairly" may translate into the number of customer complaints at the retail branch level.

In practice, this translation of the Board-level risk appetite statement is via policy documents and other statements. The risk policy documents will be reviewed by the Board on a regular basis, for example annually. This inclusion of risk appetite in policy documents – especially for some of the more qualitative risk issues – can be extremely valuable in the cascade down activity. These documents include Human Resources or

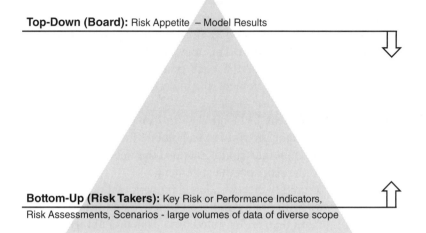

Figure 5.3   Risk appetite perspectives

Personnel manuals that describe sanctions for employee harassment or discriminatory behaviour. Other examples may include the Credit Risk Management manual, or its equivalent, that states no lending to criminal organisations. Another example may be IT policies that describe who is allowed to load software onto company computers. These are all components of risk appetite. At some point the activities prohibited in the policies or manuals may be breached (exceeding the risk appetite), requiring risk management decisions and a governance process to be triggered.

The middle, senior and executive management layers have a complex situation. Depending on the business in which they operate, they may have credit, liquidity, market and operational risk mandates as well as a revenue target to meet. They also have a risk appetite statement from higher up the hierarchy to convert into something appropriate for their reporting lines in terms of metrics and procedures. They need a governance process to enable monitoring adherence to the risk appetite and they need a documented process in case of breaches or excesses.

One of the quantitative expressions of risk appetite is the economic capital number. Overviews of the individual calculations are outlined in Part II. One of the essential features of economic capital is that it reduces the variety of information conveyed upwards through the organisation.

When cascading the top-level risk appetite down through the organisation it needs to be converted into factors that the risk takers can appreciate. Effectively, the models need to be run in reverse and increase the granularity as the information cascades down the organisation. Some of this granularity is provided by reference to non-capital business constraints, for example:

- products (no over-the-counter derivatives) and/or
- clients (only companies over a certain size) and/or
- industry (companies in telecommunications) and/or
- country segments (not subject to anti-money laundering restrictions).

These business constraints may be addressed in divisional or business policies, standards and/or procedures. In effect, the risk appetite is expressed as a combination of a metric and requirements in related documentation.

The commonest example of economic capital is the VaR (Value at Risk) result for market risk. This daily VaR calculation can then be used to monitor actual risk taking with the risk appetite allocated to market risk. Similar concepts can be applied to credit and operational risks. The total VaR figure for the group is likely to be less than the sum of the individual components due to perceived and actual portfolio effects, as measured by correlation. These portfolio effects can be important in the way that risk is managed across the firm, for example, the degree of conservativeness in correlation assumptions behind the portfolio effects within a risk type and between risk types. The most conservative would be to assume that the correlation is perfect, in other words when there is a large risk in credit there is simultaneously a large risk in market and operational risks. However, this may lead to inefficiencies when deploying resources and meeting target returns on equity for the primary stakeholders, the shareholders.

The portfolio effect issue applies at all of the intermediate layers of aggregation up to the top and disaggregation when cascading down to the bottom. At a certain level of granularity the portfolio version of risk appetite may be supplemented by alternative metrics for specific risk types. For example, interest rates in the market risk portfolio might be assessed in terms of 5-year Treasury equivalents, or the P&L impact of a parallel move in interest rates. Where multiple metrics are used to express risk appetite, it needs to be clear which metric is dominant in the event of conflicting messages. For consistency of risk appetite message and cascade down the organisation, it will normally be the portfolio metric that is dominant for credit and market risk. Liquidity and operational risk appetite metrics may be based on other measures.

Although operational risk may be expressed at the top of the organisation in portfolio terms, this is not useful information at the level of the individual risk taker, for example the head of physical security and individuals within that team. In addition, many of the individual operational risks are not within the control of the firm, such as crime. This means that having operational risk mandates, with the same scope and detail as credit or market risk, is generally not practical. The operational risk appetite metric is one that triggers risk management activities, including escalation and risk management decisions. These metrics are more likely to be in the form of loss amounts or performance criteria.

For liquidity risk, a portfolio metric equivalent to economic capital has not yet emerged. As a result, at the risk taker level, alternative metrics are crucial. These metrics may refer to ratios or volumes of assets or liabilities.

Owing to the purpose of portfolio models, to reduce variety, the same economic capital estimate can represent different underlying snapshots of risk. For example, a market risk economic capital estimate could be $Y, at the beginning of the year, with the main risk component being interest rates and later in the year the main component could be equities. As a result, the economic capital figures at the top may be supplemented by the contribution made by components, for example interest rates contribute 60%, equities 30%, commodities 5% and other market risks 5%.

Not all risks or effects experienced by the firm can be expressed in monetary terms; examples include risk to the firm's reputation, or key man. Nonetheless, these are parts of the risk universe to which the firm is exposed.

5.4.3 Dynamic Aspects of Risk Appetite

The discussion so far is largely from a snapshot perspective as opposed to something that evolves over time. This dynamic element is important for the Board as well as the risk taker. For example, a change in the central bank stance on monetary policy and quantitative easing could trigger a change in risk appetite between formal reviews.

At the Board level, the appetite should not be viewed as being constant. The risk appetite represents the Board's perspective at a point in time. If there are economic or political or regulatory or social changes, or a change in stakeholder expectations, then the Board may decide to adjust the risk appetite. This adjustment may not only be in the overall level of risk appetite, but also the allocation between the contributing risk types. These reviews and possible changes need clear and unambiguous dialogue between the Board and the Executive so that the new risk appetite can be cascaded down the firm, causing various changes down the hierarchy to the risk taker.

Some firms were not as badly affected as others by the financial crisis, and a possible factor behind this success could well have been a change in the Board's risk appetite, rather than luck. These changes in risk appetite were then cascaded down the organisation to have the desired effect.

Utilisation of risk appetite by an individual risk taker is dynamic. However, the metric determines the extent of the individual risk taker's control. A metric based on economic capital will express their contribution to the overall riskiness. For market risk the risk taker may have been allocated an appetite or threshold or limit of $M00,000. They are within risk appetite provided the riskiness of their position is less than or equal to $M00,000. However, the amount of risk that the individual risk taker contributes will be influenced by other parts of the market risk portfolio and correlations between the parts. As a result, it is possible for a risk taker's position to exceed their risk appetite not through their actions, but by the actions of others or even changes in correlation. Nevertheless, for risk appetite to serve as a discipline from the top to the bottom of the firm, adherence to the limits and business constraints needs to be maintained. That is not to say that limits may never be breached, but there needs to be a governance process that clearly describes the dominant metric and actions to be followed when there is a breach.

5.5 FRAMEWORK

Some of the preceding comments on risk appetite have mentioned aspects of the framework. For example:

- The risk appetite is not static, but dynamic.
- It may be necessary to use metrics in addition to economic capital contributions.
- Some aspects of risk appetite statements are included in policies.
- There are some sources of risk and effects for which economic capital estimates are not widely accepted, for example liquidity and reputational risks.

This section explores additional features of the appetite framework.

The risk appetite framework does not stand in isolation as the firm has to generate a return on capital and capital is related to risk. For some sources of risk the exposure to these risks is taken deliberately in order to generate a return, while for other risk sources the exposure is generated by having a business. For example, operational risk includes legal risk around contracts and in the case of liquidity risk there is a need to fund assets on a sustainable basis.

For the sources of risk that are deliberately taken to generate a return, various techniques can be applied to support decision making. The goal of the decision making may be to rank alternative uses of resources, such as allocation of risk appetite and available skills, between competing activities and projects. One of the oldest of these tools is the Sharpe ratio,[6] which looks at the excess return less the risk-free return divided by the volatility, σ:

$$\frac{r - r_f}{\sigma}$$

There are a number of variations on this theme in the literature and implemented by firms. The risk-free rate could be the cost of Treasury bills or government bonds, or could be the target rate of return on equity. If it is the target return on equity then this ratio can link into the concept of RAROC and promote consistency in decision making.

One of the issues is an underlying assumption that the returns are symmetrical, that is to say there is an equal opportunity for upside and downside outcomes. In addition, there may be the assumption that returns are normally distributed. This assumption is often embedded in estimates of credit and market risk economic capital. For some risk sources the returns are skewed, particularly on the downside (see Figure 5.4), in other words a loss is more likely than a profit, for example operational risk. For these there are downside ratios to consider, such as the Sortino ratio,[7] which focuses on undesirable outcomes rather than the volatility of returns:

$$\frac{r - t}{d}$$

---

[6] Kemp, M. (2011) *Extreme Events Robust Portfolio Construction in the Presence of Fat Tails.* John Wiley & Sons, Chichester, pp. 104–105.

[7] Sortino, F. and Satchell, S. (2001) *Managing Downside Risk in Financial Markets.* Butterworth-Heinemann, Oxford, p. 63.

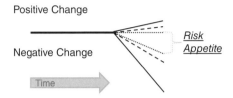

Positive Change

Negative Change

Risk Appetite

Time

Figure 5.4   When outcomes are skewed to the negative

In the Sortino ratio:

r is the expected return,
t is the target or budgeted return and
d is the downside risk – the standard deviation of returns below the
   target.

Some implementations of these ratios replace the volatility denominator with an estimate of the amount of economic capital, for example at the 99% confidence interval. This has the advantage that the denominator can be a portfolio result, for example the amount of credit, market and operational risk, using various correlations and adjustments. The numerator is the dollar return, which may be predominantly from market risk or credit risk or a combination. For the business, the formula requires decisions on managing the downside, especially for risks that do not generate a return, and the costs that entails in comparison with the returns generated.

For some risks, such as operational risk, decisions are needed on mitigation. These decisions may be part of the risk management cycle (see Chapter 4). In the risk management cycle a risk management decision is to reduce the risk or accept the risk. An element of this decision is the cost to reduce the risk as opposed to generating a return on the economic capital allocated for the accepted risk.

Some non-financial industries may use the concept of ALARP (as low as reasonably practicable). For these industries operational risk is a large, potentially dominant, contributor to their total risk profile. For the financial sector an issue will be distinguishing the risks whose consequences are met from cash flow, for example expected losses (in a non-statistical sense) as opposed to those residual accepted risks that contribute to the economic capital. The "reasonably practical" element includes the return on capital. For example, if the risk reduction went ahead, what would be the imputed reduction in economic capital assuming that the released economic capital could be deployed and make a return equivalent to the target return on economic capital, for example 20% p.a. A change in the target return on economic capital will influence the number of risk reduction projects. These interactions can be seen in the Sortino ratio.

The portfolio approach of the above Sortino ratio can be applied at various levels of the organisation. However, at the most granular levels to which risk appetite is cascaded there are issues of how to use metrics to express the downside risk. For example, when operational risk appetite is expressed as the volume of settlement fails or the number of complaints from retail customers, can these be used in the Sortino ratio? Not directly, but by reference to expected losses they can still be included in cost/benefit calculations that underlie ALARP.

The implication of the Sortino ratio and ALARP is that there is some level of return that can be used to justify taking any risk. However, the discussion on cascading risk appetite down the firm provides the possibility of establishing zero tolerances for some risks. The use of zero-tolerance risks particularly applies to operational risk. For example, if the Board-level risk appetite statement refers to establishing trust with stakeholders (including clients) then this can be translated into a zero tolerance for mis-selling. As the selling process involves people and judgement, zero tolerance does not mean that mis-selling will never happen. Zero tolerance means that there is an extensive control framework and that if there is an event then risk mitigation actions are taken to manage the consequences and further reduce the likelihood that it will materialise in the future. In cost/benefit calculations it may be desirable to amend the target return parameters for zero-tolerance risks to enable using the same decision support tools for all risk issues and motivating decisions to support taking certain risks in certain amounts.

Ultimately, risk appetite is part of a portfolio optimisation problem. Which combination of risk sources and in what amounts will most likely enable the firm to meet its return on book capital targets while keeping within regulatory capital constraints? Unlike an investment portfolio, the Board is integrating different sources of risk that have equal, or near equal, desirable and undesirable outcomes (credit and market risk), with those that are predominantly undesirable (liquidity and operational risks). There are those sources of risk over which the firm can choose the amount of risk with some accuracy and other sources of risk where external factors are the main drivers. For some of these risk sources a change in the amount of risk can be relatively quick, for example over

12 months, and for others a much longer time frame is needed. Some of these features will become more transparent in Part II.

5.6 RISK REPORTING

Reporting on risk is to enable a comparison between the current state, or a projection into the future, with the risk appetite. There are two main users of this data, the risk owners and the corporate risk functions. The requirements of reporting change between the bottom of the firm, the middle and the top of the firm (Figure 5.5).

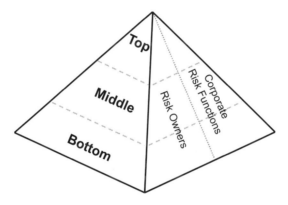

Figure 5.5   Users of risk reports

The different users of reports are based on the different information needs from the top to the bottom of the firm and the risk owners as opposed to the corporate risk functions. Internal audit, the third line of defence, is not included in this diagram as they tend to use reports as an element to be tested during their periodic audit.

In addition to the users there is also a spectrum on the content of the reports. As a minimum the reports say "something is being done" (Figure 5.6) and these reports may be rich in data, requiring interpretation by the report recipient. Some of these reports have pages of numbers

Figure 5.6   Spectrum of risk report content

and raise the fundamental question of "what am I supposed to look at?" These data-intense reports may be most suitable for the bottom of the pyramid; they probably contain KRI data that is aligned with certain activities, for example number of payments made.

In the middle of the spectrum are reports that convey the status quo and enable identification of changes in patterns. Owing to the amount of information these reports can be very visual, making extensive use of heat maps and other techniques to portray the data. For reports that are seen frequently, for example monthly, these intense reports work well as they convey a great deal of information. However, when the reports are seen quarterly or less frequently then the sophistication can interfere with the understanding. More time and effort is spent on trying to understand the report than comprehending its actual message.

At the other extreme are reports that focus on decisions. These reports are often destined for the top of the firm, whether executive management, risk committees or the Board. The focus of these reports can be descriptions of excesses, or changes in risk profiles or emerging risks. In addition to the information data content there may also be comments on implications and recommendations.

The risk owner at the bottom wants sufficient information that they can identify implications for meeting objectives. The objectives might be staying below risk appetite or losses that will reduce the likelihood of meeting revenue targets. This sort of report will include granular KRIs and related metrics. One way of providing focus is to have a traffic light colour scheme – red, amber and green. What constitutes red will be linked, explicitly or implicitly, to the risk appetite. The boundaries between red and amber can be part of the oversight and challenge role of the corporate risk functions. Red means that action is needed. The action may be to get a better understanding of the issue: is it a one-off event or something that will persist? The data used in these reports can be used to identify changes in risk over time.

As the data and information move towards the middle there is a need for aggregation. This is also where the richness of the data begins to diminish as part of the reporting process. The need for aggregation involves combining the same data from different units. This is where the search for patterns and changes in risk profile begins. For two units, reporting into the middle, are their risk profiles the same or are they different? Why should they be the same or different? These are questions that the risk owners and corporate risk functions can ask each other.

As the data continues to be aggregated towards the top of the firm, so its use starts to change. The data is viewed through tactical and strategic lenses. The relationship to the firm's risk appetite becomes more transparent. Questions such as return on economic capital start to be asked. This can be followed up by queries about how the business can be so profitable in relation to the risks being captured. Are any major risks missing from the risk reports? There have been occasions when "riskless arbitrage" has provided expensive/catastrophic lessons on risks that were not captured by the risk reports, as in the case of Barings.

At the top of the firm the risk committees, CRO and group heads of various risk functions will be seeing risk reports regularly. For this group the information content can be sophisticated. However, for this group information needs to be added to the reports so that focus can be directed. How are the topics for attention determined? Some topics will relate to the risk appetite, changes in risk profile and emerging risks. The selection of topics is made by people, so bias may be present in the line-up of issues. This is also the level at which an understanding of the business activities is needed. The mathematical components of these reports need to be supplemented by common sense and judgement.

The risk reports to the Board are the most aggregated and contain the least variety of information. Regular reports may focus entirely on economic capital metrics. Some reports will focus on decisions, for example changing the risk appetite or the impact of strategic decisions on risk appetite. These reports will be provided by the risk committees and/or the CRO and originate from group heads of various risk functions.

An additional category of reports, for the top, will be the results of stress tests and scenarios. The stress tests and scenarios may be specified at the top or by regulators. The stress test or scenario may be narrowly based, for example a reduction in market trading volumes, or Internet failure to Asia. On other occasions the stress tests or scenarios can be broadly based, as for a downturn in the economy and the impact across credit, market, liquidity and operational risks and interactions between them. These reports will include comments about potential consequences and decisions. In extreme versions the reports will include the recovery and resolution plans ("Living Wills"), which will probably focus on legal entities and subsidiaries in various jurisdictions.

The reports for the top can range in scope from solo to regional to consolidated. The solo reports are by legal entity. The solo top-level reports may be required by local regulators. For the group risk committees the scope, most usually, will be the consolidated group. Owing to potentially offsetting positions within the group, the sum of individual solo reports may show higher risks as there are fewer portfolio effects. This difference between solo and consolidated risk will affect the distribution of capital around legal entities within the same group.

There are still some technical and methodology challenges. The above model of risk reporting works for large volumes of data with or without a mathematical model, such as economic capital. However, there are risks which are difficult to model and therefore aggregate across businesses and locations. These risks may include staff resources, such as the knowledge needed to provide effective challenge, exercise oversight and advise or coach businesses. How could key man risk be aggregated and escalated? These risks can still be assessed and monitored, but they are unlikely to fit into a mathematical model.

A significant role of these risk reports is to inform and influence decisions. The management information systems to collect and aggregate the data and then the manpower to add information is expensive. In the case of some firms during the financial crisis, poor risk management information systems may have contributed to their demise. A consequence is that the regulators expect to see evidence that this information is being used in decisions from top to bottom to top again; this is the "use test".

5.7   ISSUES TO CONSIDER

- What is the current Board-level risk appetite statement?
- When was the Board-level risk appetite statement last reviewed?
- When was the Board-level risk appetite statement last changed?
- How does the risk appetite statement compare with those of peers and competitors? Where and why does it differ?
- Does the Board-level risk appetite statement need to be revised to facilitate cascade down the organisation?
- Is the Board-level risk appetite statement intelligible to the majority of stakeholders?
- How is the Board-level risk appetite allocated amongst the major risk types – credit, liquidity, market and operational?
- How is the risk appetite cascaded down the organisation?
- How are the risk appetite metrics aggregated up the organisation?
- How do the risk committees and the Board satisfy themselves that the risk reports are accurate?

- Is it transparent for which risks or events there is zero tolerance?
- Is there evidence that the risk appetite statement is effective? For example, has it resulted in amendments to change programmes such as new products, new projects and (re)consideration of outsourcing. Has it influenced strategic or tactical decisions?
- At what point are excesses escalated to the Board/risk committees? How are they escalated to the Board? What decision did the Board take last time an excess was escalated, for example increase the risk appetite or raise additional capital?
- If profits are above target how does the risk appetite respond? Is there more risk taking because there is additional capacity or less to protect the achieved returns?
- When did internal audit last provide feedback on the risk governance framework, not just on adherence to policies and procedures?

FURTHER READING

Chartered Institute of Management Accountants (2007) Corporate Reputation: Perspectives of measuring and managing a principal risk.

European Banking Authority (September 2011) Guidelines on Internal Governance. http://eba.europa.eu/cebs/media/Publications/Standards%20and%20Guidelines/2011/EBA-BS-2011-116-final-(EBA-Guidelines-on-Internal-Governance)-(2)_1.pdf

Financial Stability Board (February 2013) Thematic Review on Risk Governance: Peer Review Report. http://www.financialstabilityboard.org/publications/r_130212.pdf

Institute of Risk Management (2011) Risk Appetite and Tolerance – Guidance Paper.

International Standards Organization (2009) Risk Management – Principles and Guidelines. ISO 31000.

International Standards Organization (2009) Risk Management – Vocabulary. ISO Guide 73.

Kemp, M. (2011) *Extreme Events Robust Portfolio Construction in the Presence of Fat Tails*. John Wiley & Sons, Chichester.

Sachs, S., Rühli, E. and Kern, I. (2009) *Sustainable Success with Stakeholders: The Untapped Potential*. Palgrave Macmillan, London.

Scandizzo, S. (2011) A framework for the analysis of reputational risk. *Journal of Operational Risk* **6**(3), 41–63.

Sortino, F. and Satchell, S. (2001) *Managing Downside Risk in Financial Markets*. Butterworth-Heinemann, Oxford.

Tricker, B. (2012) *Corporate Governance: Principles, Policies & Practices*. Oxford University Press, Oxford.

6

Risk Culture

"Risk culture" is a phrase that has been mentioned often in recent years. There is some uncertainty as to its meaning and scope, but this is gradually being resolved. Risk culture is an element of organisational culture as it focuses on risk and its management. Implicitly or explicitly, all firms have a risk culture.

At its simplest, risk culture influences what individuals do with regard to risk when the situation is not covered by policies or procedures or "nobody is watching". Firms in the financial sector have extensive documentation on risk policies and procedures, so risk culture can be important even when the requirements are documented but unread or forgotten.

The aim of risk culture is for the right people to do the right thing (behaviour) at the right time regardless of circumstances. What the "right thing" is will be influenced by explicit statements of corporate values, and/or purpose and/or risk appetite.

6.1 INTRODUCTION

Risk culture is an aspect of the wider corporate culture. Top-level statements on risk culture need to be consistent with and supportive of descriptions of the organisation's values, purposes and risk appetite. Inconsistency reinforces the opportunity for confusion and surprises. For example, mentioning "sustainable shareholder return", as part of the group level risk appetite statement, indicates that some short-term decisions may be incompatible with longer-term profits and dividends.

The top-level risk culture statement needs to be made by the Board. This statement then needs to cascade down the organisation to influence the local version of risk culture and across the three lines of defence. Various levers can be used to reinforce the risk culture. Most of these levers are part of the risk oversight framework, for example the risk appetite.

When the risk culture is ineffective or inappropriate, the outcome is inappropriate decisions and behaviours by individuals leading to surprises for senior management and the Board. The effects and consequences of this behaviour can include:

- reputational risk, loss of trust from key stakeholders;
- adverse impact on credit risk ratings;
- difficulty in obtaining funds or increased costs;
- increased cost of capital;
- loss of talented staff;
- inability to attract talented staff.

Other consequences of inappropriate risk cultures are provided by Banks.[1]

With possible indirect and direct consequences, such as rogue trading, the regulators have an ongoing interest in the risk culture of a firm. Basel emphasises the role of the Board in establishing a strong risk management culture.[2] Other international regulators also have clear expectations that risk culture encourages the understanding and management of risks.[3]

When the firm has an appropriate risk culture, sustainable competitive advantages are likely to accrue. Some of these advantages include the prompt escalation of issues, increased resilience and reduced attention from the regulators.

The rest of this chapter looks at the:

6.2 Terminology
6.3 Assessing and Influencing Risk Culture
6.4 Monitoring Risk Culture
6.5 Issues to Consider

The relationship between risk appetite and risk culture can be described as symbiotic. The existence of a risk appetite statement at the top of the firm, which is then cascaded down the firm, reinforces the risk culture. The risk culture encourages adherence to the spirit of risk appetite beyond the words on a piece of paper (Figure 6.1).

Figure 6.1   Relationship between risk appetite and culture

---

[1] Banks, E. (2012) *Risk Culture: A Practical Guide to Building and Strengthening the Fabric of Risk Management*. Palgrave Macmillan (Table 5.1) © 2012 Erik Banks. Reproduced by permission of Palgrave Macmillan.

[2] Basel Committee on Banking Supervision (June 2011) Principle 1: Fundamental principles of operational risk management.

[3] European Banking Authority (September 2011) Part C: Risk Management, Section 20: Risk Culture.

6.2 TERMINOLOGY

"Risk culture" is a relatively recent addition to the lexicon of risk. As a result, a common understanding of its scope and implications is still being developed. Nonetheless, as mentioned in the Introduction, changes to risk culture are being required by regulators and society and being implemented by firms.

6.2.1 Definitions and Descriptions of Risk Culture

Risk culture, a component of organisational culture, embodies an inter-active system of values and normative behaviours.[4]

Risk culture can be defined as the norms and traditions of behaviour of individuals and of groups within an organisation that determine the way in which they identify, understand, discuss, and act on the risk that the organisation confronts and the risks it takes.[5]

Risk culture is the system of values and behaviours present throughout an organisation that shape risk decisions. Risk culture influences the decisions of management and employees, even if they are not consciously weighing risks and benefits.[6]

Risk culture is the norms of behaviour for individuals and groups within an organisation that determine the collective ability to identify and understand, openly discuss and act on the organisation's current and future risks.[7]

Risk management culture concerns the tone setting and ethical environment in place at all levels. These touch upon lines of reporting, internal and external risk management communications and policies that reinforce risk management. "It's critical to possess a risk culture in which the right people do the right thing at the right time regardless of circumstances. No matter how sophisticated the systems or controls, the underlying culture must be committed to ethical decision-making."[8]

---

[4] Banks, E. (2012) p. 22. Towers & Perrin (2008) Assessing your company's risk culture.

[5] Institute of International Finance (2009) Reform in the Financial Services Industry: Strengthening Practices for a More Stable System.

[6] KPMG (2009) Never Again? Risk Management in Banking beyond the Credit Crisis.

[7] Levy, C., Lamarre, E. and Twinning, J. (February 2010) Taking control of organisational risk culture. McKinsey Working Papers on Risk, No. 16.

[8] Extracted from 'Point of View' (December 2008) by PricewaterhouseCoopers LLP (US), http://www.pwc.com/us/en/point-of-view/enterprise-risk-management-standard-poors.jhtml. Reproduced by permission of PricewaterhouseCoopers.

Risk culture begins with fostering an open dialogue where every employee in the organisation has some level of ownership of the organisation's risks, can readily identify the broader impact of local decisions and is rewarded for identifying outsize risk to senior levels. In such cultures, strategic decision making routinely includes a review of relevant risks and alternative strategies rather than a simple return on investment analysis.[9]

Risk culture is the values, beliefs, knowledge and understanding about risk, shared by a group of people with a common purpose.[10]

Some of the common threads running through these definitions and descriptions are:

- behaviour and decisions
- individuals
- groups
- values
- tradition.

Risk culture influences behaviour at a conscious and/or subconscious level. Risk culture influences individuals in the decisions that they make and their subsequent activities. The intangible direction, provided by risk culture, is needed because not every possible risk or circumstance can be described in policies and procedures. Even if all possible risks and circumstances could be described, the documentation would then be so large that it would guarantee that few would read all of it.

Risk culture provides direction to individuals as they make decisions. The aim should be to have every decision made with implicit or explicit reference to risk and the firm's perspective on risk. These decisions are made by individuals in the context of their own experience, biases, values (including ethics), understanding and knowledge.

Decisions are seldom made by individuals without reference to the broader environment, often provided by groups. These groups can be composed of task- or function-related colleagues as well as informal networked contacts across the organisation. The risk culture of these groups can often influence the decision made by an individual. It is possible for the risk subculture, exhibited by a group through actions

---

[9] Dreyer, S.J. (June 2010) Standard & Poor's looks further into how non-financial companies manage risk.

[10] The Institute for Risk Management (2012) Risk Culture: Resources for practitioners. http://www.theirm.org/RiskCulture.html

of its members, to be inconsistent with the risk culture as espoused at the top of the firm. An example is the apparent manipulation of LIBOR rates. In this case the norms and traditions of behaviour exhibited by a very small number of people resulted in reputational damage and had an impact on retaining and attracting talented staff.

All firms and groups within firms have an explicit or implicit risk culture. For somebody joining a particular function this risk culture can be described as "this is the way that we do it around here" or "that is acceptable here". Effectively these are the norms and traditions of the particular group.

Events have identified that the risk culture displayed by some groups is inconsistent with the organisation's risk culture as intended by the Board and senior management. Improving this consistency is one of the tasks being undertaken by firms.

6.2.2   Expressions of Risk Culture

We commit to a culture that aligns risks and rewards, attracts and develops talented individuals, fosters teamwork and partnership, and is sensitive to the society in which we operate.[11]

Create a culture of risk awareness and personal responsibility throughout the firm where collaboration, discussion, escalation and sharing of information are encouraged.[12]

Barclays risk culture is based on a close alignment with our businesses to support understanding, trust and openness together with clear independence to ensure strong challenge, rigorous, analytical and objective decision making and consistency across the bank. Risk is a shared responsibility between business and risk teams with the business operating as a 'first line of defence'.[13]

Other firms do not necessarily have an explicit risk culture statement, but they may have statements underlying the principles by which they conduct business. In this context the focus is not solely upon the client, but includes teamwork and the individual.[14]

---

[11] Deutsche Bank Annual Report for 2012, p. 26.

[12] JP Morgan Chase Annual Report for 2012, p. 123.

[13] Barclays Annual Report for 2012, p. 314. Reproduced by permission of Barclays Bank Group plc.

[14] Goldman Sachs Business Standards Committee Impact Report: "The Goldman Sachs Business Principles".

A strong risk culture[15] requires awareness, at all levels of the firm, of the impact of risk – desirable or undesirable – and where it fits into the various business models. For example, it may be inappropriate for cash equity traders to take credit risk and similarly it may be inappropriate for commercial lending officers to take equity market risk. Essentially this is about which risks to take and how much to take, effectively the firm's risk appetite.

Risk culture is heavily influenced by the "tone from the top" and behaviours exhibited by the Board, executives and management. These behaviours are highly visible to the rest of the organisation and will be adopted by others. This is especially true when responding to inappropriate behaviours.

Strong risk cultures are not rigid, but have a degree of flexibility. The issue is identifying risks and escalating them to the right organisational level for a quick decision. These risks can present revenue-generating opportunities. If the decision making is slow then individuals may prefer to take the initiative themselves and "ask for forgiveness" later, when it is often too late.

The risk management functions need to be seen and treated as partners of the business. The objective is to get the business done within the firm's risk appetite. For this to happen the risk management functions need to be viewed and treated as partners with the business, and not as a function that only likes to say "No". In turn this means that the risk management functions need to have an understanding of the business and the business model. This partnership requires the free flow of information:

- between the business and the risk management functions,
- between businesses, and
- between risk management functions.

The different roles and responsibilities need to be clearly understood and appreciated. For example, if the business keeps escalating a decision until it gets the answer that it wants, then the wrong message is sent on the partnership, roles and accountabilities between the business and the risk management functions.

These features of a strong risk culture need to be obvious and reinforced not only in tough business conditions, but also during better times. This reinforcement helps to ensure that the risk culture is

---

[15] Banks, p. 31.

embedded in the firm and not turned on or off, giving rise to uncertainty as to how individuals are expected to behave.

If the intention is a strong risk culture, how do weak risk cultures arise? These are some of the warning signs that the risk culture is weakening:[16]

- Risk issues are ignored at the top of the firm, including the Board.
- Inconsistent messages on business activities and risk management.
- Displaying overconfidence in risk management skills.
- Following the herd on business strategy.
- Reliance upon bureaucratic or committee decision making on risks.
- Weaknesses in the three lines of defence.
- Under-investing in the control structure – resources and information systems.
- Lack of relationship between risk and compensation.
- Use of outdated policies and rules.
- Blame culture when things go wrong or "shoot the messenger".

While risk culture is a phenomenon of teams, groups, functions and organisations it is influenced by the attitude and behaviour of individuals.

6.2.3   The Individual

The Institute of Risk Management[17] puts significant emphasis on the individual and their characteristics and their contribution to the firm's risk culture. For the individual, their risk culture is the consequence of interactions between several layers of influence (Figure 6.2).

At the core is the predisposition of the individual towards risk at one point in time. For individuals, this predisposition may vary with their own circumstances, such as age, experience and consequences from getting it wrong. As with other aspects of personality there are techniques to assess predisposition, for example the risk compass.[18]

The risk compass has the categories listed in Table 6.1.

There are two aspects of the risk compass (Figure 6.3). The first is that individuals can exhibit attributes against all points on the compass, but to varying extents along a scale.

---

[16] Banks, p. 67.

[17] The Institute of Risk Management (2012) Risk Culture – Resources for Practitioners, p. 16. Reproduced by permission of The Institute of Risk Management.

[18] The Risk Type Compass is reproduced by permission of Psychological Consultancy Ltd and the Institute of Risk Management (2012) Risk Culture – Resources for Practitioners, p. 29.

Figure 6.2 Influences on risk culture of an individual
Source: The Institute of Risk Management (2012) Risk Culture – Resources for Practitioners, Figure 2.1.

Table 6.1 Points on the risk compass

Wary	Very low risk tolerance
	Likely to be self-disciplined, cautious, uneasy and conservative. Ultra-sensitive about vulnerability to risk, they are zealous and fervently seek control.
Prudent	Low risk tolerance
	Likely to be detailed/organised, systematic and conscientious. Primary concern is to bring order to everything and to eliminate risk and uncertainty.
Intense	Low risk tolerance
	Likely to be ardent, anxious, edgy and passionate. They invest passionately in people and projects, but are haunted by the fear of disappointment.
Deliberate	Average risk tolerance
	Likely to be analytical, investigative, calm and business-like. Calculated and sure-footed, they test the ground and never go into anything unprepared.
Spontaneous	Average risk tolerance
	Likely to be excitable, unpredictable, enthusiastic and impulsive. They are attracted to the idea of spontaneity and risk, may regret hasty decisions.
Composed	High risk tolerance
	Likely to be cool-headed, self-contained and imperturbable. Strangers to anxiety and oblivious to risk.
Adventurous	Very high risk tolerance
	Likely to be uninhibited, fearless, challenging and venturesome. Both fearless and impulsive, they are prepared to try things that no-one else has tried.

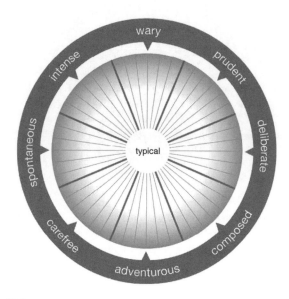

Figure 6.3   Risk compass

The second aspect is that the risk compass of a department or team can be described from the positions of the individuals in the department or team. Ideally, not everybody in a team should have the same strengths. Further, different teams need to exhibit different emphases on the risk compass due to the nature of their tasks. For example, the profile of internal audit should be different from trading. Internal audit is expected to exhibit prudence as a strong or even dominant category, whilst for trading it might be spontaneous or composed. Which points on the risk compass should dominate the Board profile?

6.2.4   Groups and Teams

Having identified that individuals are the building blocks of teams and groups, so their exhibited attitudes and repeated behaviours influence the risk culture.[19]

In this context attitude refers to the "chosen position adopted by an individual or group in relation to a given situation, influenced by perception". Perception includes assumptions made by the individual(s)

---

[19] The A–B–C culture model is copyright © 2009 Risk Doctor & Partners Limited, and is reproduced by permission of Hillson (2009), The Institute of Risk Management (2012) and Gower, Risk Culture – Resources for Practitioners, p. 22.

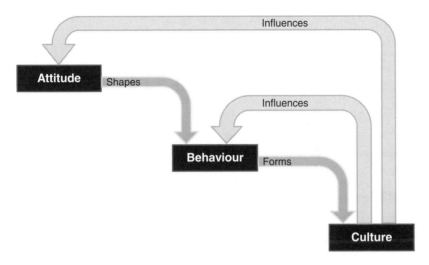

Figure 6.4   Attitude–behaviour–culture model

as to what is the right thing to do. For example, assessing a short-term gain, possibly to the detriment of the counterparty or the employer, versus considering longer-term factors such as building relationships and trust for a sustainable business.

Behaviour comprises external observable actions, including decisions, processes and communications. The focus is upon decision making, generally of issues other than the business as usual type. For example, how is harassment in the office managed? How are customers viewed and treated when there is a bona fide dispute? These observable individual decisions and their communication form the risk culture.

Figure 6.4 shows the feedback loops between attitude, behaviour and culture. Of these three components, culture is the least tangible. As a result, amending risk culture will need to start with changes in attitude and behaviour.

Within each group, team or function there will be a leader. In this context the leader can be interpreted as the individual that others in the group look towards for attitude and behaviour. The leader is usually the organisationally most senior person, not necessarily the oldest, and not necessarily the highest paid in the team.

The influence of the leader can be seen by amending Figure 6.4. The attitude of the leader will influence the behaviour of other team members and the behaviour of the leader will influence their risk culture. See

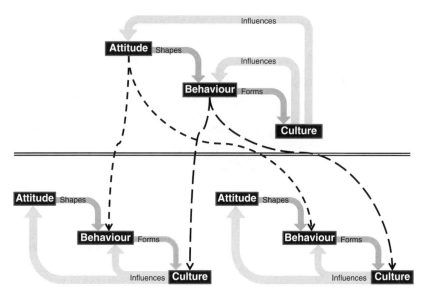

Figure 6.5   Attitude–behaviour–culture model for teams

Figure 6.5. Some of this linkage is due to implicit assumptions about success and activities that lead to success.

The attitude and behaviour of the leader will establish the group norms of behaviour. The leader will also be part of a team, for example a team of team managers, product managers, branch managers and so on. Taking this team concept to the extreme, the CEO and the Board form the most senior team in the organisation.

With this recursive view of attitude, behaviour and culture the importance of "tone at the top" becomes evident in determining and influencing the organisation's risk culture.

6.3   ASSESSING AND INFLUENCING RISK CULTURE

This section describes the assessment and then how to influence risk culture. What are the aspects or features that describe the current risk culture in various parts of the organisation? Having determined the current risk culture, how can it be changed to something more desirable? A desirable risk culture is influenced by the expectations of regulators, wider society, customers, shareholders and employees.

Table 6.2   Risk culture indicators

Tone at the top	Risk leadership
	Dealing with bad news
Governance	Accountability and governance
	Risk transparency
Competency	Risk resources
	Risk skills
Decision making	Informed risk decisions
	Rewarding appropriate risk taking

6.3.1   Assessing Risk Culture

In terms of indicators of risk culture, "tone at the top" is considered to be one of four major themes (Table 6.2).[20]

These themes and issues can be extended to form a scorecard with grades. The grades may be in the form of red–amber–green or a numeric scale. To be effective, the values on the scale need to have related behaviours clearly stated. For example, "dealing with bad news" may involve not only the timely escalation of the news, but also having an associated "lessons learned" communication to reinforce the value of the escalation and prevent the same bad news having to be reported in the future.

With these scorecards an issue is how they should be used. For example, should individuals be assessed based on the sum of the indicators? The summation could be weighted, for example are some themes more important at some organisational levels than others? One of the experiences with such scorecard models based on totals is the possibility of offsetting a weakness in one indicator with a strength in another. For example, this may mean that somebody might use strong risk leadership skills to offset poorly informed risk decisions. A consequence of linking the indicators to the exhibited behaviours and the organisation's risk culture may be considering each indicator in isolation.

The risk culture of an organisation can be mapped using two dimensions: "governance spirit" and "pressure to conform".[21] The "governance spirit" refers to shared organisational goals and common meanings for what it is trying to achieve (Figure 6.6). The "pressure to

---

[20] The Institute of Risk Management (2012), p. 72. Reproduced by permission of The Institute of Risk Management.

[21] Ibid., p. 25.

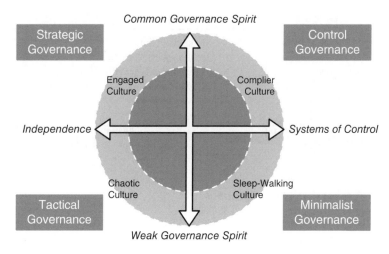

Figure 6.6   Risk aspects of risk culture

conform" includes the "buy in" to a common set of behaviours and how the organisation incentivises the adoption of shared meanings.

The control governance places particular emphasis on rules and systems to enforce those rules. For businesses that are very mature, and possibly automated, this style of governance may be appropriate. Corporate governance does not encourage questions but does encourage compliance. At an organisational level the risk is likely to be rare, but severe when it does arise. The severity arises from the likelihood of a rule being incorrect and having been followed for thousands or even millions of transactions.

The strategic governance involves challenge of the way that things are done. This can lead to continual improvements and adjustment of risk appetite in response to the internal and/or external environment. However, to be effective, this places an emphasis on high levels of competence – risk resources and risk skills – across the organisation.

Given the size and complexity of some financial firms it is possible that the entire organisation is on the spectrum between control governance and strategic governance. Where an individual part of the organisation is (or should be) on the spectrum can be influenced by aspects such as the maturity of the business model and the nature of the products or services involved. When a business is in the entrepreneurial stage then strategic is preferable to control governance. Likewise, a business that is offering highly customised service will probably find control governance sub-optimal.

A more formal link between risk culture and the organisation's activities can be found in the enterprise risk maturity evaluation.[22] The evaluation uses three lenses: professional/technical, managerial and social. The professional/technical lens considers the firm as a micro-economy and focuses upon aspects such as accountability and governance and the business model. Managerial considers the firm as an industrial system with aspects such as informed risk decisions, risk transparency (systems and controls), risk resources and skills and the free flow of information within and between businesses and risk management functions. The social lens considers the social aspects of the firm, for example risk leadership, dealing with bad news and rewarding appropriate risk taking.

These three lenses can be used to perform an evaluation of the enterprise risk maturity by scoring each lens and multiplying the results. For example, see Table 6.3.

Table 6.3   Enterprise risk maturity evaluation

	Professional/ technical	Managerial	Social
Optimise (3)	Business model designed to create value	Continuous optimising to create sustainable value	Systemically aware, value-creating collaboration
Improve (2)	Sales forces "push" product/service into the market	Continuous process improvement to de-risk product/ service delivery	Clearly defined process and improvement strategy, effective team work
Standardise (1)	Control by squeezing budgets	Standardise and maintain status quo	Command and control maintains hierarchy and status
Degenerate (0)	Serve my own interests and move on within the firm or change firms	Degenerate, politicised with in-fighting that fragments communication and risk view of the firm	Public and private statements are inconsistent

---

[22] The Enterprise Risk Maturity Evaluation is reproduced with permission from Consulting People Ltd and Institute of Risk Managers (2012). The Institute of Risk Management (2012) Risk Culture – Resources for Practitioners, p. 46.

The maximum possible score is 27 (3×3×3). However, if the situation for any one of the lenses is degenerate then the score is zero. This severe response is justified by the implications of having a degenerate ranking, for example increased likelihood of a crisis, slower escalation of risk issues up the organisation and even people leaving the firm to protect their own personal reputations.

For large complex organisations it may be appropriate to apply the enterprise maturity risk evaluation to business lines or regions and possibly drill down the organisation further.

6.3.2   Influencing Risk Culture

Having identified that there is a gap between the desired and prevailing risk cultures, a change project is needed. The duration of the project will be long to produce a common risk culture. The project cannot begin in a vacuum, for example there needs to be an existing risk management framework that can be used to monitor change and the related communication channels up and down the organisation.

A number of "imperatives"[23] have been identified that can be reviewed, amended and/or reinforced as part of the change project:

1. Defining a common risk philosophy.
2. Formalising the risk appetite.
3. Assigning accountability.
4. Developing appropriate incentives.
5. Building operational sophistication.
6. Rotating personnel.
7. Recruiting from outside the firm.
8. Establishing the right tone at the top.
9. Ensuring adequate risk skills and resources.
10. Ensuring proper business expertise.
11. Reinforcing communication, coordination and cooperation.
12. Demanding common sense, simplicity and clarity.
13. Building credibility.
14. Promoting mutual respect.
15. Developing a corporate risk memory.

---

[23] Banks, pp. 102–141.

The common risk philosophy will probably exist, for example as a listing of the firm's values, vision or business standards. As part of this philosophy there may be a statement about the businesses in which the firm wishes to be involved. Since the financial crisis and the regulatory reaction, there have been extensive examinations of the business portfolio and the relative importance of the individual businesses. Often statements about the risk philosophy will be published, for example in the annual report or as standalone documents. When combined with the risk appetite it should be clear to all stakeholders the amount of risk that the firm wishes to take, and how this amount is distributed across the different risks in the different businesses.

The assignment of accountability includes the three lines of defence and the allocation of various authorities. The three lines of defence concept has clear responsibilities for the business, the risk management functions and internal audit. While the total firm risk appetite may be set by the Board, it needs to be cascaded down the organisation to reach the various risk takers using terminology that they can understand. This accountability also includes the role of various committees at various levels down and across the organisation.

Developing appropriate incentives has undergone major change in the past few years. There is more attention on the total risks involved in generating a given return and whether the return is sustainable. Similarly, less emphasis is now put on cash and more on equity as part of incentive payments to more closely align the interests of the management with the owners of the firm. (This trend began before the financial crisis, but has accelerated since.) The concepts of deferral and claw-back are also part of this alignment with the firm's owners and recognition that actions today may have consequences several years ahead.

In the scheme of appropriate incentives the role of risk management should not be forgotten. Like the business, they need to focus on the longer-term consequences. However, their incentives should be separate from an individual business to prevent "capture" by a business and consideration of the bigger total firm picture.

Operational sophistication refers to the organisational structure and clarity over governance. To make risk governance work, the risk function needs to have a prominent profile within the firm. The foundation of this imperative is relevant, reliable and timely data. This data then needs a minimum IT infrastructure to make it useful in a timely fashion. This

IT is not a luxury, but a necessity. The factors determining what is appropriate include:

- the organisational complexity, e.g. matrix management;
- the customer segments;
- the range and complexity of products and services;
- the expectations of key stakeholders such as regulators.

Rotating personnel provides a number of benefits, including the development of the individual. There is rotation between the various risk functions and between the risk functions and the businesses. As a minimum, these rotations help to extend the important informal communication network. For the business and risk functions there is an opportunity to develop an understanding of priorities. The risk functions learn about a business and the businesses gain insights into risk issues. Both of these rotations promote a common organisation-wide risk culture.

Recruiting from outside the firm has some advantages as well as costs. It provides the opportunity to insert additional skills and energy into specific functions. During integration with the new employer there is the opportunity to challenge how things are done, potentially providing a different perspective and helping to mitigate against group-think bias.

As mentioned above, the tone at the top influences shapes and forms the attitudes, behaviours and culture of colleagues. This tone includes ethical behaviours and treatments of all stakeholders. For risk culture, the tone at the top implies using the right tone to describe the role and responsibility of the risk management function. If senior management are seen to treat the risk management functions as partners, then others will follow this attitude and behaviour.

Giving the risk functions the appropriate stature can only work if there are adequate risk resources with the best skills and expertise available. The risk expertise also needs to be embedded in the businesses and senior management as well as the risk functions. The business is the first line of risk defence and without expertise the risk management activity will be about crisis mitigation rather than operating within appetite.

Without the right level of expertise, distributed across the firm, the risk appetite becomes meaningless and it is difficult to have an effective challenge process promoting knowledge and moving forward. However, not everybody needs to be a risk rocket scientist. At the top of the firm the risk expertise is about the risk governance process, risk appetite, the relationship between risk and return, a portfolio view of risk and its measurement. Further down the firm, knowledge of risk governance is still needed alongside risk measurement and crucially knowledge of the various exposures generated by their activities.

The reference to business expertise includes business models and the impact of the external environment on the firm. The business model includes issues such as how the product is distributed, related risks and how the firm obtains value from the client relationship. For example, if the product or service is distributed via the Internet then a series of cyber security issues around theft and fraud arise. For risk managers, working in partnership with the business, an understanding and appreciation of various business models is important. Without this understanding it is difficult to have a conversation about how the business can be conducted and the value for the firm obtained whilst staying within the risk appetite.

Reinforcement of communication, coordination and cooperation requires effort to achieve the benefits. To reinforce the profile of the risk management functions, generated by the tone at the top, the risk management functions need to be in dialogue with everybody – directors, senior executives, businesses, control and support functions, compliance, regulators, risk committees and internal audit. The communication, via formal or informal channels, reduces misunderstandings and delays and promotes the sharing of facts for use in informed decision making. Some of these informal channels will be established through the rotation of personnel.

Coordination means communicating with all groups that need to know and involving them in decisions. This increases the likelihood of a "better" decision and one that is likely to gain acceptance by those that it affects. For those not directly involved in the decision, it promotes the image of control and an organisation with a clearly defined sense of purpose.

Cooperation indicates a partnership with the aim of achieving the firm's goals. Part of cooperation involves the challenge process, and this implies knowledge and expertise about risks and business models. For cooperation to be effective there has to be an understanding of the respective roles of different groups involved in the dialogue.

Operating with common sense, clarity and simplicity can be difficult. For example, common sense is influenced by the risk culture, the structure of incentives and knowledge. As a result, what is common sense to one person is uncommon to another. For a firm the emphasis should be on substance over form, adding value, keeping things as simple as necessary (but no simpler) and being transparent in preference to opacity. Some of these actions, such as being transparent, are supported by trust and having sufficient knowledge to be able to add value to the dialogue. Features such as complexity work against clarity and simplicity.

Building credibility applies to the firm as well as individuals. For the firm, credibility with key stakeholders such as shareholders, customers and regulators is a requirement. The financial crisis has diminished the credibility of some organisations.

For communication, coordination and cooperation the credibility of the individual or function is a key intangible requirement. Without credibility little comes of these efforts. Credibility arises from aspects such as technical knowledge about risks and business, preferring to be constructive rather than just saying "No", being clear, efficient, responsive and consistent when making decisions. These attitudes and behaviours go a long way to creating mutual respect. Both credibility and mutual respect take time and effort to achieve. The mutual respect between business and risk management function reinforces the risk culture.

Developing a corporate risk memory can be a formal or informal process. The formal process involves an archive of successful and unsuccessful risk-related decisions. This archive could include records of Board-level discussions as well as the reaction to risks identified by risk takers. Owing to increasing transparency and efforts of the media, the risk discussions at one firm can also be initiated by events experienced by peers.

The informal corporate risk memory involves the memories of individuals who have worked for the firm for several years. These individuals, within a department, can significantly affect the credibility of the function.

A number of features of financial firms add to the complexity of corporate memory. One of these features is that financial firms continually evolve so that transformations are achieved over 5–10 years. These changes mean that risks that materialised seven years ago may still materialise, but with a different consequence. For example, when mis-selling interest rate swaps to small and medium-sized enterprises emerged it had different consequences from mis-selling in the 1990s. Additionally, after the materialisation of a risk with substantial effects there tends to be a change in the local control environment affecting the potential re-emergence of these precise risks in the same business with the same consequences. Further, changes instigated by regulators, in response to the financial crisis, are resulting in change to the portfolios of businesses and related business models. While some of these features reduce the value of corporate risk memory, it is not as difficult to formally establish as some of the other imperatives mentioned above.

6.4   MONITORING RISK CULTURE

The consequences of having a mismatch between the risk culture and stakeholder expectations have been observable following allegations of LIBOR manipulation and other behaviours. Firms have a risk culture but without monitoring and assessing it is difficult to tell if it is the appropriate risk culture. The auditability or appropriateness of a risk culture will be influenced by stakeholder expectations and the roles of different teams within the firm. Any gap identified by the monitoring can then be the subject of change initiatives or projects.

The stakeholder expectations will vary as different stakeholders have different interests. However, all stakeholders will expect behaviours to be of the highest ethical standards. What corresponds to the highest ethical standards evolves with time, for example in the context of the history of banking; the illegal nature of insider trading is relatively recent. From a different perspective, not all national or regional cultures have the same expectations, for example interest on loans can be viewed as unethical in some locations.

For the firm, these national or regional variations can create additional complexity. Many firms are international brands, and the risk culture is part of that brand. Should a client in one location that deals with the same product or service-providing function expect a different risk culture in a different location? This means that in some situations the firm's risk culture may have to be different from the location's risk culture.

Firms are reviewing their business models following the financial crisis and the political and regulatory responses. While this is forcing changes in attitudes to various risks and short-term versus long-term objectives, some teams or functions will have to change more than others. For example, some firms had business models that focused upon the creation and distribution of new products and services. These businesses were required to be more entrepreneurial, often taking more risk. Entrepreneurial attitudes may have contributed to payment protection insurance and even mortgages, in response to changes in society that resulted in crises. However, reactions from politicians, regulators and wider society show that having an inappropriate risk culture as well as formal policies and processes can lead to extensive damage for all involved. The natural reaction is to change the business model and risk culture to be less entrepreneurial, and have a smaller proportion of gross income coming from products that have been in existence for less than two years.

Monitoring risk culture can be achieved via staff surveys and some of the consequences of having an inappropriate risk culture. These consequences include:

- ability to retain staff;
- ability to attract staff;
- profile in the media – newspapers, Internet blogs, etc.;
- customer complaints or satisfaction;
- tone of regulatory dialogue;
- staff misconduct trends;
- staff surveys.

With the relationship between risk culture and risk appetite mentioned in the Introduction, a key monitoring activity of risk culture is to look at risk appetite and its role in the day-to-day management of the firm. An unclear risk appetite statement, at any level of the firm or for any team or function within a level will not support risk culture. Likewise, if risk issues are discussed separately from business tactics and strategy then this will also affect the risk culture. If the risk management functions are not partners with the business then this also has a detrimental effect upon risk culture. These and other risk appetite-related activities influence the risk culture through transparency and communication. This transparency and communication reinforces the attitude–behaviour–culture model of teams.

6.5   ISSUES TO CONSIDER

- How would the current risk culture be described?
- What is the desired risk culture?
- Implicitly, are the risk appetite and risk culture consistent?
- How would the Board describe the "tone at the top" on risk culture?
- Are there major differences in risk culture between business units? Are these differences desirable?
- Are there major differences in risk culture between locations? Are these differences desirable?
- Are there any differences in risk culture between the risk management functions and the businesses?

- Is the firm's risk culture communicated to stakeholders, e.g. via the annual report?
- Are the broader control and support functions aware of the firm's risk culture?
- How are aspects of risk culture currently reinforced or emphasised?
- Are policies and procedures and risk culture mutually reinforcing?
- Is risk culture and its various aspects a component of performance evaluation and appraisals of businesses and individuals?

FURTHER READING

Banks, E. (2012) *Risk Culture: A Practical Guide to Building and Strengthening the Fabric of Risk Management*. Palgrave Macmillan, London.

Barclays Annual Report for 2012. http://group.barclays.com/Satellite?blobcol= urldata&blobheader=application%2Fpdf&blobheadername1=Content-Disposition&blobheadername2=MDT-Type&blobheadervalue1=inline%3B+filename%3D2012-Barclays-PLC-Annual-Report-PDF.pdf&blobheadervalue2=abinary%3B+charset%3DUTF-8&blobkey=id&blobtable=MungoBlobs&blobwhere=1330696635816&ssbinary=true

Barclays Bank (April 2013) Salz Review: An Independent Review of Barclays' Business Practices, Appendix B – What is Culture and How Can it Go Wrong? http://group.barclays.com/Satellite?blobcol=urldata&blobheader=application%2Fpdf&blobheadername1=Content-Disposition&blobheadername2=MDT-Type&blobheadervalue1=inline%3B+filename%3DRead-the-Salz-Review-report-PDF-3MB.pdf&blobheadervalue2=abinary%3B+charset%3DUTF-8&blobkey=id&blobtable=MungoBlobs&blobwhere=1330697040891&ssbinary=true

Barclays Bank (April 2013) Barclays' Response to the Salz Review. http://group.barclays.com/Satellite?blobcol=urldata&blobheader=application%2Fpdf&blobheadername1=Content-Disposition&blobheadername2=MDT-Type&blobheadervalue1=inline%3B+filename%3DRead-Barclays-full-response-to-the-Salz-Review-PDF-3MB.pdf&blobheadervalue2=abinary%3B+charset%3DUTF-8&blobkey=id&blobtable=MungoBlobs&blobwhere=1330698492832&ssbinary=true

Basel Committee on Banking Supervision (October 2010) Principles for enhancing corporate governance. http://www.bis.org/publ/bcbs176.pdf

Basel Committee on Banking Supervision (June 2011) Principles for the sound management of operational risk. http://www.bis.org/publ/bcbs195.pdf

Deutsche Bank Annual Report for 2012 (2013) https://www.deutsche-bank.de/ir/en/download/Deutsche_Bank_Annual_Report_2012_entire.pdf

European Banking Authority (September 2011) Guidelines on Internal Governance. http://eba.europa.eu/cebs/media/Publications/Standards%20and%20Guidelines/2011/EBA-BS-2011-116-final-(EBA-Guidelines-on-Internal-Governance)-(2)_1.pdf

Goldman Sachs (2013) Business Standards Committee Impact Report. http://www.goldmansachs.com/s/bsc-2013/index.html

Heskett, J. (2012) *The Culture Cycle: How to shape the unseen force that transforms performance*. FT Press, London.

Hillson, D. (2009) *Managing Risk in Projects*. Gower Publishing, Farnham.

JP Morgan Chase Annual Report for 2012 (2013) http://investor.shareholder. com/common/download/download.cfm?companyid=ONE&fileid=652147 &filekey=a734543b-03fa-468d-89b0-fa5a9b1d9e5f&filename=JPMC_ 2012_AR.pdf

The Institute of Risk Management (2012) Risk Culture – Resources for Practitioners. http://www.theirm.org/RiskCulture.html

The Institute of Risk Management (2012) Risk Culture – Under the Microscope, Guidance for Boards. http://www.theirm.org/documents/Risk_Culture_A5_ WEB15_Oct_2012.pdf

Part II
Specific Risks

Risk Management at the Top				

Ch. 1: Introduction				

Part I: Risk Oversight

Ch. 2: Risk – An Overview	Ch. 3: Risk Oversight	Ch. 4: Risk Management	Ch. 5: Risk Appetite	Ch. 6: Risk Culture

Part II: Specific Risks

Ch. 7: Credit Risk	Ch. 8: Market Risk	Ch. 9: Operational Risk	Ch. 10: Liquidity Risk	Ch. 11: Other Risks	Ch. 12: Risk Interactions

Part III: Regulatory Environment

Ch. 13: Regulatory Environment

Part II – Specific Risks describes the main risks encountered by banks. Many of these risks are also encountered by other types of financial institutions in the same or slightly altered guises. With the scale of some of these risks, a considerable amount has been invested to understand their behaviour and how they can be summarised using models.

The starting point for most of these chapters is a description of risks and where they arise amongst banking operations.

Chapter 7 looks at credit risk, possibly the most significant risk for banks of various types. Credit risk caused problems at a number of banks as economies slowed following the financial crisis. The discussion on the credit risk framework introduces the various risk metrics, including the portfolio approach, of looking at credit risk. This aligns naturally with the need to reduce the level of variety in the data and information that is reported upwards through the organisation. This chapter concludes with a discussion on credit risk management and some of the available choices.

Market risk (Chapter 8) is taken by all banks and many other firms in the financial sector. This risk may be taken in a dedicated portfolio, often described as the "trading book", or as a by-product of other activities such as interest rate-sensitive reserve assets for managing liquidity risk. It is arguable that statistical and mathematical models were first applied to market risk because there was extensive readily available data, and then spread out to be used to summarise credit and operational risks. The risk management choices are well known, although banking regulation is having an impact on liquidity.

As a formal discipline, operational risk (Chapter 9) is relatively new, but it has been managed for years. This is the risk management discipline that started with a regulatory definition and learnt from the more mature disciplines of credit and market risk management. Some of the distinguishing features of operational risk include that it is seldom taken voluntarily for additional return, it is present across the entire organisation and the indirect effects can be substantial. The range of choices available for risk management is more limited than for some other risk types, and yet firms have been transferring this risk for years via insurance.

The final individual risk is liquidity risk (Chapter 10). Banks and other groups in the financial sector have been managing liquidity funding risk since they were incorporated. However, it is only recently that the topic has been subject to formal regulatory scrutiny. Aggregating information on liquidity and funding risks is difficult; the portfolio-type models for credit and market risk are difficult to transfer. Funding as an organisational resource also needs to be priced for users – transfer pricing. This is especially important as the different parts of the firm may use the funds for different periods of time, from several hours to several decades.

While Chapters 7–10 describe the most significant risks faced by banks, these are not the only ones that fall within the scope of Board and senior management risk oversight (Chapter 11). Some of these risks stand on their own, for example business and strategic risks. Other risks arise from businesses, such as other market risk, how risks are aggregated for escalation (model risk), how business activities are executed (supplier risk) and the firm's resources. At the moment it is not clear whether reputational risk is a risk in its own right or a consequence of other risks such as the operational risk of mis-selling.

The final chapter in Part II (Chapter 12) looks at the interaction between the risks. For example, credit and market risks can be connected via certain forms of collateral. Liquidity and operational risks can be connected if an operational risk prevents funds from being received by a firm. It is not clear how these connections should be measured and monitored, but it is an increasing necessity. It is arguable that some of the events associated with the financial crisis arose from these interactions, but which is the lead risk – e.g., credit or operational – and how to show the interaction in reports are questionable.

7
Credit Risk

Risk Management at the Top					

Ch. 1: Introduction					

Part I: Risk Oversight

Ch. 2: Risk – An Overview	Ch. 3: Risk Oversight	Ch. 4: Risk Management	Ch. 5: Risk Appetite	Ch. 6: Risk Culture

Part II: Specific Risks

Ch. 7: Credit Risk	Ch. 8: Market Risk	Ch. 9: Operational Risk	Ch. 10: Liquidity Risk	Ch. 11: Other Risks	Ch. 12: Risk Interactions

Part III: Regulatory Environment

Ch. 13: Regulatory Environment

All banks and other financial institutions have credit risk. For some firms it is their primary business, for example retail banking. For others it is an ancillary risk that comes with other activities, such as market risk in the form of derivatives.

Credit intermediation is the reason that banks were created. As a result, it is not surprising that this is one of the most sophisticated areas of risk management within banks. For many financial institutions credit risk is the largest component of economic capital and revenue generation. With this emphasis come extensive supporting policy documents.

Credit risk can be found in most of a bank's businesses, for example:

- corporate finance
- commercial banking
- private banking
- retail banking
- trading and sales.

The products involved include:

- credit cards
- personal loans
- derivatives
- leases
- mortgages and property lending
- corporate loans
- project loans
- sovereign loans
- trade finance.

For banks, credit risk makes up a significant proportion of the on- and off-balance sheet positions.

7.1 INTRODUCTION

With the Board responsibility for risk oversight, a considerable part of this oversight is associated with credit risk. With the diversity of products and revenues generated, considerable attention is paid to risk and return created by credit risk. This focus is supported by an extensive risk management effort and sophisticated risk measurement processes.

The rest of this chapter looks at the:

Table 7.1 provides a high-level view of where credit risk arises in the firm. The matrix has business lines[1] across the top and products/services[2] down the side. Not all products are used by all business lines. Additionally, some products do not generate credit risk for the firm, for example deposits. The darker the shading, the more concentrated is the credit risk. For many banks the credit risk is concentrated amongst the lending activities associated with retail and commercial banking. Trading and sales may also have considerable credit risk through derivatives, especially over-the-counter and securities settlements.

7.2 DEFINITION OF CREDIT RISK

Credit risk[3] is the potential for loss due to the inability, unwillingness or non-timeliness of a counterparty to honour a financial obligation. Whenever there is a chance that a counterparty will not pay an amount of money owed, live up to a financial commitment or honour a claim, there is credit risk.

Individual firms may not use this definition exactly, but it will have similar features and components. If the "financial obligation" is omitted from the definition then the scope will include contracts with office suppliers, insourcing companies and staff. The financial obligation element may be documented explicitly in a contract or implicitly via standard market terms and conditions, for example for a forward foreign exchange trade. The scope also includes settlements that do not complete as scheduled.

A key element of credit risk is the event of default. The event of default requires that the inability or unwillingness to meet the financial

---

[1] Basel Committee on Banking Supervision (2004) International Convergence of Capital Measurement and Capital Standards – Operational Risk Appendix.

[2] Operational Risk Data Exchange – ORX (July 2012) Operational Risk Reporting Standards – Appendix. http://www.orx.org/standards

[3] Coogan-Pushner, D. and Bouteille, S. (2012) *The Handbook of Credit Risk Management: Originating, Assessing and Managing Credit Exposures.*

Table 7.1 Business line versus products/services intensity of credit risk

	Corporate Finance	Trading Sales	Retail Banking	Commercial Banking	Payments and Settlements	Agency Services	Asset Management	Retail Brokerage
Capital raising								
Corporate finance services								
FX and money markets								
Securities								
Derivatives								
Retail credit								
Commercial credit								
Deposits								
Cash management, payments and settlements								
Trust/investment management								
Investment products								
Brokerage								

obligation persists for a period of time, for example 90 days. The event of default is preceded, in the sequence of events, by impairment. Stating that an asset is impaired requires objective evidence. Impairment is used in accounting standards and is surrounded by processes and controls.[4]

The events of impairment, potentially followed by default, are key points in the process from risk management and accounting perspectives. The events of impairment and default enable provisions and/or reserves to be taken against the possible loss. The sizes of provisions and/or reserves are estimated in a highly controlled environment governed by accounting controls and standards.

The provision of credit, for example a loan, is governed by a contract. These contracts will place various obligations on the borrower in the form of covenants and warranties. One of these warranties might be the provision of audited annual financial statements to the lender within a certain period of time. A covenant might be that the total payments of interest and principal do not account for more than 75% of gross revenue before depreciation and tax or a balance sheet ratio. If a covenant is breached then technically there is an event of default as the contractual terms are no longer met, so there is a breach of contract.

It is not uncommon for companies and individuals to have multiple lenders or multiple credit facilities with the same lender. Each of these credit facilities may have slightly different contractual terms. To prevent a lender being economically disadvantaged in the event of a default, the contractual terms may include a cross-default clause. Effectively, the cross-default clause means that if one credit facility goes into default, then all credit facilities, with the cross-default clause, are also immediately in default. This puts all the lenders in the same position should there be a renegotiation of terms and conditions or a liquidation.

When establishing a credit facility it is in the lender's best interests to be "secured". This means taking security over certain assets or cash-flows. For a property loan the security may be a house or a shopping centre, when the loan becomes a mortgage. Other forms of security include debentures on assets such as equipment. If the borrower gets into financial difficulties then the lender has rights over those assets. However, the degree of protection for the lender depends upon the resale value of the asset. If the market for the asset falls, for example a downturn in the housing market, then so does the value of the security.

---

[4] IAS 39 Technical Summary (2012) Financial Instruments: Recognition and Measurement.

For the lender, this downturn in asset values may come at the same time as an increase in the likelihood of default.

Traditional products giving rise to credit risk include mortgages and loans via credit cards and loans to small and medium-sized enterprises up to firms spanning the globe. Other products may have contingent credit risk. Contingent credit risk requires something else to happen before the credit risk arises with that particular counterparty. An example would be an insurer, where the credit risk does not exist until the firm has an insurance claim (where the insurance claim probably arises from an operational risk event). Another example would be a financial guarantee from a third party. In the event that the borrower goes into default the lender can claim against the guarantee, depending upon the specific terms of the guarantee.

Another sort of contingent credit relates to derivatives. Whether a derivative creates a credit risk depends on the value of the derivatives contract. The credit risk is held by the firm that has a profitable position and is owed value from the counterparty. The derivative might be a forward, a future, a swap or an option. Estimating the credit risk requires forecasting the future value of the derivative. Identifying where the derivative is in profit in the future provides an estimate of the potential future exposure (PFE). The credit risk is then measured using this PFE. The PFE is estimated using information and techniques from the market risk calculations.

This section has introduced some of the issues that make credit risk complex in terms of risk estimation and management. The next section considers aspects of the credit framework.

7.3   FRAMEWORK

For banks it is not surprising that the credit risk framework is extensive and sophisticated. For many banks the credit risk framework is often larger and more complex than liquidity, market and operational risks combined.

Credit risk is taken in the trading book and in the non-trading book (banking book). The trading book can be considered to be a portfolio of assets that are held for sale. The trading book can include financial derivatives of various forms. Amongst derivatives, it is the OTC transactions that make a significant contribution to the total credit risk in the trading book. OTC transactions are entered into on a bilateral basis, whereas exchange-traded derivatives will generally have a central counterparty to stand between the two traders.

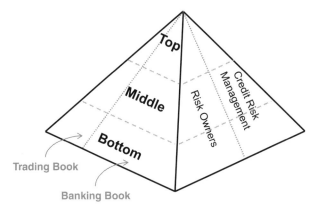

Figure 7.1   Users of credit risk reports

For most banking firms a significant proportion, if not the vast majority, of the credit risk resides in the banking book. Positions in the banking book are usually held for their natural life. For example, a 10-year loan to a company will be held in the banking book until it matures in 10 years, likewise a 30-year mortgage.

Whether the credit risk arises in the trading or banking books, the risk is owned by the business which receives the revenue stream. Credit risk management, as a corporate risk function, will have a significant advisory role with the business, in addition to oversight and challenge (Figure 7.1). These roles may include pricing and establishing minimum returns for particular levels of credit risk. This can get complicated as the relationship with a complex counterparty may touch many parts of the firm. One part of the firm may be involved in reorganising the counterparty's liabilities, another part in project finance and a third part in handling foreign exchange transactions. This can result in a matrix approach with a relationship manager and several functions executing individual transactions or providing services. The relationship manager will have a limited capacity to add credit risk for a particular counterparty and will need to have a view on future as well as current opportunities to generate revenues. Depending upon the revenue generated by individual transactions, it may be necessary for cross-subsidies to be arranged to meet the revenue targets of individual risk owners/profit centres.

One of the differences between the trading and banking books is their accounting treatment. In the trading book positions are marked-to-market, whilst the banking book approach is accrual accounting.

When recognising deterioration in the counterparty's financial position, in the banking book, the lending firm is permitted to take a reserve or provision. The taking of these reserves and provisions is governed by accounting standards such as IAS 39, which is gradually being replaced by IFRS 9. These standards require objective evidence of impairment of future cash flows from the borrower to the lender. The extent of the impairment shows up in the lender's P&L account. This process means that the progressive financial deterioration of a counterparty can be recognised, as opposed to a single write-off when the counterparty defaults. Firms have an extensive control environment around the assessment of impairment. The deterioration in a counterparty in the trading book may be recognised through a change in the mark-to-market or mark-to-model valuation. The valuation derived from mark-to-model is based on a model which may use an input that reflects the possibility of deterioration in the creditworthiness of a counterparty.

Depending upon the volume of a particular business, there may be extensive use of a credit scoring model. The credit scoring model is a decision support tool. Different scoring models will be used for different types of transactions. For example, a model for credit card limits will differ from the model used to assess the financing of a project. Some of these models will be highly formalised, for example credit cards, whilst others may be in the form of guidance, as in project finance. The outputs of these scoring models may be known as Z-scores or ratings.

The purpose of these models is to compare the revenue generated from the credit risk with the likelihood of default and the severity of any losses. Highly formalised models probably work best where there is a high volume of standardised transactions. In some cases these models are behind the on-line application engines for particular transactions, such as trade finance. The models will be developed by the businesses and are likely to be reviewed by credit risk management as part of their oversight and challenge activities. Some of the inputs may also come from credit risk management, such as the appetite for a particular form of credit risk with a particular type of counterparty. The constraints could be the duration of the transaction and implications for the balance sheet in the future, especially when an OTC derivative can have a maturity of more than 10 years and mortgages 30 years.

This multi-year view adds complexity to the management of credit risk and the associated returns. The transactions that are entered into now will have an impact upon revenues until they mature. As a result, one of the issues is the turnover of the credit risk portfolio. What proportion of the credit risk portfolio is scheduled to mature this year, how big is any increase in the credit risk appetite and what returns are currently available? Even if there is capacity within the credit risk appetite, the competition for certain categories of counterparty may drive down revenues, making certain counterparties or products unattractive. For some groups of counterparties the competition does not come from other lenders, but other sources of funds, in particular the bond markets.

Other aspects that may factor into credit decisions include country of risk, size of counterparty and industrial sectors. The country of risk can mean that a loan to an organisation in one country is funded by resources from another. This issue has increased its profile during the crisis around the euro (€) and the prospect of countries leaving the euro. This cross-border funding risk can be offset by limiting loans in a particular country to deposits sourced from the same country. This means that if there is a seismic economic and/or political change then the firm's assets and liabilities will both be affected, rather than just assets.

The available size of counterparties means credit risk can be segmented across

- individuals
- SMEs
- large companies
- governments and supra-government organisations.

Each of these counterparty groups has different risk and return profiles. Each will require different levels of resources to maintain and monitor the relationship. For example, SMEs may involve a significant amount of resources, but the returns are likely to be higher than lending to governments. The increased likelihood of impairment for SMEs in the near term may be offset by the fact that some of them will become the large counterparties of the future.

The preference for one industrial sector over another has similarities to the choice of counterparty size. Does the firm prefer credit risk with the agricultural sector, or heavy engineering or professional services?

In terms of managing the overall credit portfolio, a balance is needed between many relationships and few. The presence of few relationships indicates a concentration of exposure. This concentration may mean that while the relationship with the few counterparties is extensive, if any one of them has an impairment then it will have significant consequences for the lender. Similarly, if the counterparty decides to move the relationship to another lender then there will be an impact on future revenues. This concentration issue also applies to the industrial sector, having relationships with a few or with many. Firms usually have constraints that may be expressed as ratios of the credit portfolio, to prevent concentrations. The suitability of a particular value for a constraint may be reviewed as part of a stress testing or scenario exercise on the entire portfolio or its parts. The constraint will usually be set by credit risk management in their role of cascading the credit risk appetite down the organisation.

Owing to the number of dimensions involved in the credit risk portfolio, and related complexity, the risk takers may need a simpler approach than an allocation of economic capital. The credit risk takers, which may mean the relationship manager, may be given limits or authority expressed in simpler units, such as 5-year loan equivalents.[5] The overriding constraint is expected to be the incremental economic capital allocated to a particular counterparty, but this may only be updated monthly or quarterly. Using something like 5-year equivalents enables the relationship manager to compare the revenue generated by different opportunities. A comparison can be made between the revenues on a 6-month loan and a 5-year interest rate swap. The credit risk management function is expected to be involved in the translation from economic capital to the simpler metric, in part to promote consistency across the organisation and prevent surprises.

Some of the decisions across the various dimensions may be heavily influenced by the statement of credit risk appetite and its degree of granularity. Concentration ratios may be an explicit part of a high-level credit risk appetite statement.

7.4 RISK APPETITE METRICS

Credit risk appetite has been used for many years. The sections below cover the evolutionary path. At its simplest, the capital required to support the credit risk can be derived from:

1. Simplest metrics – credit exposure.
2. Intermediate metrics – probability of default.
3. Complex metrics – loss given default.
4. Economic capital.

---

[5] The credit risk is normalised to a 5-year horizon. This will enable more to be lent for shorter periods and less to be lent for longer periods. The 5-year loan equivalent enables aggregation.

Each of these topics is explored in more detail below.

While the regulatory capital focus may be based on a 12-month horizon, the Board will want to consider a longer time frame. This longer time frame may be the full length of the credit portfolio (potentially 30 years), or to the end of the credit cycle (possibly 5 to 7 years) or a fixed period into the future (e.g., 5 to 7 years).

The longer time frame will relate to the forecasting of capital needs and strategic planning. A question might be, assuming that the portfolio maintains its current composition, what is the maximum capital need in the future. This capital need might be higher or lower than the current figure for 12 months into the future. The peak may be in 2 or 20 years. This information helps to inform the discussion about the capacity for incremental credit risk and the current credit risk appetite.

There are a variety of credit risk capital estimation methodologies with a range of complexities and precisions. For regulatory capital purposes, permissions will be needed to apply the model-based methodologies to all parameters, and for some parameters the regulators will specify minimum values.

7.4.1   Simplest Metrics – Credit Exposure[6]

For financial institutions there are two broad categories when assessing exposure:

- loans, bonds and settlements;
- derivatives, especially OTC.

The credit exposure of a loan is the notional amount of the loan. For example, a loan of $100 will have a credit exposure of $100. From a credit risk perspective, a bond can be considered to be a loan in the form of a security. Loans and bonds can have fixed or floating rates of interest, for example 6.5% or LIBOR+1.25%. Interest payments may be made monthly, quarterly, semi-annually or annually depending upon the contractual terms. Generally, the maximum possible credit loss is the notional amount of the loan.

Credit risk from settlements arises when there is movement of cash or securities into the firm. Is the cash or security delivered when expected? Many securities markets have standard settlement periods between when

---

[6] Gregory, J. (2012) *Counterparty Credit Risk and Credit Value Adjustment: A continuing challenge for global financial markets*, pp. 121–137.

a transaction takes place and when the cash or securities are received. Generally, the settlement period is five business days or less. In the event that a settlement does not occur on schedule, there is an exposure based on the amount to be settled. It is always possible that the settlement was misdirected, in which case it should settle soon. For many transactions the focal point is that the firm pays cash or securities to the counterparty's account before cash or securities are received from the counterparty.

One of the critical times for this timing difference, between payment and receipt of cash or securities, is when a firm is put into liquidation. In the global marketplace there are a few hours in the 24-hour day when cash or securities are not being settled somewhere. The key time window seems to be between the close of New York and the opening of Sydney. This issue about timing came to prominence when Bank Herstatt, in 1974, was put into liquidation after Deutschemarks were delivered in Germany as part of a foreign exchange transaction, but before US dollars could be delivered in New York. The issue was compounded by different bankruptcy codes being applied in Germany and in New York.

Since Bank Herstatt there have been changes to the infrastructure to assist in managing the settlement element of credit risk. For example, securities can now be delivered versus payment, so that if the security (cash) is not ready and waiting then the cash (security) does not leave the account. For foreign exchange there has been the creation and operation of continuously linked settlements to dramatically reduce this risk.[7]

Determining the credit exposure of derivatives is a more complicated task.[8] The value of the derivative is dependent on the market value of risk factors that determine the price. For a single currency fixed to floating interest rate swap the value will depend on the position and slope of the yield curve. Most swaps are entered into at prevailing market prices so they have an initial notional value of zero. However, over the life of the transaction, for example 5 years, the yield curve will change and alter the value of the interest rate swap. This is an example of interaction between credit and market risks.

The components needed to estimate the potential future exposure of a derivative over its life are more complex than estimating market risk VAR. This complexity generates model risk issues, in particular the

---

[7] http://www.cls-group.com/Pages/default.aspx. In the 10 years since creation, CLS has settled US$7.7 quadrillion of payments. On an average business day it settles US$5 trillion and in a 35-minute window it processes US$14.5 billion of payments.

[8] Gregory, J. (2012), pp. 157–185.

robustness of assumptions. For some credit portfolio structures certain assumptions may have a negligible effect, but if the structure of the portfolio changes then the results may be more sensitive to the assumptions.

Although credit exposure is the simplest approach, it has a number of shortcomings:

- It isn't risk sensitive.
- It is relatively static.
- It is difficult to adapt for derivatives.

7.4.2   Intermediate Metrics – Probability of Default

The intermediate sophistication metrics involve creating cohorts based on the probability of default. The probability of default is inferred from credit ratings. The individual counterparties with a particular credit rating are collectively described as a cohort. In this intermediate stage, the cohorts may have risk weightings of 0%, 5%, 10%, 20% or 50%, or some other risk weighting. The credit exposure is scaled by the appropriate risk weighting to provide the risk-weighted asset (RWA). The RWA for each cohort can be added to produce the total RWA for the firm.

The probability or likelihood of default is a key component of credit risk. Given the number of possible counterparties, there needs to be a mechanism to group them into cohorts rather than considering each counterparty in isolation. The mechanism is linked to credit ratings, generated internally by the firm, externally by ratings agencies or some combination.[9]

Owing to the historic data available, the credit rating agencies publish material on the probability of default (PD) and the transition matrices.[10] The material gives users an insight into the probability of default for 12 months into the future for a given rating, how the credit might migrate from "AAA" to something else and how this might evolve over a number of years.

The ratings, whether internally or externally generated, have a limited number of subdivisions. For externally generated ratings the highest quality are labelled "AAA" and the lowest quality are "CCC" or something equivalent depending on the individual ratings provider. For each rating an estimate of the likelihood of probability of default over

---

[9] Moody's (www.moodys.com) and Standard & Poor's (www.standardandpoors.com) are the best known ratings agencies; there are others.

[10] Standard & Poor's (March 2012) 2011 Annual Global Corporate Default Study and Ratings Transitions.

Table 7.2 Descriptive summary statistics on 1-year global default rates

	AAA	AA	A	BBB	BB	B	CCC/C
Minimum (%)	0.00	0.00	0.00	0.00	0.00	0.25	0.00
Maximum (%)	0.00	0.38	0.38	1.02	4.22	13.84	48.68
Weighted Long-Term Average	0.00	0.02	0.08	0.24	0.89	4.48	26.82
Median (%)	0.00	0.00	0.00	0.19	0.73	3.62	22.07
Standard Deviation	0.00	0.07	0.11	0.27	1.05	3.32	12.68
2008 Default Rates (%)	0.00	0.38	0.38	0.48	0.78	4.00	26.00
Latest four quarters (Q1 2011 – Q4 2011) (%)	0.00	0.00	0.00	0.07	0.00	1.50	15.94
Difference between last four quarters and average	0.00	(0.02)	(0.08)	(0.17)	(0.89)	(2.98)	(10.88)
Number of Standard Deviations	0.00	(0.31)	(0.66)	(0.64)	(0.85)	(0.90)	(0.86)

Reproduced with permission from Standard & Poor's, a division of The McGraw-Hill Companies, Inc – Vazza, D. and Kraemer, N. (21 May 2012) *2011 Annual Global Corporate Default Study and Ratings Transitions*, Table 4. (See S&P disclaimer on page 305.)

a 12-month time horizon is generated from historical data and used in creating forecasts.

Table 7.2 shows that the probability of default for an "AAA" counterparty over a 12-month horizon is effectively 0. For "B" counterparties the long-run average is 4.48% probability of default, but has been as high as 13.84%.

Not every counterparty can be expected to have an external rating. As a result, firms need some form of internal credit scoring model. The purpose of the model might be to take balance sheet, income statement and other information and enable a mapping to a particular credit rating; this may be known as a Z-score. The model parameters may vary depending on the industry, for example agriculture, engineering or software.

These credit ratings are related to the probability of default over a particular time period, for example 12 months. However, as many credit-focused relationships with counterparties are multi-year, a 12-month timeframe only tells part of the story. If there is a 5-year loan what will be the probability of default in year 5? The evolution of the probability of default of an individual counterparty, when bundled with other similarly rated counterparties, is described as credit migration. Effectively, what is the likelihood that what starts as a loan to an "AAA"

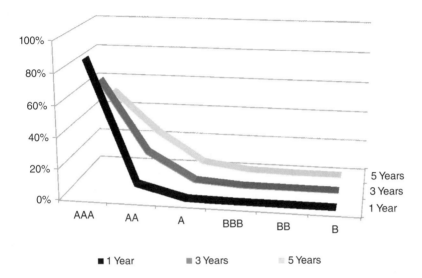

Figure 7.2   AAA transition to other ratings over various periods

counterparty today will, in 5 years, be "AAA" or "CCC" or somewhere in between.

Figure 7.2 shows that a counterparty initially "AAA" rated is 87.19% likely to be "AAA" after 1 year, but only 52.33% likely after 5 years. At the other extreme, an "AAA" rated counterparty is 0.03% likely to be "B" after 1 year, but 0.15% likely after 5 years. More details are provided in Table 7.3.

Table 7.3 provides the same data as Table 7.1 but for a wider range of ratings. Table 7.3(A) shows the migration after 1 year, Table 7.3(B) after 3 years, Table 7.3(C) after 5 years and Table 7.3 (D) after 7 years. For example, after 5 years 0.41% of the counterparties rated "B" will have improved to "A". Around each of these values there is a degree of uncertainty, which Standard & Poor's express as a *standard deviation*.

There are boundaries to the migration. The highest quality is "AAA" so for counterparties initially given this rating the evolutionary path is to stay the same or get riskier. For lower ratings, such as "B", there is the chance to improve, stay the same or get riskier. As a result, for non-defaulting counterparties (so there is a survivor bias in the sample) there is gravitation towards the middle ratings over a long period of time.

Table 7.3   Global corporate average transition ratings (1981–2011) % (Standard deviation)

(A) Over 1 year

%	To								
	AAA	AA	A	BBB	BB	B	CCC/C	D	NR
From AAA	87.19	8.69	0.54	0.05	0.08	0.03	0.05	0.00	3.37
	(9.11)	(9.10)	(0.87)	(0.31)	(0.25)	(0.20)	(0.40)	(0.00)	(2.58)
AA	0.56	86.32	8.30	0.54	0.06	0.08	0.02	0.02	4.09
	(0.55)	(4.94)	(4.01)	(0.73)	(0.25)	(0.25)	(0.07)	(0.07)	(1.92)
A	0.04	1.91	87.27	5.44	0.38	0.16	0.02	0.08	4.72
	(0.13)	(1.15)	(3.49)	(2.10)	(0.49)	(0.36)	(0.07)	(0.11)	(1.92)
BBB	0.01	0.12	3.64	84.87	3.91	0.64	0.15	0.24	6.42
	(0.07)	(0.23)	(2.31)	(4.64)	(1.84)	(1.03)	(0.24)	(0.27)	(1.82)
BB	0.02	0.04	0.16	5.24	75.87	7.19	0.75	0.90	9.84
	(0.06)	(0.16)	(0.39)	(2.37)	(4.97)	(4.70)	(0.92)	(1.05)	(2.85)
B	0.00	0.04	0.13	0.22	5.57	73.42	4.42	4.48	11.72
	(0.12)	(0.16)	(0.80)	(0.99)	(3.64)	(6.30)	(2.40)	(6.82)	(6.03)
CCC/C	0.00	0.00	0.17	0.26	0.78	13.67	43.93	26.82	14.37
	(0.00)	(0.00)	(0.71)	(1.02)	(1.30)	(8.59)	(12.68)	(12.68)	(7.32)

(B) Over 3 years

%	To								
	AAA	AA	A	BBB	BB	B	CCC/C	D	NR
From AAA	66.82	19.93	2.42	0.33	0.17	0.08	0.11	0.14	9.99
	(11.61)	(11.67)	(1.67)	(0.83)	(0.45)	(0.35)	(0.51)	(0.39)	(5.50)
AA	1.29	65.24	18.95	2.24	0.36	0.27	0.03	0.15	11.47
	(0.79)	(8.34)	(5.83)	(1.41)	(0.66)	(0.53)	(0.08)	(0.19)	(4.32)
A	0.08	4.42	67.45	11.90	1.40	0.57	0.12	0.33	13.74
	(0.11)	(2.38)	(5.96)	(2.83)	(1.14)	(0.82)	(0.16)	(0.26)	(3.69)
BBB	0.03	0.38	8.67	62.12	7.36	2.07	0.36	1.19	17.83
	(0.10)	(0.54)	(4.11)	(7.92)	(3.67)	(1.76)	(0.50)	(0.86)	(3.40)
BB	0.01	0.07	0.65	11.17	44.28	12.13	1.35	4.97	25.36
	(0.09)	(0.23)	(1.10)	(4.30)	(5.86)	(3.83)	(1.09)	(3.44)	(4.01)
B	0.01	0.04	0.32	1.00	10.71	39.49	4.54	15.25	28.63
	(0.12)	((0.16)	(0.80)	(0.99)	(3.64)	(6.30)	(2.40)	(6.82)	(6.03)
CCC/C	0.00	0.00	0.26	0.88	1.86	15.18	11.62	42.69	27.52
	(0.00)	(0.00)	(0.86)	(2.34)	(3.41)	(7.59)	(11.50)	(14.23)	(11.60)

Table 7.3   (*Continued*)

(C) Over 5 years

%	To								
	AAA	AA	A	BBB	BB	B	CCC/C	D	NR
From AAA	52.33	24.52	4.96	0.87	0.17	0.15	0.09	0.35	16.56
	(9.54)	*(9.66)*	*(2.63)*	*(1.80)*	*(0.44)*	*(0.46)*	*(0.33)*	*(0.61)*	*(6.65)*
AA	1.62	50.95	24.17	3.94	0.59	0.41	0.05	0.35	17.91
	(0.92)	*(6.79)*	*(4.64)*	*(1.79)*	*(0.71)*	*(0.72)*	*(0.12)*	*(0.38)*	*(4.86)*
A	0.10	5.55	54.06	15.07	2.19	0.85	0.18	0.67	21.33
	(0.11)	*(2.58)*	*(6.84)*	*(2.33)*	*(1.30)*	*(1.15)*	*(0.22)*	*(0.43)*	*(4.15)*
BBB	0.04	0.65	10.60	48.20	7.86	2.77	0.44	2.39	27.06
	(0.11)	*(0.68)*	*(4.34)*	*(7.93)*	*(2.47)*	*(1.83)*	*(0.58)*	*(1.30)*	*(4.36)*
BB	0.01	0.09	1.30	12.49	28.25	11.25	1.42	9.16	36.03
	(0.08)	*(0.28)*	*(1.27)*	*(4.09)*	*(5.24)*	*(3.20)*	*(1.47)*	*(4.61)*	*(4.21)*
B	0.02	0.04	0.41	1.93	10.77	22.87	2.93	21.41	39.62
	(0.27)	*(0.14)*	*(1.16)*	*(1.55)*	*(2.85)*	*(5.81)*	*(1.42)*	*(7.97)*	*(6.27)*
CCC/C	0.00	0.00	0.24	0.91	3.16	12.38	3.28	45.93	34.10
	(0.00)	*(0.00)*	*(0.84)*	*(4.15)*	*(3.22)*	*(5.56)*	*(7.92)*	*(13.97)*	*(12.18)*

(D) Over 7 years

%	To								
	AAA	AA	A	BBB	BB	B	CCC/C	D	NR
From AAA	41.59	26.98	7.35	1.68	0.21	0.12	0.12	0.49	21.44
	(7.09)	*(7.21)*	*(2.70)*	*(2.15)*	*(0.50)*	*(0.40)*	*(0.35)*	*(0.75)*	*(7.09)*
AA	1.69	40.17	27.20	5.21	0.78	0.38	0.04	0.52	24.01
	(1.03)	*(4.70)*	*(3.76)*	*(1.62)*	*(0.72)*	*(0.59)*	*(0.10)*	*(0.55)*	*(4.70)*
A	0.10	5.80	44.69	16.77	2.77	1.01	0.17	1.13	27.56
	(0.14)	*(2.08)*	*(6.30)*	*(1.78)*	*(1.40)*	*(1.25)*	*(0.23)*	*(0.54)*	*(3.69)*
BBB	0.05	0.90	10.95	39.19	7.69	2.87	0.41	3.65	34.29
	(0.17)	*(0.56)*	*(3.85)*	*(6.29)*	*(0.91)*	*(1.30)*	*(0.52)*	*(1.60)*	*(3.56)*
BB	0.00	0.09	1.76	12.19	19.58	9.72	1.10	12.99	42.57
	(0.00)	*(0.30)*	*(1.38)*	*(4.39)*	*(4.52)*	*(2.77)*	*(0.99)*	*(4.93)*	*(3.76)*
B	0.01	0.03	0.60	2.42	8.92	13.77	1.78	26.29	46.18
	(0.23)	*(0.15)*	*(1.01)*	*(2.00)*	*(2.32)*	*(3.58)*	*(0.93)*	*(7.48)*	*(6.02)*
CCC/C	0.00	0.00	0.42	1.32	3.62	8.36	1.46	48.82	36.00
	(0.00)	*(0.00)*	*(0.93)*	*(4.69)*	*(2.40)*	*(4.23)*	*(4.45)*	*(13.14)*	*(11.04)*

Reproduced with permission from Standard & Poor's, a division of The McGraw-Hill Companies, Inc – Vazza, D. and Kraemer, N. (21 May 2012) *2011 Annual Global Corporate Default Study and Ratings Transitions*, Table 21. (See S&P disclaimer on page 305.)

Over particular periods, certain industries and regions may have higher default rates and different patterns of ratings migration that deviate from the average across the total portfolio. Scenarios analysis and stress testing will assist in identifying concentrations in the portfolio. The parameters for the stress tests and scenarios are specified by the credit risk management as part of dynamic management of the credit risk appetite. Some of the stress test and scenario results may be by-products of the modelling and simulation, in other cases they will have to be specifically generated.

The probability of default with the potential for credit ratings to migrate over time adds a dynamic element to credit risk estimation. This additional complexity enables better alignment of time horizons with the strategic direction on capital and risk appetite. The missing element is the scale of impairment or loss when the credit rating does migrate to default.

Of particular note is that the credit ratings provided by the ratings agencies are opinions. These opinions are usually paid for by the issuer/borrower. Ratings are dependent upon the available information and refinement in the opinion-generating processes.

7.4.3   Complex Metrics – Loss Given Default

The more complex metrics outlined in this section build on the material above.

The Loss Given Default (LGD) is equal to 1–recovery rate. If the credit exposure is in the form of a loan with a notional amount of $75 and it goes into default, then the amount recovered might be $50. For this simple example the loss given default is $25 or 33%.

The addition of the LGD enables an expected loss or expected impairment to be estimated for a period of time.

Expected credit risk loss/impairment	= Exposure ×	Expected probability of default (PD)	×	Expected loss given default (LGD)

To get a range of possible credit risk losses or impairments, rather than an expected loss value, various values in the above equation can be replaced. For example, using the minimum and maximum values in Table 7.2.

The loss given default is connected to the seniority of the claim on the counterparty and the legal environment surrounding the transaction.

The seniority of the claim refers to the ranking of the claim in the event of a liquidation of the firm. Best positioned are senior secured claims and at the bottom junior subordinated claims, which rank close to equity in terms of potential for any recovery.

The legal environment surrounding a claim, in particular the documentation, statutes and case law, means that Bank A's particular loan or claim does not have to experience the default for Bank A's claim to be in "default". For example, the cross-default clauses in the documentation may mean that if another claim, for example with Bank B, is in default, then Bank A's claim is automatically in default as well. From a loss given default perspective this puts the various claimants on a more level playing field. The alternative is that whichever Bank, A or B, was due to receive a payment first has a default first and is in the best position to minimise their loss given default as they are first in the queue. If the claims by Banks A and B are in different jurisdictions then there may be a difference in the amounts received by Banks A and B in the event of liquidation. This difference is attributable to different bankruptcy processes in various jurisdictions. An example was the allocation of assets in the Lehman Brothers bankruptcy, with assets in multiple jurisdictions and claims also from multiple jurisdictions.

The loss given default situation can get more complicated when derivatives are involved.

- Owing to the documentation, derivative transactions are senior claims and so rank alongside many bonds and other claims.
- The derivative transactions between two counterparties can be subject to a netting agreement. This means that the net amount is paid in the event of a liquidation; it may be a payment from the solvent to the insolvent or from the insolvent to the solvent. Netting is a powerful technique.
- As many derivative transactions do not have a notional amount, the exposure has to be determined from the mark-to-market or mark-to-model value of the transaction. The valuation will vary at different points in the future as described in the material on exposure.
- Collateral.

The mark-to-model valuation will require a discount rate to be used. Which discount rate is appropriate, the risk-free rate or the risky rate? The risky rate may reflect the default risk of the solvent party to the transaction. This risk rate may be derived from yields on bonds issued by the solvent party.

Collateral is another mechanism by which the loss given default can be reduced. It tends to be used for derivative transactions and short-term borrowing in the form of repurchase agreements (Repos). As discussed below, collateral can significantly reduce the loss given default, but is unlikely to make it zero.

Determining the loss given default is not always straightforward. There is the value of the claim at the time that the counterparty goes into default (settled recovery) and there is the amount eventually recovered (actual recovery).[11] The settled recovery is represented by the price for claims affected by the default, for example the price of a bond. The actual recovery may take many months and litigation to achieve. Each have their uncertainties.

The main components for estimating the risk, exposure, probability of default and loss given default are a series of sub-models and assumptions. One of these issues is described as "wrong-way" risk.[12] Wrong-way risk refers to the link between the claim and the probability of default. A simplistic example is holding government bonds; the more bonds a government issues the more likely it is to default. Some of the wrong-way risk can be managed in loans by having covenants such as interest cover or minimum net asset value. The issue is more complex for derivatives, whether they are forward foreign exchange contracts or equity put options due to the involvement of market risk.

Part of the difficulty with estimating and monitoring wrong-way risk is the lack of historic data and the need to specify the relationship between the counterparty and the related claim. A "chicken and egg" example: when interest rates are low there seems to be an increase in defaults. Is this because low interest rates encourage more to borrow beyond their capabilities, or is it due to central banks lowering interest rates to offset the fragility of the economy. This also suggests that the relationships in wrong-way risk may involve time lags.

The use of exposure, probability of default and loss given default provides a risk-sensitive metric for credit risk. The next challenge is to extend this process from considering individual loans or claims on individual counterparties to considering the portfolio as a whole.

---

[11] Gregory, J. (2012), p. 210.
[12] Ibid., pp. 307–338.

7.4.4   Economic Capital

The discussion above has kept the consideration down to a limited number of counterparties at any one time and a limited number of claims. With all of this data there is a need to look at the credit risk of the portfolio as a whole using economic capital. Generally, it is the portfolio view that senior management and the Board are going to see:

Expected loss/impairment = Exposure × PD × LGD   *Counterparty* 1, *Claim* 1
Expected loss/impairment = Exposure × PD × LGD   *Counterparty* 1, *Claim* 2
Expected loss/impairment = Exposure × PD × LGD   *Counterparty* 1, *Claim n*
Expected loss/impairment = Exposure × PD × LGD   *Counterparty N*, *Claim n*

The summary statistic will be economic capital and relate to a particular confidence interval, for example 99.9%. The formulas above are based on expected values for PD and LGD. These expected values now need to be replaced by statistical distributions. The PD, for a given counterparty, will be the same across the loans/claims, making the assumption that there is a cross-default clause in the documentation. Likewise, the LGD will be the same across all loans/claims if they all have the same level of seniority. To make matters even more complicated, the exposure amount for claims involving derivative contracts will change with conditions in the markets, such as changes in interest rates. The output, from this model, for a single counterparty will be a statistical distribution from which the average loss, also known as the statistical expected loss, and the 99.9% confidence interval can be taken. It should be noted that the value at a confidence interval does not describe how much could be lost above the confidence interval.

One consideration when graduating from single counterparties to the portfolio view is the interaction between the counterparties. This interaction may be described as a correlation; the causal relationship may be at the industry or geographic level. For example, if world trade is reduced then shipping companies will have less revenue, in turn this may impact on their ability to make payments on loans and/or derivatives, so increasing the overall likelihood of impairments. The airline industry may also be affected by a downturn in world trade. A regional or national airline may be affected by the local economy. These connections are often implicit or informal, but have an impact on the risk/return performance of the portfolio.

Complicating the issue is that in "normal times" the correlation of defaults between counterparties may be zero, but in times of stress may be relatively high, for example 0.5 or 50%. Although what is being measured is co-movement or performance of the counterparties, this co-movement changes with the general conditions. As a result correlation, a linear function, may be a less than perfect measure and something more sophisticated, such as copulas, is an improvement. Copulas are a mathematical technique to measure co-movement over a diverse range of values of the two or more references, in this case a portfolio of counterparties and their probability and loss given default.

The economic environment giving rise to the loss is not a direct model input. However, it may be possible to amend the model parameters to reflect assumptions about the future. For example, will the next year be similar, economically, to the past year or will it be worse. One response to this situation has been an increased emphasis on stress testing. In a stress test a set of economic conditions is described, for example interest rates increase to 10% in 24 months, inflation rises and so on. The result of the stress test applied to the credit portfolio will describe the expected outcome if the conditions materialise. The stress test parameters will usually be provided by credit risk management and may have been reviewed by the senior risk committees.

For some factors it may be difficult to perform stress testing. These factors can include the probability of default and the loss given default. If based upon historic data, there is a question of how far back to take history, assuming that there are no data limitations. For example, if recent history has been benign then the values will be low and the credit portfolio will be expanded to utilise the available risk appetite and generate revenues. However, when conditions become hostile then the portfolio may be in excess of the risk appetite and actions taken to swiftly reduce the risk in the portfolio. One of the consequences of such a change, in economic environment and credit risk appetite, is expected to be less new lending. This sequence of events and reactions is described as being pro-cyclical in that the stage of the business cycle has an amplified effect upon the credit portfolio and credit risk appetite.

For some stress test results the risk management decision may require changes to the portfolio irrespective of the likelihood of the stress test conditions arising. This is a form of testing that the credit portfolio remains within the risk appetite given potential future conditions. A refinement for risk management is linking the possible outcome to an estimate of the likelihood that the conditions arise, a scenario as opposed to a stress test.

To enable senior management and the Board to rely upon the portfolio summary statistics there needs to be some form of validation. One form of validation is back testing, as commonly used for market risk. For the credit risk portfolio, back testing requires the simulation of the risk factors forward for various periods and then comparing those results with the subsequent reality. The values of the credit portfolio, at the end of a particular quarter, including probability of default and loss given default, need to be compared with values forecast the prior quarter, and the prior year. Without some form of validation it becomes difficult to rely on model outputs. While models are summaries of how the credit portfolio will behave into the future, they cannot be expected to be 100% accurate forecasts 100% of the time. However, they need to be good enough to support decisions on risk appetite, revenues and capital possibly 5 years into the future.

An issue that can arise is the difference between risk management and accounting perspectives. This can arise as the underlying assumptions for the various perspectives are different. For example, the accounting standards are generally based on the going concern concept. However, the focus of risk management may be upon minimising future volatility of returns, especially losses. The risk management approach may be based on information extracted from current market prices, for example the return required for an implied loss given a probability of default. The accounting standards generally give more weight to historic data. This can affect the volume of reserves and provisioning and may lead to adjustments in the composition if the portfolio gives conflicting signals, such as a decrease in accounting reserves and provisions even though the apparent credit risk has increased. Impairments are part of the bridge between these two perspectives. It is not expected that these two approaches will be fully reconciled soon.

For the concept of risk and return there are two broad approaches: incremental and marginal.[13] In practice, the loss given default can be influenced at the outset of the contract, for example by the seniority of the lender's claim and collateral. However, once these contractual arrangements have been made there is relatively little that the lender can do to reduce the probability or loss given default.

Incremental exposure considers the impact of the next transaction on the borrower's credit risk. The total credit risk is estimated and then the prior risk estimate is deducted to arrive at the increased risk due to the incremental transaction. For loans the change in risk may be largely additive. However, as the exposure for derivatives is dependent upon the

---

[13] Gregory, J. (2012), pp. 176–185.

forecasting of various market risk factors, the interaction or correlation between these risk factors will usually result in the total risk being less than the sum of the parts. The incremental impact of an additional derivative contract can be extended by netting arrangements.

The incremental credit risk estimate will be used by the risk takers when considering the incremental transaction. Is the return on the transaction sufficient to meet the target returns on credit risk? Based upon the complexity and sophistication of the model described above, a considerable investment in data collection, analysis, storing and calculations is required to provide information on incremental risk to the risk owners.

In summary, return on incremental exposure is useful. Owing to the portfolio effects and netting agreements for derivative transactions, there may be an incentive to enter into transactions with counterparties with an extensive lender–borrower relationship. This in turn can lead to concentrations in counterparties.

The marginal perspective on credit risk seeks to understand the source of contributions to the total figures. This can be analysed at the counterparty or the total portfolio level. The marginal contribution of individual transactions will change with time. This can be used to identify jumps up or down in the credit risk due to maturing claims/loans as well as changes in correlation between model parameters and the volatility of the individual parameters. The main users of marginal credit risk are expected to be the credit risk management function.

Looking at the marginal contributions to the exposure of a counterparty or the portfolio as a whole can assist in credit risk management decisions. Considering the model parameters and their correlations can be a perspective for stress testing. What happens to the credit risk if the correlations increase and the volatility of the risk factors jumps simultaneously? Which segments of the credit portfolio can be considered for securitisation with the most impact on the overall credit risk?

Although credit risk economic capital is the most complex approach, it has a number of advantages:

- It is risk sensitive and dynamic.
- It enables the portfolios to be viewed from the incremental and marginal perspectives.
- Stress tests and scenarios can be performed on the credit portfolio.

The main shortcoming is the complexity of the economic capital model and the data set to feed it.

7.5   CREDIT RISK MANAGEMENT

Given the prior sections in this chapter, the sophistication of credit risk management should not be in doubt. Given the size of the credit risk appetite, in comparison with the risk appetite for other risk sources, it is crucial that credit risk management fulfil the oversight and challenge roles expected as part of the three lines of defence. Some of the techniques by which oversight and challenge roles are applied have been described above. Factors driving this sophistication include:

1. The proportion of the total risk appetite that is allocated to credit risk.
2. That credit risk is inherent in the banking and trading book activities with accrual and mark-to-market valuations.
3. The range of products and transactions giving rise to credit risk.
4. Capital calculations – economic and/or regulatory.
5. The need to perform stress test and scenarios.
6. The choice of
   - counterparty size
   - industry segment
   - maturity profile
   - degree of concentration.

7.5.1   When Things are Running Smoothly

A significant part of the role of credit risk management is providing various views of the credit portfolio and its evolution. With the range and scale of the credit portfolio there is a need for various categorisation systems and metrics. Although the capital calculations describe how much risk is being taken, there is a need to monitor what risks are being taken. The data for this analysis is usually a subset of the data needed for the economic capital calculations, so the same data can be used twice.

The views of these different dimensions can then be used by credit risk management in discussions with the Board and businesses. Discussions will include the total credit risk appetite and also the implication for various dimensions. Thought experiments or scenarios may also be created to consider how the portfolio could evolve over the next few years.

At the risk taker level, for both the person entering into a transaction creating credit risk and the counterparty relationship manager, there will be a steady exchange of information with credit risk management. Credit risk management will provide regular reports showing the consumption of credit risk against the available appetite for the relationship manager. For the risk taker the report may show the amount of credit risk economic capital consumed, revenues and the actual versus required or target returns for consuming that credit risk economic capital.

To support these activities, and consistency, across the organisation there are credit policies and procedures. These policies will describe processes, responsibilities and authorities to support credit risk management across the organisation. This documentation will describe the data to be collected, the systems holding the data and the general use for the data. The documentation can also be expected to describe the credit risks that are not wanted, for example no exposure to alleged or actual criminal organisations.

There may be additional policies and procedures for transactions involving parts of the consolidated group driven by local regulatory requirements. For example, subsidiaries as separate legal entities may be required to have their own credit risk appetite, which needs to be compatible with and fit into the consolidated group appetite and processes. In the interests of efficiency the policies and procedures are likely to be the same as for the consolidated group. Nevertheless, local regulatory requirements may mean that local staff need to have a detailed understanding of these policies, procedures and economic capital methodologies even when using IT platforms rolled out across the group.

The policies and procedures for separate legal entities within the group may need to describe the extent of inter-group activity. This arises from concentrations of funding sources. While this is not a new requirement it has been given more emphasis by the need to create recovery and resolution plans ("living wills") for individual subsidiaries in the consolidated group as recommended/required by some regulators.

The policies and procedures will also describe what happens when circumstances change. One of these changes arises when a counterparty, or potential counterparty, is added to a sanctions list by a government body. Technically, failure to comply with sanctions requirements is an operational risk, but a common place to communicate and monitor business-affected counterparties is via the credit portfolio.

7.5.2   When Things are Not Running Smoothly

One way in which credit risk does not run smoothly is when there is an impairment, a reduction in the likelihood that contractual payments will be made on time and in the right amount. For a large credit portfolio impairments are expected to be a regular occurrence. The impairment review process is likely to be continuous, but there will be concentrations around quarter ends and annual accounting processes. The discussions are likely to involve the counterparty's relationship manager, credit risk management and the finance or accounting function. Once a decision has been made that an impairment exists, the discussion will move to the extent of the current impairment and finally how the impairment might evolve. For example, is the current impairment the beginning of a slippery slope that will result in default or can a rearrangement of terms and conditions limit further degradation?

The discussion on the evolution of the claim/loan may result in changes to the original transaction. For example, if a homeowner has a mortgage that requires repayment of interest and principal then it might be rearranged to be an interest-only mortgage. This rearrangement will effectively extend the average life of the credit exposure, but it may prevent the mortgage from going into default. Alternatively, the decision may be to recognise that the situation is poor and that a rearrangement does not alter the fundamental situation.[14]

Post-financial crisis these rearrangements have become a regular credit risk management activity. They provide a number of advantages for lenders, for example the loan is still generating revenue, even if at a lower rate. Any underlying security, such as a property, does not have to be transferred to the lender and then insured by the lender. If the security is transferred to the lender then the assumption is that the lender will try to sell the security, if impairment is part of a cyclical event then the market for the security will be depressed so the lender is less likely to recover full value for the security. From a society stakeholder perspective it may be preferable to initiate a rearrangement rather than default, foreclose and take possession of the security.

Whether a counterparty defaults or needs a rearrangement, teams of specialists will be involved. These teams, sometimes known as work-out teams, may be part of the business or part of credit risk management. These teams will have resources and experience of such conditions and work to achieve a successful outcome. The flexibility of these teams is governed by the initial contractual terms and how well they are executed. For example, if the mortgage agreement is incorrectly executed at the outset then the ability to manage the impairment/default may be severely limited by the courts. Crossing jurisdictions, where the lender

---

[14] In the USA there are programmes involving the modification of mortgages – Home Affordable Modification Programme (HAMP) and the HOPE for Homeowners Act, Home Affordable Refinance Program (HARP) – all encouraged by the government.

and borrower are in different jurisdictions, can make matters extremely complicated even when the choice of law and jurisdiction is part of the original contract.

In some cases legal risk has been reduced following years of experience and amending contractual terms, for example car loans. In other cases legal risk is reduced by developing industry standard contracts, such as those developed by ISDA for over-the-counter derivatives.[15] These industry standard contracts enable pooling of resources and generating contracts that are more complete and robust than would otherwise be the case. The added advantage is that industry standards reduce the need to negotiate every aspect of the contract and the focus can be upon the economic element of the individual transaction. This is an example of risk identification, assessment and management decisions to reduce the risk via the creation of an industry standard.

Although legal risk is an element of operational risk, it has the ability to make life complicated for credit risk management. The scope of legal risk includes the suitability of individual clauses, the robustness of contracts as well as the choice of law and jurisdiction. However, legal risk may only become noticeable when the claim/loan is impaired or in default. For this reason the counterparty relationship managers, businesses and credit risk management all work closely with the legal department at the outset of the transaction and whenever there is a change in its status. Errors made at the outset may only materialise years later.

Another occasion when credit risk management is actively involved is when the actual credit risk exceeds the credit risk appetite allocation or credit risk limits have been breached, this can be a serious issue. Given that the credit risk appetite may be expressed in terms of economic capital, part of the reason for an excess may be due to activities elsewhere in the credit portfolio. This is one of the consequences of using portfolio models, with correlation components, as the basis for estimating risk appetite. Credit risk management will be closely involved in exploring the reason behind the excess and making suggestions on how the situation can be normalised.

7.5.3   Reducing Credit Risk

As described in Section 7.4, economic capital for credit risk is a function of credit exposure, the probability of default and the loss given default.

---

[15] International Swaps & Derivatives Association (ISDA) http://www2.isda.org/

Amending the probability of default or the loss given default is difficult for a lender. As a result, this leaves the lender having to manage the level of credit exposure.

Some structures to reduce credit exposure are an integral part of an individual transaction, others are actions that can be taken by the lender. A mortgage, where the loan is collateralised by the value of the property, is an example of a transaction where the provision of collateral is built into and specific to the individual transaction. Other examples include forms of debentures and liens on specific assets. The easiest time to insist upon collateral is at the time the transaction is initiated, or if a rearrangement is needed.

The need to reduce credit exposure on an existing credit portfolio may arise from a revision to the credit risk appetite and business focus. This could be a need to reduce the riskiness of the entire portfolio, or a counterparty segment, for example the shipping sector, or instrument type, for example mortgages. More specifically, the need to reduce credit exposure might arise when a counterparty is at, or getting close to, the lender's appetite. Restricting the ability to do new business with a specific counterparty or group of counterparties may affect the ability of a business unit to meet their objectives.

The tactics to reduce credit exposure vary with the types of instrument. Does the risk arise from loans or from OTC derivative transactions or from settlements?

Starting with the need to reduce exposure to loans, the choices are to sell or securitise segments of the credit portfolio. The benefits include not only a reduction in credit risk, but also a reduction in the amount of funding required.

These securitisations are generically termed asset-backed securities (ABS), including mortgage-backed securities (MBS). The underlying assets can be varied and include mortgages, car leases or cash flows from toll roads.

With a securitisation the vendor may perform multiple roles. These multiple roles can include structuring the portfolio, selling the portfolio, maintaining the credit risk of the portfolio and transferring payments to the new owners. If a single firm has all these responsibilities then care is needed over potential conflicts of interest and operational risk events.

The terms and conditions of the securitisation can vary significantly. At one end of the spectrum the new owners actually own the loans and become the counterparty for the borrower. Others have the new owners effectively indemnifying the original lender for any defaults, providing funding and receiving the income from the underlying portfolio. Additionally, the securitisation may be structured into different tranches with different levels of credit risk and income or margin for each tranche.

Pre-financial crisis another tactic was to establish a special purpose vehicle (SPV) to acquire a portfolio of loans. The SPV would then fund this portfolio by issuing short-term instruments such as commercial paper. However, when funding liquidity disappeared in the wholesale markets during the financial crisis, the SPV could no longer fund itself! In some cases it was necessary for the original lender to take the assets back onto its balance sheet with consequences for capital.

Some securitisation structures result in residual exposure left with the originator of the portfolio. The residual exposure might be in the form of maintaining the credit quality of the portfolio or the provision of standby funding facilities for a SPV.

For credit exposures arising from derivatives there are alternative methods to reducing the exposure. These alternative methods include netting and collateral. OTC derivatives can be long-dated transactions, for example 10 years, which remain with the counterparty until maturity.

"Netting is the right to offset amounts due at termination of individual contracts to determine a net balance, which is the sum of positive and negative transaction values, to determine a final close-out amount."[16] Netting is facilitated by the documentation surrounding the portfolio of transactions between two counterparties, especially OTC derivatives. The documentation surrounding the portfolio of OTC transactions is known as the master agreement and will be supported by schedules reflecting the details of individual transactions.

The reduction in credit exposure, due to netting, arises from the recognition that for a portfolio of derivative transactions between two counterparties some transactions will have a profit and some will have a loss for one counterparty. The ability to consider the net exposure can lead to a significant reduction in the amount of credit risk outstanding.

Another common approach to reducing the credit risk of a portfolio is to enter into a collateral agreement.[17] Depending on the negotiating position of the two parties, the agreement may be one way or bilateral.

---

[16] Gregory, J. (2012), pp. 48, 170–175.
[17] Ibid., pp. 185–195.

Amongst major dealers the agreement is likely to be bilateral. While collateral can result in a major reduction in credit risk, it does not remove it entirely. The assumption is that at one point in time there is a zero-sum position with one counterparty's profit (loss) being the other counterparty's loss (profit). The collateral will flow from the firm with the mark-to-market or mark-to-model loss to the firm with the profit.

The collateral agreement will have a number of features, including:

• Who performs the calculation.
• The interval between revaluations and calculation of collateral.
• The time by which collateral is to be delivered.
• The minimum change in the amount of collateral.
• The acceptable forms of collateral.

The interval between revaluation of the OTC derivative positions, for collateralisation, may be every 90 days or every 10 days.[18] In a bilateral collateral arrangement the collateral moves to whoever has the profit. Revaluing the derivative positions, the credit exposure is effectively turned from a 10-year (or longer) OTC derivative into the interval between revaluations (90 or 10 days). There is still some credit exposure due to the change in value of the derivative between revaluations. The shorter the elapsed time between revaluations the less the risk, but the more movements of collateral.

The collateral agreement will also provide time for the counterparty to deliver the collateral. This effectively extends the period for which the counterparty has a credit risk beyond the interval between revaluations.

Another practical issue is the minimum change in the amount of collateral. The agreement may say that the minimum movement is $100,000. This means that if the profit of the position increases by $90,000 then there is no change in the amount of collateral until the next revaluation at the earliest.

Finally, there are the acceptable forms of collateral, cash or various securities. If the collateral reduces in value then the firm has an increased credit risk.

For the firm with the profit, receiving the collateral, the ideal form is cash. However, the firm providing the collateral does not generate a return on cash collateral. For non-cash collateral the agreement will specify "haircuts" for various securities, such as bonds. The "haircut" is

---

[18] For exchange-traded derivatives the calculation is daily.

a discount in the value of the collateral due to the nature of the security, in particular its price volatility. For example, the haircut will be less on 3-month US$ Treasury bills than 30-year US$ Treasury bonds. For the collateral receiver the price volatility on the Treasury bill is less than on a Treasury bond, but the collateral provider receives a lower return as well. Likewise, the "haircut" will be less on a liquid government security than an illiquid equity in a different currency. The information on the historic volatility in the valuation of securities provided as collateral can come from market risk calculations.

When considering the choice of collateral some care may be needed due to correlation with the market risk in the underlying position. For example, if the swap is denominated in US$ and involves fixed and floating payments then its revaluation will be correlated with the yields of US$ government securities. An increase in the profitability of the swap position, for one counterparty, may be accompanied by a decrease in the value of the collateral.

Collateral does not have to be applied to individual transactions, but can be applied to portfolios. These portfolios may also be subject to a netting agreement. The gross exposure of the portfolio of derivative transactions may be $100s millions or $1000s millions, but after netting and collateral it may be $10s millions, a considerable reduction in credit risk. The effectiveness of these processes in reducing the credit risk can increase operational and funding liquidity risks. The operational risk features include legal risk, in particular the robustness of contractual terms, the revaluation of the portfolio (model risk) and the need to move cash or securities. Some of these issues can be reduced by extending the interval between revaluations, but this increases the credit risk. The requirement to provide collateral, in the form of cash or securities, means that there are implications for funding liquidity risk management and transfer pricing for the potential amount of funding needed.

The use of netting and collateral reduces the credit risk of derivatives, however many individual transactions may be involved. The volume of transactions means that there is an opportunity for errors. Counterparties can enter into a compression process.[19] This process may also be known as consolidation. The aim is to rationalise the many trades between two counterparties to a few, while keeping the market risk the same. This can reduce the operational risk associated with these portfolios.

---

[19] Gregory, J. (2012), pp. 55–56.

A more recent addition to the credit risk management toolbox is the use of OTC derivatives whose performance is linked to credit risk. These contracts can be specific to an individual borrower or to a portfolio. Standard documentation, facilitated by ISDA,[20] has helped these derivatives to grow in volume and reduce legal risk. Once the trigger event, for example default, has been experienced then the settlement takes place. Some of the settlement processes include:

- a cash amount equivalent to the loss given default;
- a fixed cash amount (irrespective of the loss given default);
- the transfer of the defaulted loan.

These instruments are focused on default as opposed to impairment of credit. This difference was emphasised in the renegotiation of Greek € bonds.[21] Technically there was no default, but there was a renegotiation of principal, effectively impairment. This need for a specific trigger event means that the economics of the transaction may not be a perfect transfer of all the credit risk consequences.

Some of these issues may be addressed by other techniques. For example, indices are now available based upon portfolios of particular credits.[22] An issue is the imperfect relationship between the performance of the index and the portfolio undergoing a reduction in the credit risk; this imperfect relationship is known as "basis risk". For reducing the credit risk the firm may need to make a risk management decision between accepting basis risk and being able to transact in reasonably large volumes, or going for something more specific and precise, but the available volume is small.

These credit-based derivatives create a contingent credit risk. Effectively, the credit risk is being transferred to the derivatives counterparty. As a result, the derivatives counterparty needs to have good credit.

Before the financial crisis some firms specialised in taking on the credit risk from the provider of funds, in particular for US mortgages and US municipal bonds. Whilst these specialist firms had efficiencies in managing their portfolios and pricing benefits, it did mean that the market was extremely concentrated. Once one of these firms looked as though it might fail the others became "infected" as well, causing a reappraisal of the credit risk in lender portfolios.

---

[20] International Swaps & Derivatives Association (ISDA) http://www2.isda.org/

[21] Gregory, J. (2012), pp. 211–224.

[22] http://www.markit.com/en/products/data/indices/credit-and-loan-indices/itraxx/itraxx.page

7.6   ISSUES TO CONSIDER

- What proportion of the total risk appetite is allocated to credit risk appetite?
- What is the return on economic capital allocated to credit risk?
- How is the credit risk appetite sub-allocated to individual segments?
- What is the return on loans, and other sources of credit risk, expected to mature and run off the balance sheet over the next year?
- What is the return on new loans being put onto the balance sheet over the next year?
- What validation is undertaken to review the accuracy of the credit risk economic capital model?
- What are the main sources of parameters for the credit risk economic capital model?
- What was the last stress test performed on the credit risk portfolio and what was the outcome?

FURTHER READING

Bank of England (2011) Systemic Risk Survey.

Basel Committee on Banking Supervision (2004) International Convergence of Capital Measurement and Capital Standards – A revised framework (Basel II). http://www.bis.org/publ/bcbs107.htm

Basel Committee on Banking supervision (July 2012) Basel III Counterparty Credit Risk – Frequently Asked Questions. http://www.bis.org/publ/bcbs228.pdf

Bouteille, S. and Coogan-Pushner, D. (2013) *The Handbook of Credit Risk Management: Originating, Assessing and Managing Credit Exposures.* John Wiley & Sons, Chichester.

Gregory, J. (2012) *Counterparty Credit Risk and Credit Value Adjustment: A continuing challenge for global financial markets,* 2nd edn. John Wiley & Sons, Chichester.

IAS 39 Technical Summary (2012) Financial Instruments: Recognition and Measurement.

Löffler, G. and Posch, P.N. (2011) *Credit Risk Modelling using Excel and VBA,* 2nd edn. John Wiley & Sons, Chichester.

Vazza, D and Kraemer, N. (2012) 2011 Annual Global Corporate Default Study and Ratings Transitions, 21 May 2012, Standard & Poor's. (See S&P disclaimer on page 305.)

8

Market Risk

Risk Management at the Top

Ch. 1: Introduction

Part I: Risk Oversight

Ch. 2: Risk – An Overview	Ch. 3: Risk Oversight	Ch. 4: Risk Management	Ch. 5: Risk Appetite	Ch. 6: Risk Culture

Part II: Specific Risks

Ch. 7: Credit Risk	Ch. 8: Market Risk	Ch. 9: Operational Risk	Ch. 10: Liquidity Risk	Ch. 11: Other Risks	Ch. 12: Risk Interactions

Part III: Regulatory Environment

Ch. 13: Regulatory Environment

All financial firms have a degree of market risk in the broadest sense. The risk may be actively taken as when guaranteeing returns on investments, for example with annuities, or embedded in transactions involving different currencies.

Market risk measurement is closely associated with VaR. VaR is an expression of risk that is extremely useful, but as with all models there are embedded assumptions.

VaR gained its close linkage to market risk in the early 1990s. Essentially, VaR is a metric extracted from a portfolio approach to measuring market risk. The portfolio approach has become very popular amongst banks and other financial firms. VaR is not used to measure all the market risk experienced by a firm, but is focused on the market risk in the trading book and the foreign exchange and commodity risks across the entire firm.

As the roles of some banks and other financial intermediaries evolved, so market risk intermediation became an element of their activities. At the outset, market risk intermediation probably grew from financing trade with foreign exchange transactions. A logical extension to providing funding and taking credit risk is supporting borrowers in raising longer-term liabilities such as commercial paper programmes, bonds and equity. This horizontal integration, extending the range of products made available to the same customer, has led to the development of universal banks operating alongside and competing with specialist firms.

8.1   INTRODUCTION

Market risk appears in many aspects of banking and managing the risks of various banking activities. It arises from exposure to movements in prices of currencies, bonds, equities, commodities, other elements and their various combinations. The risk may be related to individual transactions or due to the broader composition of the balance sheet, for example the currency denominating assets as compared with liabilities, such as equity; this is sometimes referred to as translation exposure.

Banks of all sizes now have market risk as they all have funding liquidity risk. Managing funding liquidity risk involves the management of portfolios of regulatory qualifying reserve assets, such as government bonds. In the event that there is a shortfall in funding, these qualifying reserve assets are sold. The market risk of this portfolio of qualifying reserve assets relates to the possible future sale prices.

The management of market risk is focused on the trading book or trading portfolio. What is not in the trading book is in the banking book of a bank. To complicate matters further, these two books or portfolios have different accounting treatments. As described in Chapter 11, there are other sources of market risk in the broadest sense. Chapter 12 outlines some of the interactions between market and other risks, such as credit risk.

The first major regulatory framework for market risk in the trading book was agreed in 1996 and described as the Market Risk Amendment to Basel I (the Basel Capital Accord which was agreed in 1988).[1] The Market Risk Amendment introduced two regulatory approaches to estimating market risk, a simple formula-based technique and a portfolio approach with its VaR metric.

The rest of this chapter looks at the:

8.2 Definition of Market Risk
8.3 Market Risk Framework
8.4 Market Risk Estimation
8.5 Market Risk Management
8.6 Issues to Consider

The next section introduces various definitions before looking at the risk framework, how the risk is estimated and some of the activities of the market risk management function.

8.2   DEFINITION OF MARKET RISK

Market risk is the risk of loss due to movements in the level or volatility of market prices.[2]

Market risk can be decomposed into systematic risk and idiosyncratic risk. The systematic risk refers to the movements of markets or benchmarks such as stock indices or reference yield curves or the movement of an individual security relative to the general market. Idiosyncratic or specific risk refers to particular movements of an individual security, ignoring the general market.

---

[1] Basel Committee on Banking Supervision (1996) Amendment to the Capital Accord to Incorporate Market Risk. www.bis.org/publ/bcbs24.pdf

[2] Jorion, P. (2007) *Value at Risk – The New Benchmark for Managing Financial Risk*, p. 22.

The main sources of market risk are:

• foreign exchange rates
• equity prices
• interest rates
• commodities.

The concept of the trading book was introduced in the Basel Market Risk Amendment.[3] The trading book is a portfolio of instruments, securities and/or exposures that are available for sale or are held with the intent to trade, in other words to buy and/or sell. As mentioned above, this description includes the portfolio of reserve assets held for sale, if required to manage funding liquidity. This description is under review due to various shortcomings that became more apparent during the financial crisis.[4]

When estimating market risk, the trading book concept does not apply to exposures to currencies or commodities, for which the scope is the entire balance sheet of the organisation.

All positions in the trading book must be marked-to-market or marked-to-model daily. The results of this daily mark-to-market must appear in the P&L account of the firm.

Whenever a boundary is created there is the issue of what to do with items that span the boundary. For the trading and banking books an issue is what to do about interest rate risk. For example, the banking book may have an interest rate risk that it wishes to hedge. The hedge could be executed with the trading book. However, while the position is marked-to-market daily in the trading book, it is on an accrual accounting basis in the banking book. This issue will be recognised in the management accounts and is an added complication.

Market risk focuses on the undesirable outcomes, the potential for loss. However, as a profit centre the business is also interested in the desirable outcomes from taking risk. The focus of risk management is on gains and losses; gains to meet the revenue targets and capital to support any losses.

Figure 8.1 is similar to Figure 5.1 in Chapter 5. Although the potential returns may be symmetric around zero, not surprisingly, there is less appetite for losses than for gains.

---

[3] Basel Committee on Banking Supervision (1996) Amendment to the Capital Accord to Incorporate Market Risk.

[4] Basel Committee on Banking Supervision (2012) Fundamental Review of the Trading Book.

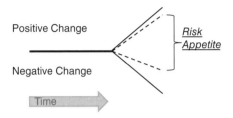

Figure 8.1   Possible returns with emphasis on the downside

For small changes in price, the returns are symmetric around zero. However, at the extreme there are some boundaries. For example, the price of an equity can only fall to zero. Likewise, interest rates seldom get above 100% p.a. There have been occasions when interest rates have been negative, but this requires a particular economic environment and it may be in the region of to –1% to –2%. These negative interest rates may persist for months.

Exposures in the main sources of market risk can be "long" or "short". When "long", the objective is for a price to increase and to sell the position or exposure at a gain at some point in the future. Being "short" can involve selling something that the firm doesn't own in the expectation of being able to buy it back at a lower price in the future and make a gain.

The concept of being long or short varies subtly according to the main source of market risk. For example, being long (short) in an equity means that as the price of the equity increases (decreases) in value the economic value of the portfolio increases, showing a gain. However, being long in an interest rate product, such as a bond, means that the economic value increases when yields decrease. For bonds, there is an inverse relationship between yields and price. Financial options add another layer of complexity as a firm can be long calls or puts giving the firm, as the owner of the option, the right to buy or sell at a given price at a specified point in the future.

As a result, the impact on economic value of the portfolio, whether bond yields increase or equity prices increase, depends on whether the portfolio is long or short. A fall in bond prices does not automatically translate into a loss as it depends on whether the firm, as a whole, is long or short bonds. As a broad sweeping generalisation, it is difficult for banks and other financial firms to be net short across their portfolio of market risk.

These exposures to market risk may be traded on- or off-exchange. For many, the image of an exchange is the New York Stock Exchange or one of the futures exchanges. In some cases the exchange is no longer physical, but electronic. Off-exchange transactions involve two parties being in conversation about the details of a transaction. There may be an intermediary in the form of a broker. Generally, these conversations occur over the telephone. These off-exchange transactions may also be described as being OTC. For example, the majority of transactions in government bonds are OTC, so is trading in foreign currency. The different trading locations, on- or off-exchange, have varying degrees of regulation, conduct requirements and possibly transaction reporting.

The internal environment in which market risk is taken is determined by the market risk framework; this is covered in more detail in the next section.

8.3   MARKET RISK FRAMEWORK

The risk management framework around market risk begins with its identification. There are two sources of market risk, those generated by transactions and those generated by the composition of the balance sheet, including off-balance sheet positions.

Transaction-related exposures to market risk involve flows of funds into (out of) the firm. Only a subset of flows into, or out of, the firm involve market risk; for example, a loan held on the banking book denominated in the reporting currency of the firm does not create market risk. However, a loan on the banking book, denominated in non-reporting currency but funded in the reporting currency, does create market risk due to a foreign exchange exposure. For example, a US dollar loan funded in sterling creates a foreign exchange risk; will the interest income from the loan offset the interest cost in sterling and change in foreign exchange rates over the life of the loan?

A translation-related exposure to market risk will be the result of the balance sheet structure. An example might be issuing a US dollar-denominated bond for long-term funding and Tier 2 capital purposes. The foreign exchange element on assets and liabilities will be captured in market risk. At a portfolio level, the foreign exchange risk from this bond might be offset by the US dollar income from the loan in the prior paragraph.

Foreign exchange risk can also arise from having revenues in one currency and expenses in another. (Some oil companies may also have similar exposures from producing oil, generally denominated in US dollars, but having expenses in other currencies.)

The majority of the market risk framework is devoted to transaction-generated exposures. All non-credit risks in the trading book and foreign exchange and commodity risk sources across the entire firm are market risk.

A significant amount of effort in the market risk framework is spent ensuring that the information flows up and down the organisation.

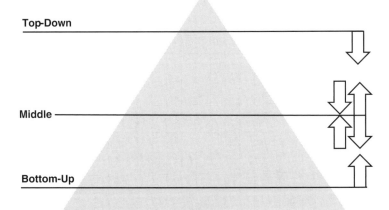

Figure 8.2   Market risk oversight perspectives

Figure 8.2 is taken from Chapter 3. The information has to flow from the top to the bottom and from the bottom to the top. As will be discussed in Section 8.4 below, the metrics used are consistent across these bands.

As Table 8.1 shows, the market risk is concentrated in the trading book, which is mapped to the trading and sales business line. This concentration of market risk enables the concentration of expertise. To promote this concentration, the firm may have a policy that any market risks acquired by other parts of the firm, for example commercial banking, have to be hedged with trading and sales. This effectively transfers the risk from commercial banking to trading and sales. Whether trading and sales decides to transfer that risk to a third party, via a hedge, is a decision for the management of business line and market risk management.

Market risk is also taken by asset management across a range of products. However, this market risk belongs to investors rather than

Table 8.1 Business line versus product/service sources of transaction market risk

	Corporate finance	Trading and sales	Retail banking	Commercial banking	Payments and settlements	Agency services	Asset management	Retail brokerage
Capital raising	�							
Corporate finance services								
FX and money markets		▓						
Securities		▓						
Derivatives								
Retail credit								
Commercial credit								
Deposits								
Cash management, payments and settlements		▓				▓		▓
Trust/investment management							▓	
Investment products							▓	
Brokerage								

the firm itself. The investors may be institutional, for example pension funds or investment plans managed by third parties, such as insurance companies. Asset management has a second-order market risk as its gross income can be based on the value of assets under management.

8.3.1   Roles in the Framework

The businesses are the risk owners and form the first line of defence of market risk management. The market risk management functions provide the second line of defence and are independent from the business. Finally, internal audit is the third line of risk management defence.

Figure 8.3 is similar to Figure 6.2 in Chapter 6. Of note is the small amount of market risk outside the trading book. This is almost the opposite of the distribution of credit risk between the two books.

In the context of market risk, the scope of the "business" is not limited to the traders. While the traders may be the front office, they are supported by the middle office and back office. The function of the middle office is to support the front office in their risk management activities such as monitoring adherence to limits and constraints of various sorts as well as performing various accounting activities. For some aspects it is required to have segregation of duties between the front and middle offices, for example in valuation of positions and attribution of gains and losses to parts of the portfolio. A control is the comparison between the valuations generated by the front and middle offices. This control can identify if there is a difference in the individual positions

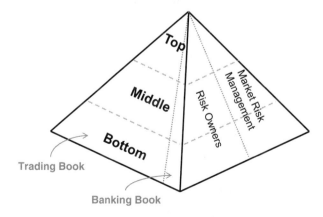

Figure 8.3   Users of market risk reports

between front and middle office records, or the positions are the same but different valuations are being used. It is this control which has been circumvented by some rogue traders. The middle office will also make the accounting entries for the transactions.

The back office function, sometimes called operations, is crucial to processing transactions. This activity is not limited to the trading portfolio, but everything that involves a transaction. The back office will look after the day-to-day management of the accounts at other institutions, such as clearing houses and custody organisations. Operations involve the matching of transactions between the firm and the counterparty and potentially notifying an additional two or three parties, such as a custodian and an investment plan sponsor. The matching is then followed by reconciliation of the accounts, for example confirming that the securities, in the agreed transaction, have actually been delivered. At the end of the day operations will also match the total position with positions held with various counterparties, taking a portfolio view as opposed to a transaction-by-transaction view.

Although part of the business, the middle and back office functions will also have reporting lines into the Board. For example the middle office in part, if not in total, may be part of the finance and accounting function. The back office can be part of operations and report into the chief operating officer (COO). As Figure 8.4 shows, the risk management functions are not considered to be part of the business and have an independent reporting line into the Board, as does internal audit. Internal audit, as the third line of defence, will review the activities of the first and second lines.

The risk management functions involved with the business will also include various compliance functions, including legal as well as market risk management. The compliance functions will be involved in activities such as the process for accepting new customers, anti-money laundering and determining which products are eligible for transactions with which types of customers. Also involved will be the business continuity team or disaster recovery team. Excluding market risk management, most of these risk management functions are involved, directly or indirectly, in managing operational risk. Some of these functions will report into the COO rather than the CRO.

One of the key issues when reporting to the Board is the consistency of information. If the front office, middle office, operations, finance and accounting and market risk management functions report different numbers to the Board for the same activity then there will be confusion.

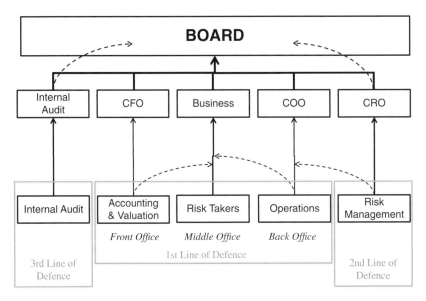

Figure 8.4 Reporting lines

The confusion will lead to a debate over which are the most appropriate numbers to be used by the Board in decision making. A considerable amount of effort can be applied to generating consistent metrics and reconciling between the books and records of the firm versus the risk management components.

8.3.2   Risk Appetite and Economic Capital

The size of the market risk appetite will be influenced by the revenue targets that have been set for the trading book. The appetite will then be subdivided into the main forms of market risk. Ultimately, they will cascade down to trading desks and individual traders or risk takers.

The trader may have two roles, price maker and position taker. Both of these roles contribute to the bank providing an intermediation service for risk other than credit or liquidity risks. As a risk intermediary, the firm is facilitating the transfer of risk from those that do not want a particular risk to those that do.

The price maker provides quotes at which the trader is prepared to complete transactions. In some firms this is known as flow business. The prices may be distributed by telephone to brokers, via sales teams, to exchanges and over the Internet via trading portals. For each instrument there will be a series of conventions, such as the price increment between bid and offer prices and the amounts that can be transacted at the bid and offer prices. In this role the trader is providing market liquidity for the instruments and is compensated by a portion of the increment between the bid and offer prices. Providing market liquidity in a bond or an equity can lead to additional business elsewhere in the firm, for example corporate finance.

The position taker role requires judgements to be made about the future price of the instrument. The time horizon may be less than 1 day up to 6 months depending on the detailed requirements of the portfolio.

While the extremes may be 100% flow business or 100% position taking, in reality many traders perform both roles to some degree. For example, if flow traders are unable to sell their inventory by the end of the trading day then it becomes a position!

For bonds and equities, the transactions are based around securities. For many OTC products, such as foreign exchange and derivatives, such as forwards, futures, swaps and options, the balance sheet position stays with the trader. To transfer the risk the trader needs to enter into an offsetting transaction. For example, a US dollar interest rate swaps trader enters into an OTC transaction with a 5-year life. In order to manage the market risk the trader may be able to use bonds, exchange-traded derivatives or another US dollar OTC interest rate swap. The bonds and exchange-traded derivatives are off the firm's balance sheet as soon as the offsetting transaction is executed. However, the OTC interest rate swap means that the firm has exposure to the counterparty for 5 years. The gross notional volume of OTC transactions can build up over time, even though the market risk is tightly controlled. As a result of this build-up the firm may enter into compression transactions with popular counterparties to reduce the gross notional volume on the balance sheet. This was mentioned as a credit risk management tactic in Chapter 7, Section 7.5.

At the level of the market risk taker the risk appetite statement may be classified as a mandate document. The mandate will include the instruments that the risk taker can use, possibly the size of the positions as well as the amount of risk that they can take. For example, a US government bond trader may be limited to taking positions in bonds with 4–6 years remaining to maturity. The mandate may also state whether the trader can use exchange-traded derivatives, which derivatives and on which exchanges. The position sizes may be linked to the market liquidity of the instrument. For example, the maximum position size may be no more than 5% of the total daily average transaction volume measured over the past 30 business days. This constraint means that price adjustments to the trader's positions will not be needed due to market liquidity. The non-risk appetite constraints, in the mandate, will be created by the middle business management layer with market risk management in Figure 8.2.

For risk takers involved with OTC products, such as interest rate swaps, there is also credit risk to consider. Rather than having a certain amount of credit risk allocated to each individual trader, the mandate will probably state that any credit risk has to be pre-approved by the relationship manager before the transaction is committed.

A firm with a large and diverse portfolio of market risk would expect to have risk takers for each type of market risk and various subsectors, forwards, futures and financial options.

8.4   MARKET RISK ESTIMATION

Market risk appetite has been used for many years. The sections below cover the evolutionary path that has led to VaR and economic capital. At its simplest, the capital required to support the market risk can be derived from:

1. Simplest metrics – exposures and stop-loss
2. Intermediate metrics – risk factors
3. Complex metrics – portfolio simulations
4. Economic capital.

Each of these topics is explored in more detail below.

The time frame to determine regulatory capital is 12 months in the future. The Board will want to consider a longer period into the future for strategic planning. However, with the liquidity in securities and risks, alongside the available data, firms monitor their market risk on a daily and, if circumstances justify, an intra-day basis.

This tension between time horizons can present challenges. For example, it is unreasonable to expect individual traders to maintain their exact positions for more than 12 months. However, it does become possible to say that if the market risk appetite is Z million then experience shows that a return of W% – Y% can be generated with an average of X%.

For the Board, a bigger issue is the potential impact of changes in the market structure when looking more than 12 months into the future.

Changes in market structure may be driven by the regulators, for example the reduction in propriety trading, the increase in capital requirements for market risk or the requirement to use centralised counterparties.

There are a variety of market risk capital estimation methodologies with a range of complexities and precisions. For regulatory capital purposes, permissions will be needed to apply the model-based simulations.

8.4.1 Simplest Metrics – Exposures and Stop-Loss

The simplest metric is to consider the size of a position in a security. This might be an individual government bond or an individual equity, such as IBM or Marks & Spencer. Each day it becomes possible to identify the gains or losses in these positions.

From a market risk management perspective, the restrictions are likely to be in the form of absolute holding size and/or stop-loss limits (Figure 8.5).

A stop-loss limit will probably be set in terms of an absolute value, for example £10,000. This limit means that when the loss gets close to £10,000 the position has to be reduced and possibly closed out completely. The stop-loss limit might be cumulative, for example, since the position was created. The alternative is an intra-day limit based on price changes since the last mark-to-market valuation. As the mark-to-market is performed daily, this effectively monitors the change in profit and loss.

The form of the stop-loss limit means that it can be aggregated and related directly to the impact on the P&L statement. It is possible to

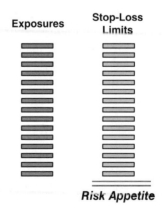

Figure 8.5   Risk appetite as exposure and/or stop-loss limits

express the market risk appetite in terms of exposures and/or stop-loss limits. Their drawbacks include:

- It isn't risk sensitive.
- It is relatively static.
- It is difficult to adapt for derivatives.

It would take a great deal of experience to be able to make stop-loss limits risk sensitive, and the easier approach is to use explicit risk factors. The stop-loss limit requires manual intervention to make it dynamic. For example, if a period of market turbulence is anticipated then each of the individual stop-loss limits would have to be reviewed. Additionally, when there are sudden and dramatic changes in price, for example a spike in market prices up or down (depending upon short or long positions), then the stop-loss limits will be broken.

The exposure metric needs to be used carefully with derivatives. The reason for the caution is that most derivatives involve more than one factor. For example, a forward foreign exchange contract requires the spot foreign exchange rate and the differential between two interest rates for pricing and revaluation. Some derivatives may have non-linear relationships; this category is dominated by financial options. As a result, the gross notional volume of a derivative may bear little relation to the risk involved.

The good thing about exposure and stop-loss limits is that their relationship to the balance sheet and profit and loss account is easy to understand.

8.4.2 Intermediate Metrics – Risk Factors

The intermediate sophistication metrics involve decomposing the source of price movement into a number of factors (Figure 8.6). The mapping of an exposure to risk factors may be one to one or one to many. Structured products and derivatives are combinations of simpler products. For example, the forward foreign exchange position can be decomposed into the spot foreign exchange rate and the two interest rates.

The risk factors may be one per risk source, or multiple as for equities. Each individual risk factor will be measured in the same units. For example, for interest rates the unit might be the present value of a change in interest rates by 0.01% (PV01), for example moving from 5.00% to 5.01%. Using this metric it becomes possible to aggregate exposures to the same risk factor. For example, government bonds, instead of having

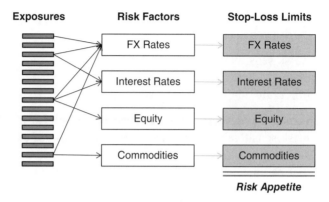

Figure 8.6   Risk appetite based on risk factors and stop-loss limits

a limit on 3-month maturity bonds and another limit on 10-year bonds it now becomes possible to aggregate based on PV01. This aggregation makes the assumption that the yield curve or term structure of interest rates moves in parallel. What the PV01 per bond would show is that the price impact of a PV01 is much less on 3-month maturity bonds than it is on a 10-year bond.

For bonds issued by non-government bodies there will be three components to the risk factor. There is the reference benchmark bond, the position of the non-government bond on the yield curve in comparison with the reference bond, and the yield increment for the non-government risk (Figure 8.7).

The yield increment for the non-government bond can be estimated directly for each individual bond. However, this will require resources. A less intensive approach is to group the non-government issuers into cohorts based on actual or implied credit ratings. This use of cohorts is similar to that used in credit risk estimation. This also means that a

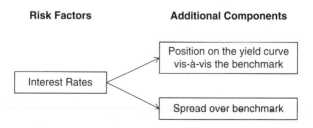

Figure 8.7   Decomposition of risk factor into components

new bond issue can be fitted into the framework using cohorts, without historical data for this individual bond.

For equities there may be two components to the equity risk factor, one representing systematic risk and the other representing idiosyncratic risk. The systematic risk represents how the market as a whole moves. These market movements are captured via movements in equity indices, such as the DAX, FTSE100 or S&P500 as representations of the entire market. The idiosyncratic component reflects how the individual equity moves in relation to the index. For example, on average does IBM change by 1.1 times the change in the index value or 0.9 times? This factor is sometimes referred to as the beta of an equity. At the extreme a firm may have exposures to all the individual equities in the index, but not necessarily in the same proportions as the index. As the index and the firm's portfolio of equities converge, so there is less idiosyncratic risk in the portfolio.

More broadly, the decomposition into risk factors enables structured products to be integrated into this framework. A structured product could have an embedded equity option, pay an interest coupon and be denominated in a different currency from the equity, as for a convertible bond. Provided the structured product can be decomposed into its components then it can be mapped to the risk factors.

The use of risk factors enables stop-loss limits to be generated for each of the major sources of market risk. For example, an exposure of X million will, on average, give rise to a loss of Y for a small change in the stock market index, for example FTSE 6500 to 6499. Once the risk factors have been estimated for a small move in each stock market index, they can be converted into an exposure limit. For example, for a move in the stock market of 1 point (6500 to 6499) the firm is willing to tolerate a loss of £X. The next step is to convert this into the number of units invested in the stock market. The position of each individual equity is generated by applying the beta of the individual stock to the stock market index.

This process means that a stop-loss limit can be generated for an equity portfolio linked to a particular market. For example, the stop-loss limit could be set at $10,000, which corresponds to a given number of units invested in the stock market index.

One of the issues around the use of stock market indices is the shape of the equity portfolio of the firm. If the firm only invests in one equity, then the idiosyncratic factors for that equity will have a more material impact on the risk than for a diversified portfolio. In this situation it is unwise to rely entirely on the market index as a good representation of risk. A role of market risk management is to advise/challenge the business on this concentration/diversification aspect.

Aggregating the risk factor coverage from a market to all markets requires some assumptions. For interest rates the objective might be to be able to aggregate the risk from bond positions denominated in US$, C$, £ and €. For equities the objective might be to aggregate exposures across DAX, FTSE100 and S&P500. The simplest approach is to assume that the different markets are synchronised in their movements, when bonds in US$ increase in price so do bonds in C$, £ and €. The further assumption is not only that they move in the same direction, but also by the same amount. The assumption is that the correlation is one. This enables the limits for each market, within a risk factor, to be added together to produce a limit for the risk factor.

The more challenging step is to consider the correlation between the different risk factors. A correlation of one means that as US$ bond prices move so will the DAX.

Correlations of one are more conservative than history shows. The challenge is in arriving at correlations other than one. Determining these correlations is usually a role for market risk management. It also supports their role of having an overview of the risk of the entire portfolio, in comparison with traders who may be limited to a small part of the portfolio, such as € bonds with a remaining maturity of 10 years.

The risk factors can be applied to derivatives as well as to bonds, equities, foreign exchange and commodities. This is a big step forward over the exposure-based approach. However, financial options do not work well or easily with the risk factor approach.

Using the risk factors as the basis for market risk measurement has resulted in a significant reduction in detail and variety when used as the basis for reporting up the organisation. Literally hundreds of individual positions can be summarised by a few figures.

The use of risk factors is not demanding on computer time. The approach is more precise than exposures, but contains a number of assumptions, such as parallel moves in yield curves. The impact of some of these assumptions can be reduced by having more components within a risk factor and adding complexity.

The downside of the risk factor approach is that it is relatively static in that it does not take into account that these risk factors move by different amounts. The PV01 is useful, but it needs to be adjusted by an estimate of the range of possible movement. Additionally, it is relatively expensive to generate and use an accurate correlation estimate and then recalculate it as the relationships between markets evolve. Some of these issues formed the impetus behind the development of portfolio approaches.

8.4.3   Complex Metrics – Portfolio Simulation

The portfolio approach makes use of concepts developed for asset management in the 1950s. These approaches make use of the variance/covariance matrix which enables diversification benefits to be recognised, via correlation, in determining the risk of the portfolio. The portfolio approach effectively states that the risk from owning two assets, less than perfectly correlated, in combination is less than the risk of owning the two assets individually.

The portfolio approach builds on the elements of the risk factor approach. The differences are additional components for the risk factors, use of historical data to determine correlations and run simulations. The result is a more accurate risk estimate as the methodology enables a more complete coverage of the risks involved and their interactions. However, it is more complex and this complexity reduces transparency. This complexity also increases the computation time required.

The model risk aspects arise from the complexity of the processes, which are explored in more detail below.[5] Other disadvantages from using portfolio approaches can include a false sense of precision[6] or accuracy and construction of sub-portfolios. Just because a risk figure can be calculated to the penny, does not mean that it is accurate to the penny. If the degree of uncertainty around the estimate was constant, for example ± 10, then this could be taken into account. However, the degree of uncertainty can be expected to vary with the portfolio composition.

With these disadvantages, why are portfolio models used? These models are used because they condense the details of thousands of positions into a single number or a small table. These models have advantages from a cybernetic perspective of condensing detail and removing variety. Monitoring and addressing the shortcomings of these models is part of the role of market risk management, for example with programmes of stress testing, scenarios and applying market liquidity adjustments.

---

[5] Alexander, C. (2008) *Market Risk Analysis IV: Value at Risk Models*, Chapter 6.

[6] Jorion, P. (2007), p. 552.

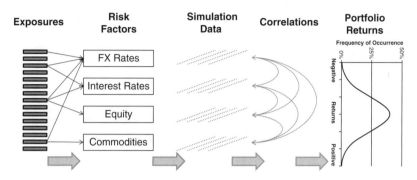

Figure 8.8   Risk appetite determined by portfolio simulation

The risk factors used in the previous section are now used as the basis for simulations of the portfolio. The data for the simulations is the actual historic data or based upon the historic data. For many of the risk factors, historical data is available going back a decade or more. Using historic data directly involves extracting the risk factor information from the historic prices and then applying to the exposures. For example, noting that on a day the benchmark US$ government bond, with a remaining maturity of 10 years, changes yield by 0.03% p.a. This change of 3 units scales the PV01 for the bond to provide the price change to the bond for that change in yield. The price change for the bond is then scaled by the exposure. Comparing the price change with the last valuation provides the return (positive or negative) from having that position for a period of time (Figure 8.8).

Using historical data in the portfolio simulation requires decisions about the length of the data series. Is a shorter period of historical data better than a longer period, is 1 year better than 5 years? A longer data series is likely to include extremes of change in the benchmark risk factors, but the longer period will have a smoothing effect. These effects mean that it is not possible to unequivocally say whether a shorter or longer period is best.

There are two main approaches to using historical data, direct and indirect. The direct approach involves using the historical data as collected for a specific day, say the values for the risk factors as of 30 January 2012. This approach has the advantage that the changes actually happened. It also means that the correlations emerge from the historic data and do not require separate calculation. The shortcoming is reliance upon historical data to accurately describe what will happen in the future. For example, changes in the benchmark bond yield only by 0.030% p.a.

and not 0.031% p.a. or 0.028% p.a., which may not have actually been experienced in the past.

To address this issue of discontinuous possible change, market risk management uses the historical data to generate statistical distributions of possible changes in the benchmark values. The statistical distributions then provide the values used in the simulation. While there may be little difference between these two approaches when changes are small, there can be differences when the changes are large. For example, during a market crash the stock market index may fall 7% in a day and the previous highest was 4.5%. However, a statistical distribution enables the 7% to be simulated as well as 6.5%, 6.2%, etc.

Using statistical distributions is not free from assumptions and other "costs". For example, what statistical distribution is appropriate to describe the changes in a particular risk factor? Does the statistical distribution provide plausible results? Additionally, it is now necessary to model correlation, or something more complicated such as copulas.

Products with non-linear price changes, in particular financial options, have been mentioned as being difficult to incorporate into exposure and risk factor approaches to estimating market risk. These financial options change their value as the time remaining to maturity, the implied volatility and the level of interest rates all vary. The implied volatility of an option represents the possible change in underlying or source prices or rates over the remaining life of the option. As maturity approaches and the current price is close to the option strike price, the option behaves in a non-linear manner. For a small movement in the price of the underlying exposure the option can have a significant change in value. Options with long times to maturity can have near linear changes in price.

These non-linear features of financial options add to the complexity of risk management. The factors driving the non-linear price changes include:

- The prevailing price of the underlying risk in comparison with the price at which the underlying exposure can be bought or sold (strike price).
- The volatility of the price of the underlying risk.
- The interest rate used in pricing the option.
- Any income, such as dividends, generated by the underlying risk.
- The time remaining to expiry of the option.
- The format of the option, for example European, American, barrier, etc.

From one day to the next, these factors may all move the option price in the same direction or have effects that cancel each other out to some degree. The processes used in the simulation and the repricing of the option make it possible to arrive at an accurate assessment of market risk embedded in these products.

The correlation feature of portfolio models becomes particularly important in the middle management layers between the risk appetite at the top of the firm and at the risk taker level. Owing to the correlation effects in the portfolio models, the sum of the individual risk appetites at the risk taker level may be more than the risk appetite expressed by the Board. This enables the risk appetite expressed by the Board to be used efficiently across the market risk activities of the firm.

The downside is additional complexity when sub-allocating risk appetite to the risk taker level. Each day the risk taken by the trader will be compared with the allocated risk appetite. This is estimated by determining the portion of the total portfolio risk estimate that is attributable to the exposures and risks under the control of that individual trader. However, due to the correlation effects in the portfolio, the trader's contribution to the total risk can change from one day to the next due to changes in other parts of the market risk portfolio.

When there are multiple constraints on the risk taker's activity then clarity is needed over which is the over-riding constraint. For firms using portfolio simulations this tends to be the dominant constraint. Other constraints may be stop-loss and size of exposure as described in the mandate.

The portfolio simulation approach reflects the market risks. The market risk estimate can now be expressed, with some precision, as a single number representing thousands of individual positions and exposures. However, the cost is considerable; market risk management needs to have knowledge about statistics and these calculations are computer intensive.

8.4.4   Economic Capital

The outcome from the portfolio simulation is a forecast distribution of returns as shown as the end product in Figure 8.8 above and in Figure 8.9.

For market risk appetite the focus is on the negative returns. This requires the data in Figure 8.9 to be reorganised and displayed differently.

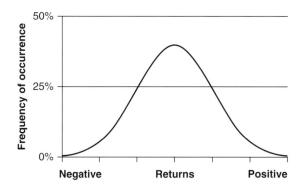

Figure 8.9   Distribution of possible returns generated by portfolio simulation

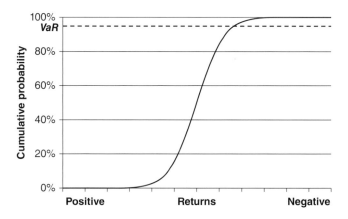

Figure 8.10   Cumulative distribution of possible returns

Figure 8.10 shows a line equating to VaR. VaR is a value associated with a particular confidence interval, such as 95% or 99%. The VaR may be expressed as $X at 99% confidence interval for 1 day. Alternatively, it says that there is a 99% probability that the firm will lose less than $X in 1 day. These are forecasts.

One of the criticisms of VaR as a measure of market risk is that it does not estimate how much will be lost with a probability of 1% (100%–99%). If VaR is estimated daily then assuming 250 business days a year and some other assumptions, the 99% VaR number should be breached 2.5 times a year.[7] If everything else is kept constant then 2.5 times

---

[7] Assuming 250 trading days a year.

a year the profit and loss will show a loss bigger than the 99% VaR. One way to address this is to raise the confidence interval, for example to 99.9%.

This issue of the possible breaching of the market risk appetite, when expressed as VaR, is widely recognised and consideration is being given to other metrics.[8] These other metrics are also being actively explored by the regulators.[9] These metrics have a variety of names, such as expected shortfall, conditional VaR, expected tail loss, tail VaR and others. The objective is to represent the average loss above the VaR-related confidence interval. If the 99% confidence interval is breached 2 to 3 days a year, on average how big might this loss be? Owing to statistical properties of the distribution of returns of the portfolio, the expected tail loss could be $X+10% or $X+50%. Use of this metric may have advantages over raising the VaR confidence interval until it approaches 100%. The use of the expected tail loss should counteract assumptions about the precision of the VaR estimate.

A VaR with a 1-day forecast horizon means the most to the risk takers. This makes the assumption that the positions are held constant for 24 hours. This assumption, about constant positions, is less robust when calculating a VaR with a 10-day forecast horizon as it assumes that the risk taker does not actively manage their portfolio during that 10-day period. Additionally, a 10-day forecast horizon may omit some of the spikes in return demonstrated in the actual daily returns. If a 1-day horizon is used then efforts are needed to aggregate and escalate the metrics up the organisation before it loses its timeliness and becomes stale.

For capital purposes, economic or regulatory, the time horizon may be more than 1 day. The VaR 1-day forecast may be manipulated, for example by using the square root of time to scale the result, to represent another time horizon. This enables a 1-day VaR to be converted into a 10-day VaR or even longer. The use of the square root of time is a further example of embedded assumptions and model risk.

VaR is an output of the portfolio simulation approach. To summarise, there are a number of features that add to the complexity of using the VaR:

---

[8] Kemp, M.H.D. (2011) *Extreme Events – Robust Portfolio Construction in the Presence of Fat Tails*, p. 15, footnote 10.

[9] Basel Committee on Banking Supervision (2012) Fundamental Review of the Trading Book, pp. 20, 50.

- decomposing positions into risk factors;
- historical data – used directly or converted into statistical distributions;
- choice of statistical distribution;
- correlation;
- sampling and simulation;
- time horizons;
- calculating VaR and/or expected tail loss.

Some of these complicating factors have been known for a long time, such as the choice of time horizon. Other complications have become evident from experience when the VaR and values at other confidence intervals do not correspond to subsequent reality.

The purpose of this significant effort is to reduce the uncertainty in the market risk estimate. When aggregating data from the bottom up, VaR reduces detail and the uncertainty in the amount of risk being taken at a point in time for a particular horizon. From the top down it has implications for the market risk appetite figure and whether there will be an unpleasant surprise.

8.5   MARKET RISK MANAGEMENT

The market risk management function has key roles in the framework and oversight of the market risk estimation model and processes. This is part of their role as the second line of defence, challenging, supporting and overseeing the business. As part of these roles a portion of their resources is dedicated to addressing various shortcomings in risk estimation and consistency of risk-adjusted performance measurement.

One of these shortcomings is what to do about market risk in the banking book. Issues such as foreign exchange and commodity risks are already part of the market risk estimation process. The main issue is likely to be interest rate risk in the banking book. This risk may be transferred from the banking book to the trading book by an internal transaction. This is achieved by the banking book purchasing an appropriate hedge from the trading book. Once in the trading book, the interest rate risk becomes more transparent due to decomposing positions into risk factors.

8.5.1   Performance Measurement

For the firm, market risk has upside and downside possibilities. The majority of market risk estimation is focused on the downside possibilities, the consequences when something goes wrong. However, as part of the firm's planning and budgeting processes consideration needs to be given to the upside.

At the Board level the upside and downside considerations are important. For an allocation of a given amount of total risk appetite, how much profit can be anticipated? When considering the possible or even actual return on risk appetite there needs to be completeness of coverage. While one risk taker may outperform another in terms of generated profits, is the ranking still the same when considering return on allocated risk appetite or utilised economic capital? Does the allocated risk appetite or utilised economic capital reflect all the risks, such as credit, liquidity and operational risks or just market risk?

This perspective can be reinforced by a process described as profit and loss attribution analysis. In this process the profit and loss is mapped to various risk factors, and other risk sources such as credit risk. The advantage of the risk mapping process is that it supports the allocation of risk appetite at the risk taker level. The process also serves as a risk identification control; if there is a portion of profit that cannot be attributed, then where is it coming from?

8.5.2   Back Testing

As overseers and possibly operators of the market risk estimation process market risk management has a responsibility, with the business, to monitor and address shortcomings. Some of the shortcomings were mentioned above and result in increased complexity in the risk estimation process. There are other shortcomings that may be difficult to address in the risk estimation process, or it may be more desirable, for transparency, if they are addressed separately.

One of the processes used to identify these shortcomings is referred to as back testing. In back testing the firm compares the number of times that the profit and loss exceeds the forecast given by the confidence interval used in VaR. If the number of excesses is higher than expected then there is an investigation. The investigation may result in changes in the risk factors, the statistical distributions, the estimation of correlation, or some other element.

One of the decisions relates to the confidence interval used for back testing. For example, if it is at 99% then that may generate losses that exceed the forecast VaR two to three times a year. The next question becomes one of when an investigation should be triggered, for example when the excesses reach 5? If there is a lower confidence interval, such as 80%, then there will be more events to test and the investigation process will become a regular activity rather than an exceptional activity, but it will require resources.

Back testing can not only test that the individual positions are comprehensively mapped to the risk factors, but also the behaviour of the risk factors themselves. Do the risk factors behave as the statistical distributions in the risk estimation process predict? This can be assessed not only by the number of excesses, but also by the size of the excess. The performance of a fat-tailed distribution will differ markedly from a normal distribution the further into the higher confidence intervals the test is applied. The difference will be more noticeable at 99.9% confidence interval than 95% or 90%. But this is counteracted by the number of data points involved. This consideration of the severity of the excess supports the use of expected tail loss over VaR as a risk metric.

When conducting back testing at the risk taker level there is a question over which risk estimate should be used. If the benchmark is an allocation of the total portfolio economic capital then correlation and diversification benefits need to be taken into account. The allocation may reflect the contribution that the individual risk taker makes to the total risk, and this includes diversification benefits across the total portfolio. If a direct estimate of the risk taker's portfolio is generated then it will be a more accurate comparison, but more expensive to implement.

8.5.3   Market Liquidity of Positions

Market liquidity risk is the risk that a firm cannot easily offset or eliminate a position at the market price because of inadequate market depth or a market disruption. Market liquidity risk can become an issue due to the composition of the firm's portfolio or due to external factors. The extent of market liquidity varies over time, sometimes liquidity increases and sometimes it decreases.

Issues around market liquidity are present at the beginning of the risk estimation process, in particular the mark-to-market or mark-to-model valuation and the time horizon. The mark-to-market valuation is intended to reflect the proceeds that would be realised from offsetting or hedging the position. If the position is twice as large as the daily transaction volume then it is unlikely that the position can be offset over a 1-day horizon. For these large positions an adjustment may need to be made to the starting valuation and/or the risk estimation.[10] These largish positions may be present in the portfolio of a single risk taker, or the summation of individual positions held in the portfolios of several risk takers.

The external source of market liquidity risk is beyond the control of the firm. This is where the daily transaction volume falls. One of the causes of changes in liquidity can be regulatory and/or political. For example, if a particular instrument suddenly becomes eligible for retirement savings programmes then liquidity will be expected to increase due to demand. If an instrument or an issuer is downgraded then there may be a burst of activity as positions are sold or risk is hedged followed by a reduction in liquidity as demand falls. A regular source of liquidity issues is when an equity moves in or out of a stock index; moving in increases the liquidity, moving out decreases the liquidity. This is caused by the number of investors that hold the stock index and the scale of that investment.

This external market liquidity risk may affect a single issuer in a single risk taker's portfolio or it may affect whole categories of instruments across the firm's entire portfolio.

8.5.4 Discontinuities

This refers to discontinuities in the histories of risk factor performance. The discontinuity arises from new situations. One of these new situations could be a macro-economic change.

Macro-economic change may relate to something new, such as the creation of the euro, or a change in an existing regime. Some currencies trade in a limited range around a reference currency. However, from time to time the trading range may be reset, creating a discontinuity. For this type of discontinuity there is no history so expert judgement may be needed on assessing the jump to the new trading range and price fluctuations within the new range.

One of the outcomes from the macro-economic discontinuities can be a surge in selling pressure. This results in price drops and an increase in volatility. The increase in volatility feeds through into the risk estimation

---

[10] Alexander, C. (2008), p. 392.

data and probably creates a jump in the economic capital. If there is a jump in the economic capital then there may be pressure to reduce the amount of risk, which creates further selling pressure, a positive feedback loop. Although the risk estimation process is risk sensitive, the consequences can lead to further volatility and losses.

8.5.5   Stress Testing

A tool in the market risk management armoury is stress testing. Stress testing can be applied to any aspect of the risk estimation process. Stress testing is particularly useful when considering longer-term horizons such as 3 or 6 months, or even strategic horizons.[11]

Both stress tests and scenarios are based on extreme but plausible events. For scenarios there may be a probability associated with the occurrence of the events that produces a particular impact. For stress tests the assumption is that the sequence of events will occur. For some stress tests inspiration may come from history, for others it needs some input from experts. However, it should be remembered that experts come with their own biases, especially anchoring to events that they themselves have experienced.

While these tests focus on extreme but plausible events, the variety of events falling into this category varies over time. Twenty years ago few would have contemplated using passenger jets as weapons against the USA. Ten years ago the idea of an entire category of instruments being mis-rated was unlikely to have been considered plausible. The outcome of these stress tests may be an adjustment to the market risk appetite and/or the creation of a "playbook" for when the events, or something close to them, materialise.

The outcome of these stress tests is fed into the discussions on risk appetite and its sub-allocation down to risk takers. Not all of the stress tests and scenarios explored will be reported to the Board, some may be aimed at the senior executives sub-allocating their portion of the market risk appetite.

An outcome of the active involvement of market risk management is that the market risk appetite is not a static number. While formally it may be reviewed annually as part of the budget and planning process, it is actually regularly reviewed. These reviews can take into account the

---

[11] Alexander, C. (2008), Chapter 7.

results of stress tests, the evolution of market conditions and opportunities and result in adjustments to the market risk appetite.

8.6　ISSUES TO CONSIDER

- When was market risk appetite last reviewed by the Board?
- How is the market risk appetite sub-allocated to risk sources?
- What is the return on the utilised market risk appetite?
- Is the market risk appetite consistent with the revenue targets for the business?
- When did market risk management last amend the market risk appetite allocated to various risk sources?
- When was the last breach in total market risk appetite notified to the Board or the Risk Committee?
- Are breaches of market risk appetite notified to the Board or Risk Committee to assure them that the process is functioning?
- Is market risk management adequately resourced?
- How does the Board or Risk Committee assure itself that the market risk estimates are reasonable?
- Does the Board or Risk Committee see the results of back testing?
- What market risk stress tests are performed on the trading book? Have the stress test results amended the market risk appetite?
- How are interest rate risk, foreign exchange risk and commodity risk in the banking book managed?
- If the anticipated revenue for the year is achieved 9 months into the year, what happens to market risk appetite for the last 3 months? Is it increased or decreased?
- How does your VaR compare with that published by peers?

FURTHER READING

Alexander, C. (2008) *Market Risk Analysis IV: Value at Risk Models*. John Wiley & Sons, Chichester.

Basel Committee on Banking Supervision (1996) Amendment to the Capital Accord to Incorporate Market Risk. www.bis.org/publ/bcbs24.pdf

Basel Committee on Banking Supervision (2012) Fundamental Review of the Trading Book (Consultative Paper). http://www.bis.org/publ/bcbs219.htm

Hull, J. (2011) *Options, Future & Other Derivatives*, 8th edn. Pearson Education, Oxford.

Jorion, P. (2007) *Value at Risk: The New Benchmark for Managing Financial Risk*, 3rd edn. McGraw-Hill, New York.

Kemp, M.H.D. (2011) *Extreme Events: Robust Portfolio Construction in the Presence of Fat Tails*. John Wiley & Sons, Chichester.

Markowitz, H. (1991) *Portfolio Selection: Efficient Diversification of Investments*, 2nd edn. Blackwell, Oxford.

Markowitz, H. (1991) *Mean–Variance Analysis in Portfolio Choice and Capital Market*. Blackwell, Oxford.

McNeil, A.J., Frey, R. and Embrechts, P. (2005) *Quantitative Risk Management: Concepts, Tools, Techniques*. Princeton University Press, Princeton, NJ.

9

Operational Risk

Risk Management at the Top

Ch. 1: Introduction

Part I: Risk Oversight

Ch. 2: Risk – An Overview	Ch. 3: Risk Oversight	Ch. 4: Risk Management	Ch. 5: Risk Appetite	Ch. 6: Risk Culture

Part II: Specific Risks

Ch. 7: Credit Risk	Ch. 8: Market Risk	Ch. 9: Operational Risk	Ch. 10: Liquidity Risk	Ch. 11: Other Risks	Ch. 12: Risk Interactions

Part III: Regulatory Environment

Ch. 13: Regulatory Environment

Operational risk is a relatively recent description for a collection of individual risks that firms have been managing for years. With Basel II, operational risk in banks began to attract a regulatory capital requirement. This regulatory focus resulted in a burst of analysis and development that continues.

Depending on where boundaries are drawn between individual risk sources, it is conceivable that poor operational risk management has contributed to more failures in the financial industry than credit and market risk combined. Operational risk accounts for many of the newspaper headlines.

9.1   INTRODUCTION

Operational risk is not only encountered by the financial industry, but is present in most corporate and personal endeavours. This is attributable to its definition. Perhaps surprisingly, operational risk was one of the first risks to be explicitly defined by the banking regulators. The definitions of credit and market risks are largely implied from the scope and methodologies of regulatory requirements.

The management of operational risk can affect the firm's reputation or brand value, with long-lasting consequences. This arises from operational risk events that affect customers, for example software failures affecting networks of ATM machines, mis-selling products, data security, etc.

Unlike credit or market risks, operational risk is seldom taken by financial firms with the objective of generating a return. A refinement is that some firms undertake activities where the dominant source of risk is operational; these firms have a business model based on their operational risk management capabilities, for example custody services.

Figure 9.1 also appeared in Chapter 5. It emphasises that operational risk rarely generates a return in compensation for taking the risk.

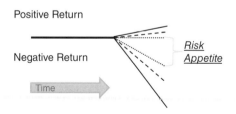

Figure 9.1   Returns from operational risk

The rest of this chapter looks at the:

9.2 DEFINITION OF OPERATIONAL RISK

Operational Risk (OR) is defined as the risk of loss resulting from inadequate or failed internal processes, people and systems or from external events. This definition includes legal risk, but excludes strategic and reputational risk.[1]

A review of the definition shows that there are very few activities or processes undertaken by a financial firm that are not subject to operational risk. The affected activities range from regulatory and financial reporting to the security guard on the front desk to payments and everything in between.

Legal risk is explicitly included in the definition of operational risk. However, the scope is not intuitive.

Legal risk is the risk of loss resulting from exposure to

(1) non-compliance with regulatory and/or statutory responsibilities and/or

(2) adverse interpretation of and/or unenforceability of contractual provisions.

This includes the exposure to new laws as well as changes in interpretations of existing law(s) by appropriate authorities and exceeding authority as contained in the contract.[2]

One of the features of operational risk that distinguishes it from credit or market risks is the duration of the period at risk. For example, with credit or market risks the exposure generally disappears when the risk has been removed from the balance sheet or has matured. However,

---

[1] Operational Riskdata eXchange (2012) Operational Risk Reporting Standards – Text, Section 3.1.1.

[2] Ibid., Section 3.1.2.

operational risk associated with tax, certain legal risks and divestment of businesses can persist for several years after the transaction has been completed.

To support the understanding of operational risk and the scope of the definition, the industry and regulators produced a list of seven event categories:[3]

- Internal Fraud
- External Fraud
- Employee Practices & Workplace Safety
- Clients, Products & Business Practices
- Natural Disasters & Public Safety
- Technology & Infrastructure Failure
- Execution, Delivery & Process Management.

Most of these categories have at least one subcategory.

Operational risk, whether human error, act of nature, technology failure or something more malign, can affect any of the processes employed by the firm.

An understanding of the business scope of operational risk can be gained from Table 9.1. It affects all business activities. No variation in shading has been used to indicate varying intensities of operational risk as nearly all of the business lines have had their low points in the past 10–20 years.

A way of thinking about operational risk is to consider it as a preventable risk or an external risk.[4] Preventable risks are those over which the firm can exercise preventative control, for example employee practices and workplace safety. External risks are those outside the sphere of influence of the firm, for example natural disasters. The controls mentioned in Chapter 4 were allocated to categories of prevention, detection and mitigation. The suitability of one or more of these control types will be influenced according to whether the risks are preventable or external. There is very little that a firm can do to prevent a natural disaster, but financial firms have extensive control frameworks to prevent external fraud.

The definition of operational risk is useful in creating a boundary with other risk types. If operational risk was defined as "everything that is

---

[3] Operational Riskdata eXchange (2012) Operational Risk Reporting Standards – Appendix, derived from Basel II.

[4] Kaplan, R.S. and Mikes, A. (2012) Managing risks: A new framework. *Harvard Business Review*, June.

Table 9.1 Business line versus product/service sources of operational risk

	Corporate finance	Trading and sales	Retail banking	Commercial banking	Payments and settlements	Agency services	Asset management	Retail brokerage
Capital raising								
Corporate finance services								
FX and money markets								
Securities								
Derivatives								
Retail credit								
Commercial credit								
Deposits								
Cash management, payments and settlements								
Trust/investment management								
Investment products								
Brokerage								

not credit, liquidity or market risks" then the issue would be where to stop. For example business risk, with its emphasis on cost and revenue structures, is not part of operational risk. However, some may decide that individual aspects of operational risk are parts of the "cost of doing" business.

9.3 OPERATIONAL RISK FRAMEWORK

The regulators expect financial firms to have an operational risk framework that is proportionate to the organisation. Effectively, the more complex and sophisticated the organisation then the more sophisticated the operational risk management framework. The regulators are in a position to make these comments on the frameworks as they see how they are implemented in a variety of firms.

For business activities, it is not unusual for operational risk management support to be embedded in the business. The individual or team may specialise in operational risk, or operational risk may be one element of their risk management responsibilities, such as in addition to compliance. This person or team will usually have a reporting line to the business and a dotted line to the corporate operational risk management function.

The specialists embedded in the business have advantages over the corporate operational risk management function. Being in the business, they are in a good position to identify emerging risks as well as those that may be getting close to thresholds. This requires knowledge and the active support of the business. Without this knowledge it is difficult for the risk management cycle to operate and provide data for aggregation and communication upwards through the organisation.

The dual reporting line, of these specialists, facilitates the introduction and implementation of policies, standards and procedures of the corporate operational risk management framework. The corporate policies need to be implemented to enable consistent data and information to be reported up through the organisation. Without consistency there will be a comparison of "chalk and cheese" and users of the data may not be aware of the differences.

For operational risk, the concepts of risk-taking authority, allocations and limits have slightly different meanings. Credit and market risks are largely acquired in pursuit of return. There are instruments that enable the credit and market risk exposures to be managed, sometimes quite quickly. For operational risks, although some may be preventable, it does not mean that the control operates with 100% effectiveness 100% of the time. As an example, a system may have a maintenance programme, a preventative control, but an element of the system can still fail unexpectedly. The expectation is that the maintenance programme will reduce the number of unexpected failures. By having a regular process the total cost will be less and the level of uncertainty reduced as opposed to managing and mitigating several unexpected events.

Given these conditions, limits cannot mean that a threshold will never be breached. For operational risk a better approach is to consider that once a threshold is breached then action will be taken to bring the risk back under the threshold. This has similarities with risk management activities for credit, liquidity and market risks.

For operational risk a key level of responsibility relates to authorising remedial reaction. For example, if there is a breach of appetite then the issue is escalated to the appropriate organisation that can authorise remedial action. The part of the firm that identifies the operational risk issue may not have budgetary responsibility.

The business needs to be involved as it is their objectives that are directly or indirectly compromised by the operational risk event. In addition, the business has the budget to initiate remedial action. If remedial action is uneconomic then the risk needs to be accepted and capital set aside for the risk, and this requires a level of authority.

In addition to the reactive stance mentioned above, a proactive stance can be taken towards operational risk. This proactive stance may involve looking at the business objectives and working backwards to operational risk events that can prevent achievement of those objectives. For example, an objective might be to increase market share. Increasing market share can be influenced by brand value as appreciated by the customer segments. Achieving this appreciation may require additional communication and managing exceptions, such as customer complaints. This in turn leads to an analysis of the complaints and working on the causes of these complaints. In this context the total volume of customer complaints may be an operational risk KRI that relates to the objectives of the business.

The definition of operational risk as provided above is broad. There is a need to distinguish between certain events and related responses. The most common categorisation is by loss frequency. Does the event produce a high frequency of losses or a low frequency of losses? Issues such as data quality can result in high-frequency low-impact events, while a natural disaster is likely to give rise to a low-frequency high-impact

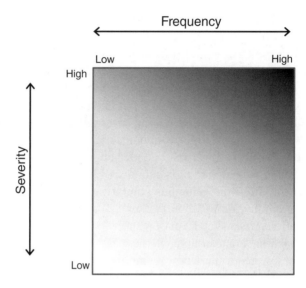

Figure 9.2   Operational risk heat map

event. Owing to exposure, a process error can result in a high-impact con-sequence. An example is a process error affecting millions of customers.

The approach to reducing the risk may vary between high-frequency and low-frequency events. For low-frequency high-impact events, insurance can be a cost-effective mitigant even if it does not prevent the event from occurring.

Figure 9.2 shows an operational risk heat map with dimensions of severity of the events and frequency of the events. Firms tend not to exist for very long if they are located in the top right corner of high-frequency events with high-severity impacts.

Often the high-frequency low-impact events are categorised as expected losses, Figure 9.2 bottom left. This use of "expected" has a non-statistical meaning and can be interpreted as "losses that are expected". For some, these losses are part of the cost of doing business. Nevertheless, these losses should be collected as they act as a drag on the business profits. Without data collection a risk analysis cannot be undertaken and decisions on whether to reduce the risk or continue to accept cannot be made.

The low-frequency high-impact events are in the unexpected loss category. These events can have several effects, including consumption of capital as well as use of management resources, regulatory intrusion and impact upon the firm's reputation.

The level of operational risk across the organisation can be monitored using KRIs as well as capital calculations. Given the range of possible operational risk events and organisational scope it is possible to arrive at a large number of KRIs. These KRIs may be linked to individual elements of the operational risk appetite, or be specified by the businesses and their support functions. For the business, the perspective may be events that can hinder achieving business objectives, irrespective of whether a loss is generated or not. Such a business objective might be the length of time that it takes to process a transaction, or the average of transactions that have not been processed within the normal time frame. The longer that a transaction has not been confirmed by a counterparty, then potentially the more expensive it is to correct any errors when they are found. The cost of these errors flows into the P&L of the business.

One of the features of the flow of information up through an organisation is the reduction in variety. Without this reduction in variety it would not be possible to provide a picture of operational risk across the firm that would be comprehensible. The issue is that many of the KRIs differ according to the business and the importance of a KRI may vary according to the process that is affected. For example, staff turnover may be a KRI on the assumption that having high staff turnover can lead to more errors. For activities that are reasonably standardised across the industry high staff turnover is less of an issue than where highly specialised expertise is needed, for example in anti-money laundering. An approach to aggregating KRIs is to use a scaling system to determine their relative importance. This scaling system can also be used to convert different individual metrics, such as staff turnover or the average time that transactions have been unprocessed, to a common metric, such as 1–5. What is a "1" and what is a "5" will depend on the business.

At the most granular organisational level, the individual values of the KRIs will add transparency. However, when aggregating the data as it flows up the organisation there are some issues. For example, when aggregating the KRIs should they be averaged or added together? In either case the aggregation process may hide adverse developments.

KRIs can be identified from a number of sources. The first line of risk management defence, the business and its support functions, may identify KRIs that have the potential to hinder the achievement of business objectives. Another source is via self-assessment of risks and controls, performed by the business, specialist functions and embedded operational risk management teams. Internal audit, as the third line of defence, may also identify KRIs through its risk-based audit process.

The support of business objectives is likely to reduce resistance to pay for the collection of KRIs by the businesses. The use of these indicators also helps to promote the risk culture of the organisation. An outcome is the increased likelihood of preventing something disagreeable, rather than mitigating the consequences. This prevention is also cheaper for the organisation.

The only KRI that does not have these aggregation issues is losses. However, losses tend to be backward looking and encourage a reactive approach to operational risk management, as opposed to a forward-looking and proactive approach. Losses are also likely to have their own escalation path. When a loss gets to a certain size then it will be notified to a particular group of people and if large enough will be escalated to the CRO and even the Board. These escalation levels are equivalent to risk appetite; thresholds in credit, market and liquidity risks.

Firms may want to set these loss-based thresholds for individual events and also for cumulative losses. The individual losses that get escalated will be the unexpected losses. The losses that are accumulated will be the expected losses. The difference between the unexpected and expected losses may be one of size, for example all losses below £1 million are expected. Thresholds and action triggers can be set for both of these loss types.

An additional refinement is to link the loss amount and the event type to the escalation trigger. For example, the firm's appetite for losses from duplicate payments will normally be higher than its appetite for internal fraud. This additional level of detail means that issues are brought to the attention of decision makers, without distracting them with a forest of numbers.

Event escalation is expected to occur up through several channels, as shown in Figure 9.3. One of the channels will be the business, another channel will be operational risk management. The third channel may be up the organisation of specialist control and support functions. For example, an internal fraud issue may be escalated up the chain of command within human resources. The minimum escalation levels and thresholds will be agreed between the business and operational risk management. The use of multiple channels ensures that issues do not get lost and those that need to know are informed.

Figure 9.4 shows the issue of aggregating and reporting operational risk information up the organisation and the flow of information down the organisation. For risk-taker and business perspectives, capital proxies contain insufficient detail. For monitoring at this level the tendency is to use KRIs.

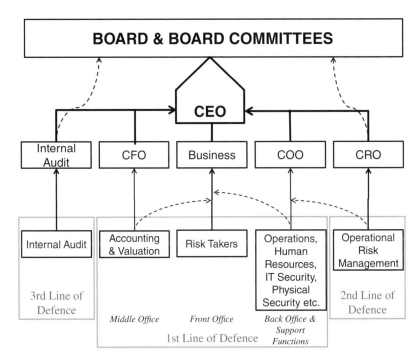

Figure 9.3   Lines of defence and communication channels

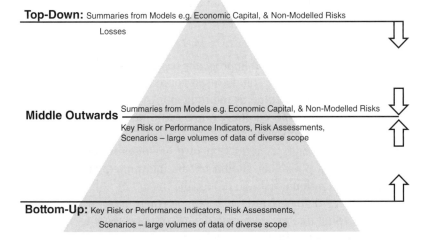

Figure 9.4   Data and information flows up and down the organisation

However, for the Board and senior executives, KRIs are often too granular when setting the firm's risk appetite, the portion allocated to operational risk and estimating the RAROC.

9.4 OPERATIONAL RISK ESTIMATION

Operational risk estimation, in terms of capital, occurs in a context that is heavily influenced by the regulators. There are two broad approaches:

1. indicators
2. models.

Indicators are much simpler to apply than models. There are incentives to migrate to the more sophisticated model approaches, for example integration with the operational risk management framework.

There is one objective for these capital-based metrics – to estimate the amount of risk for a period into the future.

Estimating the amount of risk is necessary as part of the risk appetite monitoring activities. Is the risk within the risk appetite? The amount of risk, in relation to the risk appetite, determines whether the exposure or control environment needs to change to get the level of risk within the risk appetite. Historic losses, expected and unexpected, will describe the actual risk of the recent past. However, it should be noted that for some operational risk events it can take years for the loss to emerge and materialise. Even when the event has materialised, the finalisation of the loss may require litigation which can take years.

9.4.1 Indicators

There are two risk estimation approaches based on indicators, the basic indicator approach and the standardised approach (see Table 9.2). Both approaches use gross income as the indicator. A consequence of using gross income is that the capital estimation is not risk sensitive. The fact is that it is not possible to reduce the capital amount except by reducing gross income. A reduction in gross income through a poor quarter or even a poor year should *not* be interpreted as leading to a reduction in operational risk. To reduce the impact of volatility in gross income, the regulators require a 3-year average using positive gross income on capital figures. Although the use of gross income may not be risk sensitive, it is cheap.

For these two approaches, the average gross income is scaled by a factor to arrive at the capital estimate. The use of gross income makes

Table 9.2 Basic indicator and standardised approaches to operational risk estimation

Business line[a]	Basic indicator factor[b]	Standardised factor[c]
Corporate finance	15%	18%
Trading and sales	15%	18%
Retail banking	15%	12%
Commercial banking	15%	15%
Payment and settlement	15%	18%
Agency services	15%	15%
Asset management	15%	12%
Retail brokerage	15%	12%

[a]This differs from the list in Table 1 from ORX, which has additional business lines for private banking and corporate items.
[b]Basel Committee on Banking Supervision (2004) International Convergence of Capital Measurement and Capital Standards – A revised framework (Basel II), p. 137, paragraph 649.
[c]Basel Committee on Banking Supervision (2004) International Convergence of Capital Measurement and Capital Standards – A revised framework (Basel II), p. 140, paragraph 654.

the assumption that the size of the loss is linked to the scale of the activity of the firm and that the scale of activity is adequately captured by gross income.

Migrating from the basic indicator approach to the standardised approach requires certain criteria to be met. The regulators are the gatekeepers to the various approaches to estimating regulatory capital and need to be convinced. The criteria used by the regulators include:[5]

1. The board of directors and senior management, as appropriate, are actively involved in the oversight of the operational risk management framework.
2. The bank has an operational risk management system that is conceptually sound and is implemented with integrity.
3. The bank has sufficient resources in the use of the approach in the major business lines as well as the control and audit areas.
4. The bank must develop specific policies and have documented criteria for mapping gross income for current business lines and activities into the standardised framework. The criteria must be reviewed and adjusted for new or changing business activities as appropriate.

---

[5] Basel Committee on Banking Supervision (2004) International Convergence of Capital Measurement and Capital Standards – A revised framework (Basel II), p. 141, paragraph 661.

5. As part of the bank's internal operational risk assessment system, the bank must systematically track relevant operational risk data including material losses by business line. Its operational risk assessment system must be closely integrated into the risk management processes of the bank. Its output must be an integral part of the process of monitoring and controlling the bank's operational risk profile. For instance, this information must play a prominent role in risk reporting, management reporting and risk analysis. The bank must have techniques for creating incentives to improve the management of operational risk throughout the firm.

6. There must be regular reporting of operational risk exposures, including material operational losses, to business unit management, senior management and the board of directors. The bank must have procedures for taking appropriate action according to the information within the management reports.

7. The bank's operational risk management processes and assessment system must be subject to validation and regular independent review. These reviews must include both the activities of the business units and of the operational risk management function.

Collectively, meeting the above criteria is a significant amount of work. The good news is that criteria all contribute to the operational risk framework of the firm. The alternative view is that for improvements in the operational risk framework there may also be reductions in the regulatory capital requirements.

Although a bank may be on one of the indicator approaches for the purpose of regulatory capital calculation, this does not prevent the firm from using a model to estimate economic capital.

9.4.2 Models

Models involve a reduction in the variety of information. Therefore, the risk estimates based on indicators are also models. However, in the context of estimating operational risk "models" generally refers to advanced measurement approach models. The phrase "Advanced Measurement Approach" (AMA) has its origins in the Basel II papers.[6] These models are statistically complex and require specialist skills in

---

[6] Basel Committee on Banking Supervision (2004), p. 142, paragraphs 664–679.

their design and operation. The AMA models are risk sensitive, which is an advantage over the indicator-based models.

AMA models generally have some form of simulation as a major feature of their calculations. For operational risk, these models fall into two categories; those used to estimate economic capital and those used to estimate the regulatory capital requirement.

For efficiency purposes it is best if the economic and regulatory capital models are closely related in terms of construction and inputs. This is also an advantage for the regulators as the firm then has an inherent interest in the inputs and outputs. This reduces the total cost to the firm of operating both models. Additionally, the regulators may want to see new features implemented, for a period of time, in the economic capital model before considering their integration into the regulatory capital model. However, some firms may use an AMA model for economic capital purposes, but not be permitted, by the regulators, to use it to estimate regulatory capital. This divergence may be due to the accumulated experience of the firm in using AMA models, or some aspect of the operational risk management framework.

The regulators have specified the data types that must be considered when developing the methodology to produce the risk estimate:

- internal loss data
- external loss data
- scenario analysis
- business environment and internal control factors.

These data types will all be used in the framework and risk management of operational risk. Firms will usually be collecting loss data as part of their operational risk framework. The external loss data will help the firm be aware of the range of loss events and their possible sizes. The business environment and internal control factors will largely be sourced from KRIs. The variety of data is intended to address various shortcomings in each data type.

The internal and external loss data needs to be reviewed. Part of the review includes an assessment of the relevancy of the data in comparison with the firm's current activities and the period ahead. For internal loss data the firm will be expected to have a process that assures the quality of the data, especially timeliness, accuracy and completeness. This quality assurance process is one that the Board will want to know has been established for the risk data that is being reported to them, especially losses.

The external data is intended to inform the firm of risks to which it is exposed, but has not yet experienced, as well as potential size of loss. However, there may be certain biases in the data depending upon its source. One bias relates to the size of the loss and the size of the firm. For example, if the scale of a loss is linked to the number of retail bank accounts then the source of exposure will influence the severity of the equivalent event at another firm. In general this level of exposure information is not widely available, so it becomes necessary to resort to readily available proxies for scale of activity, such as gross income.

The shortcoming of internal and external losses is that they are essentially historical data. If this was the only source of data used in AMA models then the assumption is that the future is an exact replication of the past.

Scenario analysis relies extensively upon expert opinion. The experts may be business, control and support functions, or risk managers. The goal is to generate the frequency and severity of extreme but plausible events, with a story about the events. Operational risk scenarios can have a background in various industries where they may be described as failure modes and effect analysis (FMEA) or hazard analysis or probabilistic risk analysis (PRA).[7] These techniques are used by the aerospace, nuclear and oil industries as well as the military.

The shortcoming of scenario analysis is the reliance upon experts. Experts suffer from biases, a human trait. For scenarios the biases that can have an effect on risk management are underestimates of the frequency of occurrence and underestimates of the severity. The willingness to consider events which have not yet been experienced by the firm is another bias. For these reasons the scenario process may use external loss data during scenario creation as a source of inspiration or validation.

Business environment and internal control factors are intended to consider change to the operational risk profile. This information may be in the form of KRIs used at the risk-taking levels. Changes in some KRIs may indicate possible changes in frequency of operational risk events in the future, but may be less good at indicating changes in severity. Other metrics may focus on sources of exposure, such as the number of retail customers, the number of staff, the value of buildings, etc. These exposure metrics may be collected by the business as a measure of activity.

---

[7] ORX, KPMG (2011) Preparing for the Unexpected – Leading Practices for Operational Risk Scenarios.

How these various data types are used in arriving at the risk estimate is not prescribed by the regulators. For some models the dominant input is loss data, so these are referred to as loss distribution approaches (LDA) models. For other models the dominant input is scenarios.

For the LDA and scenario-based operational risk estimations the outputs are the same, a loss amount for a particular confidence interval for a specified time horizon. The confidence interval will usually be 99.9% and the time horizon 12 months.

The portfolio-based approach to operational risk estimation has similarities to the approaches used in credit and market risk. The operational risk estimation model is likely to be designed and operated by the operational risk management function. The model validation can be performed by an independent group inside or outside the firm.

A common starting point for modelling portfolios of operational risk is a matrix of the business lines as in Table 9.1 and the seven event types in Section 9.2. One of the issues that this raises is the alignment of this matrix with the way in which certain risks are managed within the firm. For example, if there are common human resources policies across the firm then should employee practices and workplace safety be looked at by business line? If the risk measurement is too divorced from the risk management approaches then they begin to be seen as separate activities rather than different perspectives on the same risk.

At the core of this model is correlation. Some of the correlations will be influenced by risk management decisions. For example, if there is a large loss event then the firm may change its control environment to reduce the frequency and/or severity of possible repetition. Likewise, the environment for 12 months into the future may be different from the recent past. These issues have related counterparts in credit and market risk, although they may have a longer sets of data. One of the big differences between operational risk and the other sources of risk is that as firms get better at managing operational risk so there will be less loss data to use in models. It is expected to be several years before this becomes a limiting factor.

The contribution that the different data types make to the risk estimate is not prescribed. For example, it would be possible for a specialist firm to say that available external loss data is not relevant to their operational risk profile and so has a 0% weighting in their AMA model.

Another factor to consider is the feedback loop to the business for improvements in the control environment. This feedback loop influences behaviour, for example via the risk-adjusted return on capital calculations (RAROC). A business will want to see a capital benefit from applying resources to reduce the level of operational risk. This feedback loop is also behind some of the risk management decisions to reduce the frequency or severity of a risk or to accept it. This feedback loop may use changes in the KRIs to make adjustments to the input data or an intermediate risk estimate result.

A number of firms take into account risk transfer, especially insurance, when arriving at their risk estimate. This is an area where a firm may include this data in their economic capital estimates, but may not be endorsed for use in generating regulatory capital estimates.

The regulators are one of the few groups that have the opportunity to see more than one AMA model in operation. As a result they may have observations that other groups cannot provide. It is unlikely that a single approach to AMA will become dominant; more likely are trends and incremental changes in the contribution that a particular data type makes to the risk estimate.

9.5   OPERATIONAL RISK MANAGEMENT

Unlike credit or market risks, operational risk is not generally taken with the aim of generating returns. The distribution of outcomes of operational risk is generally undesirable and potentially catastrophic. However, managing operational risk to zero is neither economic nor possible.

9.5.1   Operational Risk Management Objectives

The purpose of managing operational risk is to facilitate the business in achieving their objectives as set by the Board. This objective is wider than the definition of operational risk as it can also include indirect event effects such as the impact on reputation and trust that stakeholders have in the firm.

The objectives of the businesses will be heavily influenced by the performance assessment framework of the firm. The performance framework will cascade down the organisation and separate between revenue- and non-revenue-generating functions. At the various levels the detailed operational risk management objectives may vary. The operational risk management needs of a business division head may differ from a front-line risk taker. Communication about the current and possible situations enables action and change at these various organisational levels.

For the revenue-generating functions an aspect of communication is "no surprises". That is no surprises in terms of impact upon the revenue stream. This has implications for the focus of the risk management cycle and investment in risk reduction activities.

Part of the issue around organisational levels is that not every operational risk event type can be pushed down to the individual risk taker. While sales teams will be expected to actively prevent mis-selling to customers, they are probably not the right organisational level to manage the consequences of a natural disaster.

For some firms facilitating the business meeting their objectives have extended into issues such as capacity management. From a risk management perspective this may be preventative control, as without sufficient capacity the volume of high-frequency events may be expected to increase once certain capacity levels have been exceeded.

9.5.2   Sources of Risk Information

Data and information on operational risks comes from a number of sources:

- risk and control self-assessments
- loss data
- scenarios.

Risk and control self-assessments are often conducted by local experts with the support of embedded operational risk specialists and possibly the corporate operational risk management function. The assessment is to consider the business and its enabling processes, the various risks and the effectiveness of various controls. To assist in aggregation of the data, one of the scales used might be expressed in terms of revenue. For example, a low-impact risk may be equivalent to 1 hour of revenue while a high-impact risk may be 24 months of revenue. Framing the analysis in this way also helps understanding of the risk's impact on the business.

This analysis can be used to construct a picture, for example a heat map with red, amber and green zones. Pictures can then be constructed for the same business in different locations or even different businesses in the same location using similar scales or benchmarks (see Figure 9.5). These self-assessments can also generate KRIs as a by-product of the analytic process and the individuals involved. These risk and control

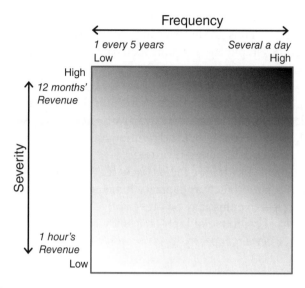

Figure 9.5   Operational risk heat map with scale

self-assessments have some similarities with the work conducted by internal audit.

The internal loss data collected is a rich source of information. While the loss amounts and various dates are useful, more information is needed to enable change in the internal environment, e.g. controls. For example, the more precisely the loss can be located in the firm the easier it is to identify the change required. The location of the event can be supported by collecting product and process information. Which product revenue stream is going to be affected? Is the product correctly priced to compensate for the risks? Which process step gave rise to the issue, and which process step identified the event? For example, if the process step that went wrong was at the beginning of the transaction chain and it was only found at the end of the transaction chain then more costs have been incurred than if the error was found soon after the error occurred. This might be a data quality error that occurs when settlement instructions are provided but not found until trying to settle the transaction. Identification of the process step also helps to identify the appropriate control and support function with a role in specifying and operating the controls.

Ultimately, controls are implemented against causes. For example, training is a control over insufficient knowledge that leads to errors. While there are industrial approaches to root cause analysis, they do not appear to be easily adopted by financial firms. Allocating everything as human error is not especially constructive.

Scenarios can be particularly useful. The risk and control self-assessment has similarities with scenarios, but without the story. Scenarios enable emerging risks to be explored as a thought experiment, arriving at opinions on their quantification. For emerging risks the story can be more important than the estimation of frequency and severity, given difficulties with lack of data and bias. The story component of a scenario enables the businesses and risk management to discuss a possible emerging risk at the early stages, rather than after it has emerged and given rise to losses.

A variant is the "reverse scenarios". In reverse scenarios a business is given a potential loss amount, for example 6 months of revenue, and asked to identify the activities and circumstances that could give rise to the loss. This analysis requires an understanding of the sensitive points in the business model, the supporting processes and various exposures. With the potential size of the loss, careful consideration is given to risk reduction or risk acceptance.

One of the roles of the risk management function is to ensure that information is communicated. For operational risk there is a particular need to share insights across the organisation, especially between businesses. This can take the form of "lessons learned" based on internal or external events or emerging risks. This communication improves efficiency and awareness of risk issues, also promoting risk culture.

9.5.3   Operational Risk Focal Points

In addition to the operational risk management activities across the businesses and the organisation there are also focal points. The focal points tend to be related to change around products, processes and even acquisition and divestments. The change itself is not the source of the risk, but the efficacy of the supporting processes assuming that the individual risks are identified in the first place. For years financial firms have operated new product approval processes. The aim of these approval processes is not to prevent the business from developing new products or client segments, but rather to ensure that the risks are known and kept within risk appetite. The outcome of poor approval processes can be undesirable surprises. With new process approval, there is an opportunity, at an early stage, to take into account operational risk issues either pre-existing or that arise out of the implemented process.

9.5.4   Risk Transfer

For operational risk management there are limited buyers of this risk, in turn this limits the opportunities to transfer the risk. This is in contrast to credit and market risks where there are a variety of buyers of the risks and a number of mechanisms to achieve the transfer.

The only readily available operational risk transfer mechanism, at the time of writing, is insurance. Firms bought insurance for operational risk events, such as flood damage, long before the operational risk discipline had a name. Insurance only transfers the financial impact of the operational risk event. The firm still experiences the event, resources are applied and management time is consumed. One of the issues that may surface due to buying insurance is that of moral hazard. Does the behaviour of the firm and its employees, etc. change because the firm has insurance? This moral hazard issue also arises with individuals and their purchase of insurance for cars, houses and possessions.

In purchasing insurance, it is relevant to consider which losses are most appropriate for insurance, the unexpected and catastrophic events or the low-impact losses. The low-impact losses should be capable of being met from cash flow. It may also be cheaper, as the insurance premiums will include the incremental cost of the risk for the insurer, their processing costs and generating their return on capital.

For firms using RAROC components in performance measurement, it becomes possible to consider the cost of insuring the risk against the cost of providing capital for a risk that has been accepted. This raises the issue of if and how insurance should be reflected in the operational risk appetite process and statement from the Board.

Insurance is market driven; as a result, insurance costs and available capacity will vary over time. Some of this variation can be reduced by increasing the threshold at which insurance starts to pay (the deductible) or capping the maximum amount to be paid by the insurer. Another way of looking at insurance is as a form of risk sharing. In risk sharing the firm and the insurance company may decide to share the financial impact, for example the firm takes 20% of the loss and the insurer pays 80%. Risk sharing may extend the maximum loss covered, even if a portion of the risk is accepted by the firm, and it contributes to managing the moral hazard as the firm will still incur a loss, even if reduced in size. A few of the insurance buying strategies are outlined in Figure 9.6. The strategies where the insured and insurer share the consequences are intended to manage moral hazard. The sharing of the consequences means that the insured has "skin in the game".

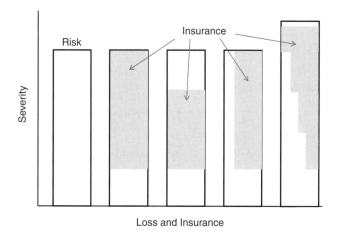

Figure 9.6   Possible insurance buying strategies

Incorporating the risk transfer effects of insurance into the AMA model is not easy. Issues to consider include mapping insurance terminology into operational risk events and causes. By having insurance there is a contingent credit risk – will the insurer be there to pay when the firm has a claim? As the AMA is to estimate the risk for 12 months into the future, what happens if there are several modelled insurable events that in total exceed the capacity of the insurance contract?

However, as the businesses are charged – directly or indirectly – for insurance premiums and the cost of capital, then trying to avoid double counting will be appreciated.

9.6   ISSUES TO CONSIDER

- What is the current operational risk appetite?
- Is the operational risk appetite before, or after, the inclusion of insurance?
- When was the operational risk appetite last reviewed?
- How does the Board assure itself of the reasonableness of the operational risk estimate?
- How is the internal operational risk estimate validated?
- What is the sensitivity of the risk estimate to statistical assumptions such as correlation?
- What is the sensitivity of the operational risk estimate to new large internal losses?

- What is the sensitivity of the operational risk estimate to new large external losses?
- What is the process for escalating individual operational risk losses to the Board?
- How are the businesses motivated to stay within the operational risk appetite?
- How are operational risks outside the businesses aggregated and reported?
- Is there a "lessons learned" process and what was the last item it was used for?
- How do operational risk management and the insurance purchasing function interact?
- Does the firm participate in an industry group on operational risk to share experiences and accelerate learning?

FURTHER READING

Ashby, S., Clark, D. and Thirlwell, J. (2011) Waking the sleeping giant – maximising the potential of operational risk management for banks. *Capco Institute Journal of Financial Transformation*, no. 33.

Barnier, B. (2011) *The Operational Risk Handbook for Financial Companies: A guide to the new world of performance-oriented operational risk.* Harriman House, London.

Basel Committee on Banking Supervision (2004) International Convergence of Capital Measurement and Capital Standards – A revised framework (Basel II). http://www.bis.org/publ/bcbs107.htm

Blunden, T. and Thirlwell, J. (2010) *Mastering Operational Risk: A practical guide to understanding operational risk and how to manage it.* Financial Times/Prentice Hall, London.

Chernobai, A.S., Rachev, S.T. and Fabozzi, F.J. (2007) *Operational Risk: A guide to Basel II capital requirements, models and analysis.* John Wiley & Sons, Chichester.

Hoffman, D.G. (2002) *Managing Operational Risk: 20 Firmwide Best Practices.* John Wiley & Sons, Chichester.

Kaplan, R.S. and Mikes, A. (2012) Managing risks: A new framework. *Harvard Business Review*, June.

Operational Riskdata eXchange (2012) Operational Risk Reporting Standards – Text and Appendix. http://www.orx.org/standards

Operational Riskdata eXchange (2012) ORX Data. http://www.orx.org/Pages/orxdata.aspx

10

Liquidity Risk

Risk Management at the Top					

Ch. 1: Introduction

Part I: Risk Oversight				
Ch. 2: Risk – An Overview	Ch. 3: Risk Oversight	Ch. 4: Risk Management	Ch. 5: Risk Appetite	Ch. 6: Risk Culture

Part II: Specific Risks					
Ch. 7: Credit Risk	Ch. 8: Market Risk	Ch. 9: Operational Risk	Ch. 10: Liquidity Risk	Ch. 11: Other Risks	Ch. 12: Risk Interactions

Part III: Regulatory Environment
Ch. 13: Regulatory Environment

Accessing liquidity is a core competency of banking, and of financial institutions more generally. The provision of credit, one of the original activities of banks, is dependent on the availability of funding, the liability side of the balance sheet.

Although a core competency, liquidity has recently been subject to the same level of regulatory scrutiny as applied to credit, market and operational risks. Some of this focus arises from painful lessons during the financial crisis.

A firm can have a positive market value or break-up value being solvent, but be illiquid and unable to fund its activities. The asset side of the balance sheet can have a higher value than the liability side, but the assets may not be saleable in the short term and so are illiquid. As a result, if depositors withdraw their funds (as in "a run on the bank") or interbank lending is not renewed, the firm may have difficulty funding its assets. A number of firms no longer exist in the post-crisis world, in part, or entirely, due to shortcomings in their funding liquidity risk management.

The measurement of liquidity risk differs from credit, market and operational risk. As described elsewhere, these non-liquidity risks can be estimated using various forms of capital calculation. For liquidity risk, risk estimation is based on ratios of liquid reserve assets and ratios of maturities of long-term assets and liabilities. A capital metric for funding liquidity risk has yet to be developed and gain broad-based acceptance.

10.1   INTRODUCTION

As liquidity risk management enables the firm to fund its activities, it is of concern to the Board. Without a thorough understanding of liquidity risk issues it is difficult for the firm to contemplate strategic or tactical initiatives. The regulators have further raised the profile of liquidity risk management by creating risk management requirements and regulatory reports. This focus upon liquidity risk management, alongside the regulatory scrutiny, is forcing firms to reconsider their business models and long-term forecasts of profitability.

The rest of this chapter looks at the:

10.2 Definition of Liquidity Risk
10.3 Liquidity Risk Framework
10.4 Liquidity Risk Measurement

10.5 Liquidity Risk Management
10.6 Issues to Consider

The next section introduces the definition of liquidity risk before considering various aspects of the risk management framework and risk measurement.

10.2 DEFINITION OF LIQUIDITY RISK

The regulators[1] have formalised two definitions of liquidity risk:

> Funding Liquidity Risk is the risk that the firm will not be able to meet efficiently both expected and unexpected current and future cash flow and collateral needs without affecting either daily operations or the financial condition of the firm.

> Market Liquidity Risk is the risk that a firm cannot easily offset or eliminate a position at the market price because of inadequate market depth or market disruption.

Most of this chapter refers to funding liquidity risk. Market liquidity risk is mentioned below, and also in Chapter 8. The two aspects of liquidity risk come together when a firm is unable to meet its expected and contractual outflows either because it is unable to raise liabilities at a reasonable cost or unable to sell assets at a reasonable price.

The time frame of funding liquidity risk ranges from intraday payments to long-term contractual maturities associated with mortgages and bonds.

The focus of funding liquidity risk management concern is the mismatch of maturities between liabilities and assets. Funding a 30-year mortgage requires long-term access to funds. Some firms fund long-term assets via liabilities, such as deposits, from the wholesale funding market. These liabilities might have maturities from 24 hours to 12 months or longer, but 30 years are unlikely. As a result, there is an assumption that the wholesale market will make the required volume of funds available for a reasonable price for the foreseeable future. The foreseeable future is unlikely to be as much as 30 years into the future. In the financial crisis the assumption, about being able to access the wholesale market for deposits, proved to be non-robust and some firms

---

[1] Basel Committee on Banking Supervision (September 2008) Principles for Sound Liquidity Risk Management and Supervision, p. 1, footnote 2. Reproduced by permission of Bank for International Settlements (BIS).

were unable to fund their assets. Simultaneously, the demand for certain types of assets shrank rapidly. For a minority of firms the consequences were catastrophic.

This maturity transformation process, of having assets with maturities longer than the liabilities, is one of the core activities of banks. As a result, managing the maturity gap between assets and liabilities, funding liquidity risk management, is a core competency of banks. (The mismatch of interest rates, for example floating rate assets but fixed rate liabilities, is an element of market risk and can be managed using various derivative contracts.)

The wholesale funding market is composed of banks, other financial institutions and various other participants. This market is subdivided into deposits (cash) and short-term tradable securities. The securities can take the form of certificates of deposit or commercial paper or their equivalents. These securities may be purchased by money market investment funds. These investment funds are dominated by US investors. As a result, if there is a credit rating downgrade to a country, or to a firm, then the securities may no longer meet the investment criteria of funds and that source of funds disappears.

Another main source of funding is from retail investors making deposits. These liabilities differ from the wholesale funding market as significant proportions do not have a defined maturity. Some types of retail bank deposits can be withdrawn immediately or "on demand"; others may require 30 or more days' notice. Nevertheless, these deposits are generally "sticky" in that the deposits tend to stay with the bank for a considerable period of time. Even retail deposits with a fixed maturity, "term deposits", tend to be renewed or rolled over. The volume of retail deposits can ebb and flow with the time of year and economic cycle. For funding liquidity risk management purposes these liabilities can be given a "behaviourally" implied maturity.

Inevitably, some of these retail deposits are less "sticky" or persistent than others. For example, deposits gathered via the Internet distribution channel are expected to be less sticky as they are made by individuals or small companies seeking to optimise yield and take advantage of introductory marketing offers. When the offer expires then the funds move on to the next offer, generally from a competitor.

As can be seen from Table 10.1, funding liquidity risk involves nearly all the products, assets and liabilities and business lines. The least risk is in asset management, where customer funds are used.

Table 10.1 Business line versus product/service sources of funding liquidity risk

	Corporate finance	Trading and sales	Retail banking	Commercial banking	Payments and settlements	Agency services	Asset management	Retail brokerage
Capital raising								
Corporate finance services								
FX and money markets								
Securities								
Derivatives								
Retail credit								
Commercial credit								
Deposits								
Cash management, payments and settlements								
Trust/investment management								
Investment products								
Brokerage								

10.3   LIQUIDITY RISK FRAMEWORK

The funding liquidity risk management framework begins with identification of change at the business portfolio level and works outwards. At a more aggregated level there are the firm-wide contingency funding plans. At a more detailed level there are the funding requirements generated by individual products and their weighting in the business portfolios.

The firm has the ability to decide upon the funding requirements created when it changes the mix of on- or off-balance sheet assets. This has some similarities to making changes in the composition of credit and market risk portfolios. At the portfolio level, funding liquidity risk management is looking for changes in patterns. For example, on the asset side of the balance sheet extending the maturity of commercial loans from 5 years towards 7 years, or on the liability side of the balance sheet investors withdrawing from 7-year bonds in preference for 5-year maturities. These would constitute changes in patterns.

For shorter maturities, the risk identification stage also seeks potential imbalances between payments and receipts on an intraday basis. Some changes in patterns may be seasonal, and also affected by the economic cycle.

Risk management looks at this change in pattern and compares it with the available sources of funding. Managing this risk requires coordination between those businesses that acquire assets, those that acquire liabilities and those that do both, such as retail banking.

A firm may have a centralised funding desk with "satellites" in the major business units. This centralised funding desk may or may not report to the liquidity risk management team. One of the influential factors is whether the centralised funding desk is viewed as a service centre or a profit centre. If it is a profit centre then there may be potential conflicts of interest with the objectives of liquidity risk management, serving as the independent second line of risk management defence. Some firms have had problems, possibly exacerbated by profit motives, with investing surplus liabilities in unsuitable assets.

The centralised funding desk can observe patterns in the demand for and usage of funds across both sides of the balance sheet. From an oversight perspective these changes should be aligned with the strategic business direction endorsed by the Board.

On a day-to-day basis the funding desk has access to the projected demand for funds on an intraday basis out to 30 days and beyond. Thirty days is a natural horizon as it matches the time frame for the regulators' liquidity coverage ratio. To be able to provide this oversight, funding liquidity risk management and the funding desk need high-quality daily information from across the firm – not a trivial objective. In times of crisis they may need this information on an hourly basis.

The funding desk needs access to this information in multiple currencies. Internationally active banks will have assets and liabilities in different currencies. While the aim may be to fund the assets in a specific currency with liabilities in the same currency, this may not always be possible. For most of the time this gap can be bridged by using the forward foreign exchange markets. This uses markets where funding is readily available, for example US dollars, and enables it to be converted into a currency where funding may be less available, for example Malaysian ringgit. However, using the forward foreign exchange markets creates an additional credit risk exposure. While the foreign exchange markets provide some flexibility in the source of funding, the maturity mismatch between assets and liabilities needs to be comprehensively managed.

Some of the more difficult risk management aspects include assets with embedded optionality. These are real options as opposed to financial options. These real options give the borrower the opportunity to draw down funds within certain conditions. An overdraft, for a retail or commercial banking customer, is an example of a product with embedded optionality. Irrespective of whether such products involve taking credit risk, they create funding liquidity risk. Customers may draw down on these overdrafts with little or no warning and these draw downs need funding.

10.3.1   Roles in Funding Liquidity Risk Management

The most senior committee focusing on funding liquidity risk is likely to be the Asset & Liability Committee (ALCO). This may report into the Board or into the Board-level Risk Committee. Participants on ALCO are likely to include the:

- Chief Executive Officer
- Chief Financial Officer
- Chief Risk Officer
- Treasurer for the firm
- Head of Retail Banking
- Head of Commercial Banking
- Head of Money Market Trading.

This broad membership of ALCO reflects the importance of funding liquidity risk to the firm. In addition to the Group Treasurer, treasurers for different regions may also participate. Table 10.1 provides an indication of the range of businesses and products involved in managing this risk.

ALCO will make recommendations to the Board on:

- the appetite for funding liquidity risk;
- issuing long-term liabilities, such as bonds;
- the maturity profile and composition of capital.

ALCO is expected to take strategic and tactical views. The strategic views will include the maturity profile and composition of capital for the firm. Bonds of the right designation, for example junior subordinated bonds, can contribute to regulatory capital as well as provide long-term funding. ALCO may also have a role in discussions on retained earnings as opposed to dividend payments for their impact on the capital and long-term funding.

The ALCO tactical views will include involvement in discussions on how the business will apply their credit and market risk appetites and implications for the demand on funding and currency of funding. This can result in deliberations on the need to increase capital or issue long-term debt; part of the scope of ALCO.

ALCO may delegate approval for large transactions to the Treasurer, for example funding a large syndicated loan. The Head of Money Market Trading is to provide feedback on the state of the firm's ability to raise liabilities from the wholesale market.

The assumption is that Treasury acts as the second line of defence for funding liquidity risk, similar to credit and market risk management. In this role they need to be independent of the business, but able to support and challenge the business. Activities such as stress testing and scenarios are also expected to be allocated to Treasury as part of the oversight role. Treasury will also have responsibility for drafting various principles and policies, for endorsement by ALCO, prior to cascading them throughout the firm.

10.3.2   Cost of Funding

The only group that can gain a complete perspective of both sides of the balance sheet is Treasury. A framework needs to be established to align the interests of businesses that gather liabilities and those that apply them to fund assets. This can be achieved by a transfer pricing

Table 10.2   Broad funding (liability) categories with interest costs

Retail on-demand deposits – core	No interest
Retail on-demand deposits – fluctuation	No interest
Retail term deposits	Managed interest rate
Corporate deposits	Market interest rates
Bonds, etc. issued	Market interest rate
Equity	No interest
Retained earnings, etc.	No interest

framework.[2] The transfer pricing mechanism is a process that more accurately charges the users of funds and rewards those that collect funds. It can also support various decisions by ALCO alongside the principles and policies.

As can be seen from Table 10.2, a number of categories of funding have no explicit interest costs. Retail term deposits carry a rate set by the firm that will be influenced by competition and the use of these funds. Corporate deposits and bonds have interest rate costs that represent the current market rates at the time the funds are obtained.

The transfer pricing framework ensures that business users of funds adequately compensate the firm for consuming this resource. A firm would normally be expected to charge a customer more for a 7-year loan than a 5-year loan. Some of the incremental charge will be related to the extended credit risk; however, the risk in maturity of the funding obligation also needs to be recognised. Without this recognition, risk-adjusted performance measurements would be incomplete.

Similarly, products with embedded optionality – such as standby lines of credit, which place a burden on the firm – should be charged for this optionality. While arranging the facility may generate a fee for the business, it also generates an obligation to provide funding at a timing that suits the borrower. This creates a contingent obligation on the funding desk and needs to be factored into the pricing. Without factoring in contingent funding obligations the risks to the firm will be understated.

On the liability side of the balance sheet, extending the average effective maturity of deposits or other funds is generally perceived to be desirable. For retail deposits this may require subdivision into core

---

[2] Grant, J. (2011) Liquidity Transfer Pricing: A guide to better practice. Financial Stability Institute Occasional Paper 10.

and fluctuating volumes of deposits. The goal becomes increasing the volume of core deposits, increasing their "stickiness" or reducing the proportion of deposits that fluctuate.

To achieve these changes in retail depositor behaviour, some form of incentive may be required. The extent of the incentive can be seen when looking at yield curves, for example government bond yields from 3 months out to 30 years. In general, the yield curve is positively sloping so that longer-maturity deposits get a higher return than shorter-maturity deposits. Other yield curves include the interest rate swap curves that are available for many currencies and are dominated by bank-to-bank trans- actions. Another approach may be to change the perspective of the firm in the eyes of the depositor; this is not a short-term approach. In reality, firms will be trying to do both and adjust them on a near continuous basis.

The internal transfer pricing needs to take into account this normally upwardly sloping yield curve for the longer maturities. The internal transfer pricing passes the cost of the longer maturities onto the users of funds. The internal pricing may be based off the interest rate swap curve with increments related to the maturity of the funding commitment, whether assets or liabilities.

One of the issues is the speed of change of internal transfer pric- ing. The interest rate swap curve may change daily, but retail deposit rates cannot. As a compromise, the maturity-related transfer pricing increments should probably be reviewed monthly or even quarterly.

Having an internal transfer pricing mechanism also enables strategic issues to be taken into account. If the firm decides that it has an uneven balance in its funding sources, then it might decide to provide a greater reward to businesses with retail depositors. This might be part of an incentive campaign to win a greater percentage of the available retail deposit market, or an incentive to make the existing deposits "stickier". This retail banking incentive may be funded by "penalties" for use of funding from the wholesale deposit market over a certain threshold determined by ALCO.

10.4   LIQUIDITY RISK MEASUREMENT

Funding liquidity risk needs to be measured, as with other risk types, to determine whether:

- the situation is getting "riskier" or "less risky", and
- whether the firm is still within risk tolerance and risk appetite.

Unlike credit, market or operational risks there is no economic capital framework for funding liquidity risk (yet). As a result, there is a dependency on ratios covering assets and liabilities of various maturities. The simplicity of these ratios reduces the extent of model risk in the process, but does make it more difficult to summarise in a few numbers.

Although financial firms have been managing their funding liquidity risk for years, it is only relatively recently that the regulators have standardised some of these ratios.[3]

10.4.1 Short Term

The liquidity coverage ratio (LCR) looks at the gross and net flow of funds scheduled for the next 30 days – the short term. This is effectively a measure of the funding gap. The objective of the ratio is to identify the largest shortfall in cumulative funding over a 30-day horizon. This is illustrated in Figures 10.1 and 10.2.

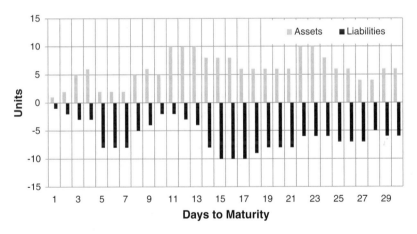

Figure 10.1   Gross cash flows over a 30-day horizon

Figure 10.1 shows illustrative cash flows over a 30-day horizon. Assets may be in the form of loans and liabilities are in the form of various deposits. The assets and liabilities are plotted by their contractual maturity dates and interest payment dates over the next 30 days. A 5-year

---

[3] Basel Committee on Banking Supervision (2010) Basel III: International Framework for Liquidity Risk Measurement, Standards and Monitoring.

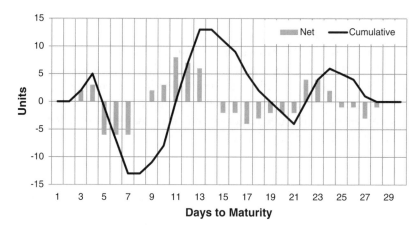

Figure 10.2   Net and cumulative cash flows over a 30-day horizon

maturity asset loan may pay interest every 6 months, and a 3-year maturity liability may pay interest every 3 months.

The LCR focuses on net cumulative outflows. For example, repay-
ing the interest/principal on a liability before a matching payment of
interest/principal on an asset also creates (all things being equal) a net
cumulative outflow. This is shown in Figure 10.2.

Figure 10.2 shows the net cash flows on a day-to-day basis and the
cumulative effect. On day 3 there are more assets maturing than liabilities, so the firm will have surplus funds to invest, for example making
an overnight deposit in the wholesale market. However by day 5 there
are more liabilities maturing than assets. As the volume of liabilities
maturing is more than the cumulative surplus from days 3 and 4, the
firm has a funding gap. This negative trend continues and then reverses
so that by day 30 the volume of assets and liabilities, cash inflows and
outflows, is equal.

The issue is how to meet the cumulative shortfall of funds beginning
on day 5 and continuing to day 12. It repeats itself, to a smaller extent, on
day 20. To meet the shortfall the firm could liquidate some securities that
it has been holding for exactly this purpose. These securities are liquidity
reserve assets. The regulators have criteria for what is a regulatory
qualifying reserve asset, for example government bonds. Key criteria
include acceptance of the securities by the lender of last resort, alongside
deep and liquid markets.

The information conveyed in Figures 10.1 and 10.2 needs to be prepared for each currency in which the firm makes or receives payments.

As mentioned above, the bridge enabling a liability in one currency to fund an asset in a different currency is through the forward foreign exchange market. As a result, the net and cumulative cash flows need to include these forward foreign exchange transactions as inflows or outflows. The complexity becomes clearer when considering that a firm can easily have payments and/or receipts in more than 20 currencies.

10.4.2 Very Short Term[4]

The liquidity coverage ratio covers the period from tomorrow to 30 days. However, funding issues can emerge intraday. The focus is on funds that are available to a firm to facilitate payments occurring during the day. This might include the repayment of overnight deposits while waiting for the proceeds of a sale of securities to arrive.

The outflows of funds may include one or more of the following:

- repayment of overnight deposits;
- payments to other participants in payment and settlement systems;
- emergency drawdown of funds by a payment or settlement system to facilitate their activities;
- contingent intraday funding facilities made available to customers;
- obligations from providing correspondent banking services.

The inflows of funds may include one or more of the following:

- cash balances and reserves held at the central bank/lender of last resort;
- eligible collateral pledged with the central bank/lender of last resort;
- secured or unsecured, committed or uncommitted intraday credit lines;
- cash balances held with correspondent banks;
- payments received from other participants in payments or settlement systems;
- return of overnight deposits.

As with other funding liquidity risk metrics, monitoring the intraday payments relies upon simple metrics. The day may be subdivided into bands of an hour, covering the time that certain payment and settlement systems open and close. The earliest band will be the amount in the

---

[4] Basel Committee on Banking Supervision (2012) Monitoring Indicators for Intraday Liquidity Management (Consultative Paper).

firm's account at a bank for that currency from the previous day. Not all firms have access to payment systems in every country in which they have cash inflows or outflows. As a result, Bank X will establish a bank account with Bank Y to enable payments in Country Z in which Bank Y is a member of the payments system. Bank X's account at Bank Y enables Bank X's payments to be made in Country Z. These accounts will have a positive balance overnight to enable payments to be made. However, the positive balance is unlikely to generate income so a goal is to keep the balance as small as practicable to minimise the lost revenue.

The intraday metrics considered can include the net flow of funds within hourly bands and the timing of critical intraday payments. Other information may include the total value of payments made in a day with various subcategories, such as correspondent bank activities and securities settlements. As with the liquidity coverage ratio, the focus is on the maximum net cumulative position during the day and if necessary, arranging an intraday overdraft to enable a payment to be made.

These metrics need to be tracked to monitor changes in patterns. Such changes may arise from strategic business initiatives, seasonal effects, such as tax payments, or position in the economic cycle.

The investment in systems to collect this information, on an end-of-day and intraday basis, is considerable. This issue is magnified when considering that it needs to be available on a currency-by-currency basis.

10.4.3   Long Term

The ratio for long-term funding is the net stable funding ratio. The goal is stable funding over the next 12 months.

The ratio looks at the funding requirement over the next 12 months and stable sources of funding for the same period. For assets, this includes contingent assets as well as on- and off-balance sheet positions. For regulatory purposes, various factors are used to weight the assets and liabilities; a level of complexity not seen in the liquidity coverage ratio.

The liabilities that can be used to meet the funding needs over the next 12 months include core retail deposits, equity capital, as well as securities issued by the firm. Retail deposits are included, even though they may be repayable on demand, due to their "stickiness".

The assets under consideration include mortgages and loans as well as standby credit facilities such as trade finance or project finance. Table 10.3 provides an indicative list of long-term assets and liabilities.

Table 10.3   Assets and liabilities with maturities more than 12 months

Assets	Liabilities
Vehicle loans and leases	Equity
Mortgages – residential	Retained earnings
Mortgages – commercial	Bonds/securities with a residual maturity of more than 12 months
Commercial loans and leases	Loans with a residual maturity of more than 12 months
Project finance	Retail deposits (core)
Trade finance	
Corporate investments	

Corporate investments can include items with no fixed maturity, such as equity-type investments in other companies. This category can also include fixed assets, such as buildings and equipment.

The items in Table 10.3 are all "on-balance sheet" products. However, long-term "off-balance sheet" products can also create cash flows years into the future. Some of these "off-balance sheet" products, such as interest rate swaps, may have originated in the trading book for taking or hedging market risk. The gross volume of these off-balance sheet products can be very large in relation to the market risk. These positions accumulate as the market risk position is closed out, but being over-the-counter products their cash flows remain. In some cases the method for closing out the market risk will also create offsetting cash flows.

By focusing on the net stable funding ratio, the aim is to move away from significant reliance on the wholesale deposit market to meet long-term funding needs. The financial crisis has shown that there is uncertainty when funding a 5-year loan with a sequence of 3-month maturity interbank deposits from the wholesale market. When needed, those interbank deposits may not be available.

Other aspects that should be considered as part of funding liquidity risk measurement include the concentration of depositors, especially non-retail deposits and tools to monitor the firm's ability to access funds in the wholesale funding markets. It takes time to influence the customer segments acting as a source of funding.

10.5   LIQUIDITY RISK MANAGEMENT

Some elements of the liquidity risk management framework have been mentioned above, for example ALCO, Treasury and internal transfer pricing. Other aspects include the expression of risk tolerance and risk appetite using various metrics, including those introduced in Section 10.4. The Board has to approve the risk tolerance and risk appetite statements for funding liquidity risk, as for other risk types. In turn, the risk tolerance and risk appetite statements need to be supported by policies, standards and data collection.

The related policies and allocation of funding will be studied with great interest by the businesses. For some businesses, a significant portion of their income is derived from the internal transfer pricing of deposits that they generate. For other businesses, the result may limit the range of products that they can offer. Even the ability to execute securities transactions may be affected by the intraday limitations.

The material below looks at some of the actions undertaken by Treasury as the second line of risk management defence. Some of the risk management actions available to other risk types are not possible for funding liquidity risk. Also, there may be greater reliance upon stress tests.

10.5.1   Overview

Away from the transaction-level activities, Treasury will be involved with ensuring that there are contingency funding plans. These contingency plans are effectively the risk management activities as it is difficult for Treasury to:

- reduce the frequency of events;
- reduce the severity of events;
- transfer/transform the risk;
- accept the risk.

Accepting the risk is not a sustainable proposition for funding liquidity risk. In reality, the only choices left are reduction in severity and transfer/transform the risk.

The ability to transfer the risk is very limited. The concept of hedging funding liquidity risk is being explored but is still to be fully developed. The structures nearest to a hedge are probably prearranged contingent funding and standby facilities. Also in this category are standby facilities from parent companies, and other subsidiaries in a group. Arrangements with individual central banks and regional central banks, such as the ECB, may be available and will change in structure, for example from conducting repurchase programmes to outright sale of securities. There have been a few transactions in liquidity swaps, but it is not clear if these are receiving regulatory recognition as a means of managing funding liquidity risk.

The limited scope for risk transfer just leaves reduction in the frequency and severity of events through policies, procedures and information. Access to accurate, complete and timely data is a key element to managing funding liquidity risk.

When wholesale and/or retail funding shrinks in relation to the volume of assets, whether on- or off-balance sheet, the firm has a limited number of choices:

(a) increase reliance on an existing source of funding;
(b) develop a new source of funding;
(c) sell some assets;
(d) a combination of the above.

Which of these actions are taken and the order in which they are taken will be part of the contingency funding plan developed by Treasury with various businesses. The contingency plan needs to be reviewed on a regular basis due to changes in market conditions.

For example, prior to the financial crisis the securitisation of assets helped to reduce the firm's funding requirements. The assets might be in the form of mortgages which were then bundled, securitised as a portfolio and sold to investors. This process enabled the firm to reduce its funding needs.

However, since the financial crisis, the ability of firms to securitise various assets has reduced significantly. A consequence is that firms have to find longer-term sources of liability to maintain their net stable funding ratios in line with the maturity of their assets. An example of these longer-term liabilities is to issue bonds.

A tactical approach to generating funds includes the sale of assets. Assets could be categorised in terms of their disposability. This tactic should take into account the capacity, any price penalty and the speed with which a sale can be arranged; the equivalent of market liquidity risk for securities. For example, some securities do not meet the criteria for regulatory qualifying liquidity reserve assets, but are saleable over a longer time horizon.

The assets that could be sold are not limited to securities; other assets may be saleable, and these might be held in the corporate investments portfolio. An extension of the sale of assets releasing funds is "sale and leaseback" of fixed assets. In this process the firm may sell an office building for a lump sum and instead make regular lease payments.

A tactical or even strategic approach to increasing funding resilience might be to extend the sources of funds. This might involve trying to persuade an existing customer segment to increase the volume of deposits and/or extend the period of time that they are willing to make deposits. A more ambitious project would be to develop a new source of deposits, for example sovereign wealth funds. However, for these deposits to be available when needed it may be necessary to use them, even when not needed, so that the credit line and processes can be established. Making these changes can take more than 12 months. In some cases the businesses gathering deposits may need additional income, via internal transfer pricing, to offset the cost of expanding into new customer segments.

10.5.2   Stress Testing

A key element of the contingency funding plan will be stress testing. Stress testing is similar to scenarios, with the exception that under the stress test it is assumed that the events will occur with certainty. The firm-wide scenarios and stress tests will usually be prepared by Treasury and overseen by ALCO.

The stress tests should cover a variety of events. Some events should focus on the intraday liquidity needs while others might be firm, industry – national or international – effects that persist over a long time.

A short-term stress could be if one of the firm's systems failed and was not able to receive payments. What impact would this have on the intraday movement of funds? Alternatively, what would be the impact if a settlement system was unable to make payments for a period of time? These events might not arise from solvency or liquidity issues, but because of a hardware or software failure. At the onset of one of these failures there is no certainty whether it will last for 10 minutes, an hour or 24 hours or more. In addition to considering failures of the firm's own systems, consideration can be given to system failures at correspondent banks.

A stress test covering a longer period of time could be downgrading the credit rating of the firm. How would this affect the ability of the firm to get deposits from the wholesale funding market? Would some customer segments no longer be willing to take the firm's credit risk? This might not affect the current funding of assets, but might seriously affect the ability to fund additional assets.

At the extreme are issues that affect the industry at a national or international level. At a national level it might be that the downgrade of a country's economic or political outlook means the funds are withdrawn from one country and deposited in another, including the individual firm. (This phenomenon can lead to negative interest rates when banks with a surplus of deposits have insufficient volume of assets that need funding.)

Another response to a national or industry-level downgrade might be purchases of government securities. For example corporates, instead of placing surpluses with banks, may choose to invest in government securities. This additional demand will increase the price and decrease the yield on the securities. These are the same securities that are used by the banks as reserve liquid assets. To compound the effects, the cost of issuing long-term bonds may increase at the same time, resulting in a squeeze on revenues.

When the stress test assumes a national or international effect, the contingency plan responses of other industry participants need to be considered. For example, the tactical response from one bank may be to increase its share of the retail deposit base. However, this is unlikely to be a complete solution when many, or even all, firms in a given country are adopting the same tactic. Under these circumstances a range of responses is more likely to be successful than total dependency on a single reaction.

As mentioned above, these contingency plans can be complex due to the need to consider different currencies and the possible reaction of different jurisdictions.

10.6   ISSUES TO CONSIDER

- How often does the Asset Liability Committee meet?
- How often does the Asset Liability Committee report to the Board?
- Is Treasury a service centre or a profit centre?
- What behaviour is incentivised by the internal transfer pricing for funds?
- How often are the funding contingency plans reviewed?
- What is the quality of the data available to Treasury and the various funding desks?
- How does the Board assure itself that the data is accurate, complete and timely?
- When were stress tests last run and what changed as a result?
- What are the existing sources of contingent funding and how much is the firm paying for them?

FURTHER READING

Basel Committee on Banking Supervision (2008) Principles for Sound Liquidity Risk Management and Supervision. http://www.bis.org/publ/bcbs144.htm

Basel Committee on Banking Supervision (2010) Basel III: International Framework for Liquidity Risk Measurement, Standards and Monitoring. http://www.bis.org/publ/bcbs188.htm

Basel Committee on Banking Supervision (2012) Monitoring Indicators for Intraday Liquidity Management (Consultative Paper). http://www.bis.org/publ/bcbs225.htm

Choudhry, M. (2011) *An Introduction to Banking: Liquidity Risk and Asset–Liability Management.* John Wiley & Sons, Chichester.

Fiedler, R. (2011) *Liquidity Modelling.* Risk Books, London.

Grant, J. (2011) Liquidity Transfer Pricing: A guide to better practice. Financial Stability Institute Occasional Paper 10. http://www.bis.org/fsi/fsipapers10.htm

Matz, L. and Neu, P. (2006) *Liquidity Risk Measurement and Management: A practitioner's guide to global best practices.* John Wiley & Sons, Chichester.

de Weert, F. (2010) *Bank and Insurance Capital Management.* John Wiley & Sons, Chichester.

11
Other Risks

Risk Management at the Top

Ch. 1: Introduction

Part I: Risk Oversight

Ch. 2: Risk – An Overview	Ch. 3: Risk Oversight	Ch. 4: Risk Management	Ch. 5: Risk Appetite	Ch. 6: Risk Culture

Part II: Specific Risks

Ch. 7: Credit Risk	Ch. 8: Market Risk	Ch. 9: Operational Risk	Ch. 10: Liquidity Risk	Ch. 11: Other Risks	Ch. 12: Risk Interactions

Part III: Regulatory Environment

Ch. 13: Regulatory Environment

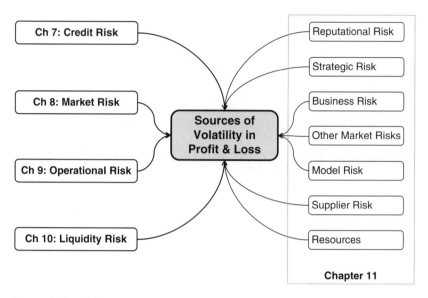

Figure 11.1   Risk types encountered by financial firms

The earlier chapters of Part II focused on the sources of risk that tend to get most attention – credit, market, operational and liquidity risks. This chapter discusses some of the other sources of risk to which financial firms are exposed. See Figure 11.1 for an overview.

The risks mentioned in this chapter need a degree of artistry in their management. Although they may be recognised as risk, their measurement is difficult. For some of these risks it is difficult to isolate their effects from other activities. Nevertheless, mismanagement of these risks can, in the extreme, result in a firm being taken over or very tough discussions with stakeholders.

11.1   INTRODUCTION

The risks mentioned in this chapter can be expected to appear on the Board agenda for discussion and decision. However, owing to their nature it is not always possible to quantify effects with clarity or precision. In comparison with the main risks – credit, market, operational and liquidity risks – these other risks have a common issue in terms of lack of data; where the data is available it tends to be sparse. The best that might be possible is being directionally correct on the impact when the event materialises. For some industries the other risks outlined below may be the major risk, for example reputational risk and the impact on the brand for a service firm.

The first step towards managing these other risks is awareness of their existence and scale of potential impact. The three lines of defence may not be as obvious for the main risks, but generally they are present. Even though a firm may not have a Group Head of Business Risk, there are roles for the CRO, businesses and specialist functions such as Finance & Accounting.

The rest of this chapter looks at the:

11.2 Reputational Risk
11.3 Strategic Risk
11.4 Business Risk
11.5 Other Market Risks
11.6 Model Risk
11.7 Supplier Risk
11.8 Resources
11.9 Issues to Consider

11.2 REPUTATIONAL RISK

Reputational risk is the possibility of losses, or underperformance, due to damage to the brand value of part of – or even all – the firm. An example is where an event in one part of the firm leads to departure of customers from the same or another part of the firm.

There are questions about whether reputational risk is a risk in its own right or a consequence of the other risk types. Is it possible to damage the firm's brand without incurring one of the main risk types, for example operational risk? One view is that reputational risk is similar to pouring petrol on an existing fire. The reputational damage may arise from the event itself or the way in which the event is managed.

The impact of damage on the brand is not restricted to the departure of customers. For example, the impact could be upon the firm's stock price. The consequences include disgruntled investors, implications for compensation packages involving stock and the ability to raise capital at a reasonable price. Other consequences can include the ability to attract high-quality resources, ranging from the graduate intake to senior managers.

In some cases the loss of market value of the firm can be multiples of the impact of the main risk, such as market risk. A firm may lose €1 billion due to a main risk materialising and yet its market value falls by €10 billion or more. This effect on the market value may be "temporary", but it may take months if not years for the market value of the firm to recover in relation to its peers or the wider market.

This impact on market value may be due to surprise, but more importantly a reflection of how well the firm is managed by the executive management team. Whether or not a risk event is a surprise is heavily influenced by perspective. This is where the range and variety of stakeholders can complicate the issue. An event that a firm may consider to be extreme, but not entirely impossible, can be interpreted as being catastrophic from a different perspective.

A change in the investor rating of a company can have strategic consequences. For example, a depressed stock market valuation can cause an increase in the cost of raising capital. The knock-on effects can influence the strategic plans for the firm. This may lead to the sale of business portfolios or entire businesses to release capital or retaining earnings rather than paying dividends, as alternatives to raising additional capital from the market.

Other consequences of a reputational event include Executive time. As a minimum, the Board and the Executive will have to spend more time with key shareholders. Other stakeholders, such as regulators and politicians, may also need to be informed of the details and the firm's response to the events. This can divert the attention of the Executive from the day-to-day task of running the firm, with potentially negative impacts on oversight and managing other activities.

Studies are done on how "crises" are managed by firms and by governments. This is a reactive stance involving the management of consequences. These are lessons that can also be applied in the financial industry. One of the key lessons seems to be the communication process and who has what role in that process. An example might be the communication processes adopted by car manufacturers when issuing a product recall.

A more pro-active approach is to raise the possibility of reputational risk as part of the strategic and tactical decision-making process. For example, is reputational risk considered explicitly as part of new product approval? However, an excessive focus on reputational risk can prevent progress and evolution.

11.3   STRATEGIC RISK

Strategic risk is the mismatch of objectives and activities with stakeholder expectations over a period of time. Strategic risk may be referred to as "change-the-firm" decisions. The stakeholders may be customers, staff, politicians, regulators and others, or a combination. The mismatch of activities with expectations can lead to a gradual reduction in market value of the firm in comparison with peers and the market as a whole.

The decisions that fall into this category range from acquisitions or disposal of businesses to major investment in systems. Investment in systems may have a relatively short time span, such as 2 to 5 years, but the amounts to be invested in these systems make them strategic in nature.

Changes in systems can be incremental or they can be step changes. For example, the implementation of a new general ledger accounting system would normally be viewed as a strategic decision. Decisions to enhance a risk estimation process may be incremental, but if the wrong choice is made then certain business activities may not be possible until a remedial project has been completed.

Related to these change initiatives are various project risks. There is a boundary between project risks and operational risk. Project risks can be summarised as:

- delivering the required functionality,
- within the agreed time frame, and
- within budget.

By managing these project risks, some of the change-the-firm issues are addressed. There is still the migration from current to future state. This might be at the level of business divisions or individual working practices.

The degree of strategic risk can be influenced by the firm's tactics relative to its peers and market place. Is the firm a leader, a fast follower or a laggard? The leadership position is equated with being first-to-market and the rewards, for being first mover, such as market share, compensate for the additional costs involved. The additional costs may be new leading edge (or bleeding edge) technology and false starts or going down dead-ends. On some occasions the demand for the product or service is not going to be as large as anticipated and it may not be possible to recover the investment. The laggard waits to see if a market develops and it is possible to take market share from the first mover, or further expand the total size of the market – second mover advantage. The expectation is that by this time the technology will have settled down so the implementation costs should be lower than for the first-to-market, but the rewards will also be lower. The fast follower is somewhere in-between.

For a large complex firm, different parts of the firm may adopt different tactics. Retail banking, for example, could be a first-to-market in its approach, while private banking could be a laggard. One of the possible areas for particular Board scrutiny is when a business that has been a laggard decides that it wants to be first-to-market.

At the extreme, when the management of strategic risk goes wrong then the firm can cease to exist. More usually there is an unexpected diversion of resources to put things right. These projects might be a cost reduction initiative, or automating a poorly understood process. This diversion of resources might result in the cancellation of a system, part way through completion, the write-off of various costs and investment in a new replacement project. In addition to the write-off and the additional costs there may be opportunity costs due to the late delivery of change-the-bank projects.

Some aspects of strategic risk can be managed via the correct implementation of known processes, such as due diligence when buying or selling businesses. Other aspects may require adoption of processes used in other industries for strategic-level change-the-firm investments. An example is real option techniques as used by pharmaceutical companies when developing drugs. Real option techniques enable various uncertainties to be taken into account when estimating the net benefits and have been shown to be superior to only relying upon net present values when considering strategic alternatives. The real option framework assists in identifying aspects that can be influenced, for example the creation of proof of concept before building a production standard system.

The first line of defence is part of the responsibility of the change sponsors. These change sponsors may be businesses or some of the other functions of the firm, for example Finance & Accounting. Another change sponsor is the Board itself.

The CRO can only provide support and advice in their role of the second line of defence if they are involved in the strategic decision-making process. While the CRO can push to be involved, the request for CRO input by the Board can go a long way to making the skills and knowledge available to decision makers. For some of the decisions, such as those involving systems, the Chief IT Officer needs to be involved with the change sponsors.

11.4   BUSINESS RISK

Business risk is the risk that a loss will result from a fall in business activity. While at the extreme this is obvious, the issue is: when does the loss occur and what can the firm do to manage it?

Business risk relates to the structure of the profit and loss account. If all the costs were variable in nature then as business volumes fall so do the costs. In reality, the cost structure of a business is a combination of:

- fixed costs
- semi-fixed
- semi-variable
- variable costs.

This characterisation of costs is in comparison with a time horizon, for example 12 months. Fixed costs are those that cannot be altered within the time horizon, while variable costs are those that can be altered quickly, for example in less than 3 months. Semi-fixed and semi-variable are in-between. As some of these costs relate to staff, what may be a semi-variable cost in one location may be semi-fixed or fixed in another location. Also, a change in compensation structure can result in cost migrating from semi-variable to semi-fixed, reducing the flexibility of the firm to respond to changing conditions.

With the relatively high level of investment in computer systems in the financial industry, some might find that the majority of their costs are fixed. This means that for a reduction in customers there is little that the firm can do to restore profitability in the short term. However, the investment in systems can enable the firm to cope with a significant increase in volume before additional capacity is needed. The increase in profits arises from not having to meet the increase in variable costs as volumes increase.

One technique that may transform fixed into variable costs is outsourcing. Depending on the outsourcing arrangement, the insourcer may be willing to charge on a variable cost basis while incurring fixed costs. However, such a risk transformation can result in increased control issues and operational risk. The increase in these non-business risks may be larger than the benefits from outsourcing.

As a result, the Board may require each business to be charged for economic capital for business risk. The economic capital estimate could be based on the cost structure mix of a business and periods of time. Estimating the economic capital could involve stress tests and scenarios around the cost/income ratio and its constituents. For example, a stress test could be the impact of an instantaneous and persistent 20% reduction in customer activity and the ability of the business to reorganise to the new level of activity over a period of 12 months.

Some caution is needed as the reduction in income may not just come about from a reduction in customer activity, but also non-customer sources of income, such as market risk. Similarly, the customers may be there, but at a level of return at which the firm does not want to do business, which may happen with credit risk.

In some cases the stress test may posit that the reduction in customer activity arises from competitor actions. In other industries, such as food retailing, this might be addressed, in the short term, by an advertising campaign. Repositioning a firm in finance is likely to be more difficult and/or take longer depending on the business and nature of the customer segment, for example retail versus government agencies.

The business is the first line of defence. The business will be supported by Finance & Accounting and various change-the-firm projects. The estimation of economic capital for this risk will focus attention on the cost structure and encourage its management.

11.5   OTHER MARKET RISKS

This section discusses a manifestation of market risk that is outside the trading book and banking book, such as pensions. Effectively, the risk is underperformance of investments to meet long-term liabilities.

Some firms may provide pensions that are based on defined contributions, whilst others provide defined benefit plans. The majority of this form of market risk is associated with firms providing defined benefit pensions to their staff. For some firms the pension liability is so large in relation to their balance sheet that they are considered to be pension funds with an operating division. The more usual view is of an operating company with a pension fund.

In the defined benefit pension plan the employer agrees to provide a pension that may be based on a combination of the number of years with the employer and the final salary. There has been discussion about the increase in pension liabilities as people live longer and investments provide lower returns.

The focus of this section is market risk in the performance of assets to meet pension liabilities. The firm and the investment manager will be advised on the gap between the assets and liabilities and even the composition of the assets. Should the assets be predominantly invested in bonds or equities or a combination that changes as the profile of outflows from the pension fund alter? These reviews may occur annually, once every 3 years or even every 5 years.

The assumptions in this process involve how the asset portfolio will perform, even if the profile of the liabilities remains unchanged. Bond yields make assumptions about the return on reinvested payments of interest and principal. Long-term equity yields make assumptions about the reinvestment of dividends. The risk is that the reinvestment assumptions, such as 7%, are a long way from the prevailing reality, for instance 1.5%, creating a shortfall. There may also be assumptions about the performance of the equity market, for example generating a real return of Y% over a particular horizon, that proves not to be robust when the level of the market remains unchanged over 5 years, resulting in an asset shortfall against the targeted inflation linked liabilities.

These shortfalls, which may border on making the pension fund insolvent, need to be met by the firm. It is possible for a firm to have to contribute millions on a regular basis to meet the shortfalls in the pension fund. When compared with the market risk appetite for trading and other activities, the pension fund risk appetite can be significant or even dominant.

For firms, an issue is that although the pension shortfall is still market risk, the time frame is longer than the 1 or 10 days for the trading book. As a result, the risk management choices are also limited. Reducing the amount invested in equities and increasing the amount invested in bonds may limit any future shortfall, but it also reduces the upside and the likelihood that the firm will be able to take a "pension contribution holiday" at some point in the future. Changes in assumptions on longevity are also difficult to hedge.

For the Board, there are additional complicating factors. One of these factors can be the different pension obligations in different countries. Other issues can be the difficulty in forecasting market conditions to achieve a balance of returns with the possibility of a shortfall and the frequency of reviews.

The first line of defence will be specialist pension plan managers, who may be part of the Human Resources division. These managers may be supported by external experts, such as actuaries, and investment managers. Some of the issues have similarity with budgeting for the trading book, for example for a given amount of market risk appetite what will be the return? As a result, other sources of relevant internal expertise may include market risk management and management of the trading book.

11.6   MODEL RISK

With the extensive use of statistical and mathematical models in the financial industry, firms have established procedures to manage associated risks. These procedures are grouped together under the title of model validation.

Models are used to represent reality, often providing a summary. Part of the process of using a model is a reduction in the variety, the degree of complexity and richness of the situation being described. An example is GDP, which is derived from a simplified version of the economy and for which GDP is used as a summary statistic. Other examples of models are economic capital models, whether estimating credit, market risk or operational risk. The other broad category of models is mental models where, as individuals, we use a simplified version of reality in decision making. Some of these models have biases but all reduce the level of detail to a greater or lesser extent.

During and since the financial crisis, models have come under significant scrutiny. These models, including regulatory capital models, have to balance conflicting requirements. On the one hand they need to more accurately reflect the complexity of the real world. On the other hand they need to be more transparent and better understood by the users of the model outputs.

The statistical and mathematical models used in financial firms fall into two broad categories, those used to price products and those used to summarise portfolios of risks. Product pricing models have two key functions, the first is to price products and the second is to assist in identifying the risk factors used by some of the risk summary models. For some products, such as derivatives, the price is largely determined by models, even for high-volume products such as forward foreign exchange, other over-the-counter derivatives as well as exchange-traded derivatives. When a product does not trade regularly during the trading day it may be necessary to rely on a model to determine the value, effectively marking-to-model, especially if the position is held in the trading book. The components used as inputs to pricing models also serve to identify the various risk factors used by models that summarise risks, including credit risks.

The broad risks around models are:

1. fit for purpose
2. assumptions
3. implementation
4. data inputs
5. usage of the model outputs.

The issue of "fit for purpose" is likely to evolve as the model is used in situations that differ from when it was designed. For example, a fixed-income portfolio model may not be appropriate for a portfolio of commodities. For a product pricing model, the example might be the extension of a bond pricing model to reflect call options embedded in a different type of bond. The outcome may be an amendment to the bond pricing model to more accurately reflect the complexity of the call options embedded in the bond.

Some of these issues may be identified via the model validation process, but it is better if the request for change comes from the users or the model designers as they are closer to the model and its purpose. For product pricing and risk portfolio summarising models, the business is the first line of defence with the risk management function acting as the second line, supporting and challenging the business.

Often, the reduction in variety and complexity is achieved using assumptions about the real world. One series of assumptions to be found in pricing models relates to the liquidity and frictionless trading. Other common assumptions include efficient markets and an arbitrage-free environment relating to the distribution of knowledge amongst market participants.

For the risk summarising portfolio model the assumptions might be the shape of the distribution of returns or losses. The use of the normal or lognormal distribution may be inappropriate if extreme events seem to occur more frequently than anticipated by these distributions.

An approach to confirming that models do what they say they do is to have a model validation process. The model validation can be the independent construction of a model for the same purpose and then conducting a comparison to identify differences and understand them. This approach requires that the modelling skills are duplicated within the firm. This "contest of the models" requires that both teams have the requisite computer skills.

An alternative approach is to have a separate group test the proposed model against a range of situations and assess the results. Of the potential errors in portfolio models some can be cancelling errors. For example, a risk portfolio model with long and short positions may have cancelling errors in the choice of distribution. However, when the portfolio is predominantly long or short, there is nothing to offset the incorrect assumption. This also requires skilled and knowledgeable testers and a suitably diverse range of sample portfolios and variety of market movements.

Issues around the implementation of these models can be the same as for any other system. Does the computer code do what it is supposed to do? An approach to identifying these issues is through the testing of the pre-implemented model with the implemented model. Any issues around the computer code should appear in the design stage, when the prototype is independently tested, and in the pre-production testing when the results are compared with the approved prototype.

The saying "Garbage In gives Garbage Out" relates to input errors. For the portfolio models these may be closely related to "fit for purpose" above. Product pricing models may have this issue systematically where the input instructions are incorrect, for example using the risk-free or risky interest rate. When product models are dependent on a price feed from a third-party supplier, an unrecognised change in the price feed can have the same consequences as a systematic error in the input instructions. For both of these situations there may be a period of time before the error is identified. For some products the fact that there is an issue may be identifiable by obtaining a competing quotation from a competitor firm for the same product. However, a high degree of reconciliation between prices can result in a comparison of models. A detailed comparison of models with competitors may not be possible as some of these models are proprietary, but some are widely known and understood.

Models are expensive to design, implement and maintain. As a consequence, there is a possibility that models may be used for inappropriate purposes. The regular risk portfolio model may not be the correct one, but it may be available and tempting to use.

With these various risks in modelling it ultimately becomes a cost/benefit decision about how much to invest in the model construction, implementation and independent validation.

11.7   SUPPLIER RISK

The focus here is on default in the form of a supplier not meeting contractual terms, as opposed to omissions, possible or actual, around the flow of funds or securities. These contracts cover a range of activities from employment to outsourcing to partnerships. Depending on the activity, the firm will manage these contract issues via the Human Resources or Procurement departments or within the business.

For non-financial firms these contracts govern the relationships with key partners in the supply chain. Although financial firms may not have the same sort of supply chain, there are key partners. Given the nature of banking, many of these key partners will be involved in providing:

- data
- software
- IT hardware
- services that have been outsourced
- office space that is leased or rented.

Data could be in the form of credit scores or ratings or end of day prices for revaluing the trading book.[1] Software ranges from Microsoft Office installed on desktops to intranet to the general ledger and activities in-between. Hardware includes the communications equipment as well as personal computers, servers and mainframes.

The risks and uncertainties relate to what happens if one of these suppliers breaches their contract. The contract may be to deliver 200 personal computers, but if after partial delivery the manufacturer fails then the only choice is to find another supplier, which can be a laborious, time-consuming and expensive process. Such a change may not only affect the performance, but other physical characteristics – such as whether it can fit in the existing storage space – may cause issues. While there are several manufacturers of personal computers, there

---

[1] Data could also include expectations around publication of data, including financial benchmarks such as equity or interest rate or other indices.

are only a limited number of suppliers of software for general ledgers or communications equipment to meet the needs of internationally active firms.

The impact of failure by a supplier may be limited to the one firm; for other suppliers it may have implications for a number of firms within a location or even across locations. A supplier failure affecting many firms simultaneously could be a cut in power supplies.

As soon as the firm enters into a contract for services or products then there is an exposure. While the contract is being devised, consideration will be given to remedies or redress for either party if it does not go according to plan. The ability to execute these remedies is dependent on the counterparty still operating and not under administration or being wound up. Effectively, the cost of the service provided by the supplier includes not only the day-to-day costs when everything is going well, but also the costs of remediation when things do not go well.

For some services, such as the publication of benchmarks or indices, there is not a one-to-one relationship between the publisher and the user of the information. The ability of the publisher to meet expectations may be dependent on other service providers such as stock exchanges or experts. In these circumstances it can be difficult to obtain redress for additional costs incurred.

The analysis of the risk needs to take into account the likelihood of occurrence and the impact on the firm. Some of the impacts arise from the management of operational or business risks by the supplier. A hardware failure may prevent the publication of an index at an expected time or the processing of a number of transactions. In some situations the risk management tactic can be to have more than one current supplier of the service.

For some contracts, such as outsourcing, it is possible to require risk management data to be provided to the service purchaser. Such data may relate to the financial strength of the service provider or the operational risk management conducted by the supplier. This data is intended to provide an early warning so that solutions can be explored and developed before it becomes an issue of reacting to a crisis.

The range of risk management decisions may depend on the analysis of likelihood and severity before events materialise. For some contracts it will be possible to have multiple suppliers or require the supplier to operate from multiple locations. In either situation the cost of managing the contract and service provider(s) will increase. The outcome may be more contracts to review and monitor or a larger service fee.

The risk management action will be influenced by risk appetite for such disruption. The risk appetite may be an element of the credit risk appetite for the skills in assessing performance under contracts, or the operational risk appetite for the potential disruption to the purchaser's activities or even a specialist dedicated risk appetite.

Some of the remediation plans are categorised as "Disaster Recovery Plans" or "Business Continuity Plans". Some of these plans can involve moving teams of people, for example a trading room and support staff, up to a hundred miles away to an alternative site. Other plans can involve having multiple telecommunication feeds coming into the building from different sides.

The first line of defence is the user of these supplied activities, for example IT purchasing, or Finance & Accounting or many other purchasers. They will be supported by a disaster recovery or business continuity team. This team may be able to provide "war stories" of things that have gone wrong in the past or be able to support the development of simulations, for example if there is a security cordon around the building and employees cannot enter. For most of these supplier-related risks the second line of defence will be operational risk management. However, it is unlikely that the firm will be able to achieve zero risk. Sometimes back-up generators do fail.

11.8 RESOURCES

This topic refers to having the right number of people with the appropriate level of knowledge at the right place at the right time. Some firms may categorise this as "key man" risk. However, "key man" risk is often assumed to be limited to the top executive management layer as opposed to throughout the organisation. Other firms may categorise having the right knowledge in the right place as a feature of the risk management and control environment and not a risk category in its own right.

The issue around knowledge arises from two sources; the pace of change and the industrialisation of finance. These two changes have been noticeable since the initial Basel Accord, but more particularly since the market risk adjustment to the initial accord. The change in the range of activities undertaken by firms has resulted in increased expectations of risk management activities by various stakeholders. The industrialisation became a response to complexity by creating specialists and experts in some very narrow fields and the demise of the generalist. Although the historical start may be linked to banking developments, other sectors such as fund management and insurance have gone, and continue to go, through similar changes.

This increasing specialisation can make some tasks more difficult, lead to tensions around boundaries and result in confusing conversations. For example, if a risk analyst does not understand the impact of a sequence of events on a business then it is difficult to perform a risk assessment. The issue of understanding the business, including the business model, is important in identifying and escalating risks, whether they are well known or emerging. Consequences of resource issues include the possibility of more undesirable surprises and inefficient processes.

A response to this industrialisation is to broaden the availability of knowledge. This can be achieved in a number of ways. Training, in various forms, is the most obvious approach.

A more tactical approach to industrialisation is to have career progression planning and ensure that individuals get exposure to a variety of issues. This might involve a prospective COO for a business in a location spending 6 months with the operational risk management function. However, this type of approach requires a level of resourcing to permit this planned progression to occur.

Recruiting from outside the firm may be one solution to the numbers and knowledge issue. For small firms there may be no other choice. For firms large and small there may be no choice when the required skills are very specialised. However, for larger firms that rely solely on recruited specialists there may be additional costs. These costs include the lack of an informal network across the firm, the lack of familiarity with the organisation's culture (risk or otherwise) and probably the increased costs of recruiting an expert. If the understanding of employees is that the firm would rather recruit externally than develop internal talent, then the talent will adopt the same approach – it will leave for career development.

The advantage of recruiting for knowledge is that it provides an opportunity for a new way of thinking about topics, effectively helping to mitigate various biases including groupthink. Sources of external talent include the traditional consulting firms on projects as well as interim executives and specialists.

Inevitably, there is a balancing act between the costs of adequate resources and returns. In some cases the resource issue may be addressed by automation of processes; from a different perspective this also results in semi-variable being transformed into fixed costs.

The first line of defence in managing resource issues is the business and every department head. Without adequate resources the departments cannot function efficiently as there is the increased likelihood of unpleasant surprises. The first line of defence will be supported by the Human Resources team providing oversight, challenge and advice. A lack of a resource management plan can lead to increases in other risks, such as operational risk. Some of the consequences of resource issues may materialise in a short period, others will have a longer gestation, possibly years.

11.9   ISSUES TO CONSIDER

- Is reputational risk explicitly considered at Board level as part of decision making?
- What factors are monitored to indicate the emergence of reputational risk? For example, share price, bond ratings, cost of funding in the wholesale market?
- When was the "crisis management handbook" last reviewed? What changes were made? Does it include social media initiatives?
- How well does the firm manage significant projects? Have they been implemented on time, provided the desired functionality and been within budget?
- Doe the firm have the resources to manage multiple significant projects?
- Have there been any changes to the project management process from past projects that failed and those that succeeded?
- Do the businesses have a vision of their ideal cost structure given their sources of revenue and level of activity? How does the business risk influence strategic change in the firm?
- What proportion of the risk management budget is allocated to the independent validation of pricing and risk summarising portfolio models?
- Are there succession plans to mitigate "key man" risk?
- Are secondments between the business and other functions part of the resources development programme?

- What are the resource hot spots and what are the implications for achieving the firm's objectives as set by the Board?

FURTHER READING

Morini, M. (2011) *Understanding and Managing Model Risk: A Practical Guide for Quants, Traders and Validators*. John Wiley & Sons, Chichester.

12

Risk Interactions

Risk Management at the Top

Ch. 1: Introduction

Part I: Risk Oversight

Ch. 2: Risk – An Overview	Ch. 3: Risk Oversight	Ch. 4: Risk Management	Ch. 5: Risk Appetite	Ch. 6: Risk Culture

Part II: Specific Risks

Ch. 7: Credit Risk	Ch. 8: Market Risk	Ch. 9: Operational Risk	Ch. 10: Liquidity Risk	Ch. 11: Other Risks	Ch. 12: Risk Interactions

Part III: Regulatory Environment

Ch. 13: Regulatory Environment

Earlier chapters have focused on individual risk management frameworks, including risk appetite. However, as expertise increases in managing the individual risk sources (first-order effects) there is increasing appreciation of the interactions (second-order effects).

The way in which these sources of risk interact is not always transparent to those receiving summary data as it flows up the organisation. These interactions can be sources of variety and information that get filtered out in the reporting process. As risk management and risk measurement precision improves within each of the risk source silos, so the contribution made by these interactions (second-order effects) becomes more noticeable to the risk takers and analysts.

One of the implications of these second-order effects is that the knowledge needed by risk management is wider than just their risk silo. For example, credit risk management will need to be aware that market risk or operational risk can influence the severity of credit risk losses. Also, operational risk management needs to be aware that the severity of some events can be influenced by market risk.

These interactions between risks can lead to boundary issues and tensions over jurisdiction and responsibility. With boundary issues there is the potential for some aspect to "fall between two stools". These interactions can also lead to queries over the scope of risk appetites for each of the risk silos. The overall principle should be that the risk is measured once, for example by economic capital, even if it requires more than one risk management function to manage it.

12.1   INTRODUCTION

The interaction between risks adds a layer of complexity to the risk management processes, including risk appetite. For clarity and efficiency the risk needs to be measured once, for economic or regulatory capital purposes, but may need inter-silo cooperation to ensure that it is adequately managed.

Some of the complexity arises from the evolution of risk management in financial firms. For many firms credit risk was the first to have an explicit dedicated risk management function and this was probably followed by liquidity and market risk. Operational risk is the most recent arrival on the risk management scene.

This sequence does not tell the entire story, as there have been spikes of activity leading to surges in sophistication. If the regulatory framework is used to provide the timeline, market risk management had a burst of increased sophistication in the 1990s. This was followed by an increase in sophistication for credit risk with Basel II in 2005 and the arrival of operational risk as an umbrella risk management concept. Most recently, funding liquidity risk has taken a leap forward. Before these regulatory leaps, firms had been implementing various theories and making incremental enhancements.[1]

One outcome of this evolutionary process is that the regulatory definitions around the individual risk silos have differing degrees of specificity.

Credit risk is the potential for loss due to the inability, unwillingness or non-timeliness of a counterparty honouring a financial obligation. Whenever there is a chance that a counterparty will not pay an amount of money owed, live up to a financial commitment or honour a claim, there is credit risk.

Market risk is the potential for loss due to movements in the level or volatility of market prices.

Operational risk is the potential for loss due to inadequate or failed internal processes, people and systems or from external events. This definition includes legal risk, but excludes strategic and reputational risk.

Funding liquidity risk is the potential that the firm will not be able to meet efficiently both expected and unexpected current and future cash flow and collateral needs without affecting either daily operations or the financial condition of the firm.

These definitions describe the cause of the loss, for example counterparty default for credit risk. However, the severity of the loss may be influenced by market risk. In this context market risk is a severity driver for the credit risk loss. Some of these interactions are the result of tactics to mitigate a particular risk, for example taking collateral to reduce the exposure to credit risk.

Some of these definitions raise issues around boundaries. For example, the list of operational risk events includes external fraud. As a result, if there is a mortgage fraud is it credit risk or operational risk? If it is credit risk, then presumably operational risk influences the severity of the loss as a result of the fraud.

---

[1] Regulators often follow industry leaders. A new regulatory regime may be signalled via consultative papers 2 or 3 years ahead of being finalised. Once finalised, the regulators will give the firms a period of time, usually several years, ahead of the compliance date.

The rest of this chapter looks at the:

12.2 Risks as Frequency and Severity Drivers
12.3 Risk Interactions
12.4 Implications for Risk Management and Measurement
12.5 Issues to Consider

From a firm-level risk management perspective, being able to transform other risks into market risk is useful. This value arises from the market being able to quickly absorb and redistribute some of these risks. However, not all risk variants of all risk sources can be converted into market risks. Operational risk, even with insurance, is one of the more difficult risk sources with which to achieve this sort of transformation.

12.2 RISKS AS FREQUENCY AND SEVERITY DRIVERS

Of the risks defined above, three (credit, market and operational) can be measured and economic capital estimated. The definition for each of these three risks starts with "the potential for loss due to....", a causal construct. (For funding liquidity risk the definition is based on a consequence.) The causal construct enables the identification of what is within scope and what is outside. For example, what is credit risk and not market or operational risk?

This causal construct can be used to define the scope of the risk appetite and related economic capital. In turn, this determines the risk management function that "owns" a particular risk event. For example, if collateral is provided to reduce the impact of a possible credit risk event and the value of collateral varies due to market risk, there is no credit risk event until there has been an impairment or default. At the point of default, market risk may result in a higher credit risk write-off than anticipated. Between the time that the collateral is lodged and when the counterparty defaults and the collateral is liquidated to offset the due payment, there is an opportunity for market prices to change. The potential for default means that the event will be overseen by credit risk management not market risk management. In turn, this means that it will be included in the credit risk capital calculations, whether economic or regulatory.

For risk appetite and economic capital estimates it is important to know not only the cause of the loss event, but also its severity. In an extreme case, where all of a firm's credit risks are mitigated by collateralisation, these factors drive the amount of economic capital for would-be events of default (to determine the frequency of credit risk events) and market risk (to determine the severity of loss when there is a default). As a consequence, market risk considerations should be involved in determining appropriate discounts or haircuts for the collateral.

From a risk management perspective, the frequency of this event is driven by credit risk, but the risk analysis may need to take into account market or operational risks. Operational risk can influence the severity of the credit loss due to legal risk around the contract. These severity drivers need to be taken into account when considering the risk management choices of:

- avoid
- reduce
- transfer/transform
- accept.

Some of these severity drivers, not linked to the frequency of the event, will be involved around decisions related to the reduce and transfer/transform choices and actions. In making decisions to manage the severity of the loss associated with a given risk source, as determined by the frequency driver of the event, the specialist may need to call upon knowledge and skills from other risk source specialists.

Other examples of divergence between frequency and severity drivers include issues of funding liquidity risk when a counterparty fails to make a scheduled payment or delivery of securities (a possible early indicator of a credit default). The relationship between funding liquidity risk (frequency) and credit risk (severity) can also relate to the credit risk of the firm as a borrower, for example a ratings downgrade of the firm. Operational risk, as it encompasses data quality, can drive the severity of funding liquidity risk as decisions have to be made on incomplete or even inaccurate data. Some of these interactions are shown in Table 12.1 and reviewed in more detail in Section 12.3 below.

The owners of the risk are the business, the risk arises from their activities. These activities and risk mitigation decisions will influence the extent to which the severity driver is different from the frequency driver. The business, as the risk owner, is often in the best position to assemble the experts from various disciplines when arriving at a risk management decision that is optimal for the firm.

Table 12.1 Interaction frequency and severity drivers

	Frequency drivers/risk management			
	Credit risk	Market risk	Operational risk	Funding liquidity risk
Severity drivers **Credit risk**				Counterpart misses scheduled payment
Market risk	Collateral values		Data quality fraud	Value of reserve assets
Operational risk	Legal risk fraud	Model error		Data quality
Funding liquidity risk	Own credit deterioration	Spreads rise at the time of greatest funding need	Conflicts of interest for depositors when assets are sold	

Table 12.1 shows some of the interactions, with examples, between the frequency drivers and the severity drivers of loss events.

Here is a story about a single transaction, a risk that it generates and the risk management decisions. The firm makes a 5-year loan with floating interest rates. The business is charged for fixed-rate funding by the funding liquidity policy. The banking book, where the loan sits, now has an interest rate mismatch, fixed versus floating interest rates. In line with the firm's policy, the risk arising from the interest rate mismatch is transferred to the interest rate trading desk in the trading book. The interest rate trader has a choice to retain this market risk or hedge it. The trader decides to hedge the risk. Should the trader hedge it using an over-the-counter product, creating an additional credit risk with the trader's counterpart, or use exchange-traded interest rate products? Using exchange-traded products to reduce market risk, will lead to incremental operational risk due to the daily movement of margin. Is this incremental operational risk allocated to the trader?

In this story, what is optimal for the firm is not easy to identify. In practice, individual transactions cannot be followed at this level of detail. The different businesses will have their allocated risk appetites for credit, market and operational risks for comparison with the amount of risks that they are taking at the time. As a result, the emphasis is on managing to the various risk appetites.

12.3   RISK INTERACTIONS

This section goes into more detail on the interactions mentioned in Table 12.1. The section starts by considering how the different frequencies and severities arise. The interactions cannot be considered comprehensive as new examples and combinations continue to emerge.

Some of these combinations arise from trying to manage the exposure associated with the frequency of the risk. Other combinations arise from the operating environment, internal and external, and counterparties. For example, where there is the possibility of wrong-doing, as in the case of fraud, either by staff or by counterparties, this is connected to operational risk.

One approach to bringing more certainty to transactions is to enhance the contractual documentation. These enhancements will be in response to identified shortcomings, actual or potential. This risk-mitigating action could be in response to a new type of transaction, or a new distribution channel for an existing transaction type, such as mobile phones for small credit card payments. Ultimately, the improved contractual documentation will have some uncertainty until supported by case law. Until then, opinions from qualified experts are the best that is available to anticipate the outcome from litigation. As a result, even if the underlying source of risk might be credit, the amount of legal risk (a subcategory of operational risk) or uncertainty may be reduced, but is still present.

The sections below look at the interactions between some of the sources of risk in more detail.

12.3.1   Credit Risk with a Market Risk Severity Driver

One of the simplest examples of interconnections between sources of risk is the use of collateral in connection with credit risk. The purpose of collateral is to reduce the net amount of credit risk. One of the commonest examples of this arrangement is the house as collateral for a mortgage. Another common form of collateral is in the form of (usually tradable) securities. However, due to the fluctuation in market prices for securities there is a need to reduce uncertainty around their value at the point they will be needed, when there is a default. To achieve this aim the lender will usually have a list of securities permitted for use as collateral, require a discount to the value of the securities to offset the credit exposure and specify a frequency of periodic revaluation. These requirements interact, so a security that has smaller price fluctuations will be able to have a lower discount and less frequent revaluation. These factors may be influenced by knowledge accumulated from the market risk economic capital calculations based on VaR. This use of collateral has effectively converted the credit risk severity driver to market risk.

Other aspects to be considered when using collateral include operational risk. Operational risk includes failures in processes and systems. For example, if the process fails to revalue the securities held as collateral at the specified frequency, for example it occurs monthly instead of weekly, then this could affect the severity of the loss when there is an event of default. However, for this process failure to have an impact on the severity there needs to be an initiating credit default.

These interactions make the accurate estimation of LGD more complicated. Whether the interactions need to be explicitly modelled or taken into account via historic losses will be influenced by the pace of change in the business and the extent to which collateral has been used/will be used to reduce the severity of credit risk losses.

Another interaction between credit and market risk is when derivatives are involved. These may be exchange-traded or over-the-counter. The change in market price drives the value of the contract. For exchange-traded derivatives the daily change in end-of-day valuation determines the margin flows resulting in very short-term credit exposures. For over-the-counter products, the mark-to-market or mark-to-model creates a revision in the value which creates a change in the profit and loss account.

The credit exposure is the extent to which the derivative is in profit for one counterparty, but in loss for the other counterparty. The potential credit exposure, the amount that it can be in profit during the life of the contract, is driven by the market risk of the underlying risk, for example commodity, credit, equity, foreign exchange or interest rate.

This fluctuation in value of derivatives is part of the *raison d'être* behind the existence of central counterparties. These central counterparties have developed with exchange-traded derivatives, for example agricultural commodities. Each principal counterparty actually transacts with the central counterparty for the amount and price agreed between the principals. Although facilitating the transfer of market risk, the central counterparty has no market risk exposure as it has two offsetting contracts, one with each of the principals. However, the central counterparty does have credit exposure. Whichever principal is on the losing side of the transaction creates a credit exposure for the central counterparty. To minimise its credit risk the central counterparty imposes daily margin calls with the principals, so on a daily basis the principals have to adjust their collateral position with the central counterparty.

The two principals, wishing to adjust their market risk profile, have created a potential credit risk, albeit with a centralised counterparty. The extent of the potential credit risk depends on the volatility of the market price of the underlying risk. The centralised counterparty requires daily adjustment of collateral, placing and meeting this obligation requires process and systems to run smoothly: operational risk. However, to offset this volatility between the end-of-day valuation and when it receives the collateral, the central counterparty will insist on an initial margin. The daily movements in collateral are to maintain the level of the initial margin. The central counterparties will review and revise the level of initial margin given changes to market volatility.

This sequence of events describes how a market risk is converted into a credit risk. The potential size of the credit risk is determined by the volatility of the underlying market risk and value of collateral. To minimise the credit risk the central counterparty requires daily adjustment of collateral. From the perspective of the central counterparty, its credit risk in the form of missing adjustment of collateral will be mainly due to an operational risk event in or by one of its principal counterparties, for example a system failure.

Whether this transformation of risk, from market into credit and operational risk, is a real reduction in risk depends on the relative competencies of the firm. Is there a reduction in total risk for the same return or an increase in return for the same total risk? Is there a real reduction in economic capital, or is the apparent reduction due to some aspects not being captured in the economic capital calculations?

12.3.2 Credit Risk with an Operational Risk Severity Driver

This section explores operational risk as a severity driver for credit risk. The scope of operational risk is not limited to failures in processes or systems, it also includes legal risk, fraud and process failures.

In some situations a lending decision will be supported by the results from a credit scoring model. This credit scoring model has various model risks. These credit scoring models will use a series of inputs to support decisions on the likelihood of default and possibly the severity of default. For lending to individuals such inputs may include industry, salary and a number of other factors. From these factors and default histories of populations a credit scoring model will be constructed. As more data becomes available about individuals and increasing sophistication is applied to its use (data mining), the models become more accurate in their predictions.

Like other models, the credit scoring model will have explicit or implicit assumptions. If these assumptions prove to be incorrect then the frequency or probability of default will deviate from expectations. Similarly, the severity or LGD may also deviate from expectations. Part of the difficulty is in determining when the outcome is consistent with the assumptions in the model and when there is an error in the model and its use. These outcomes might be deviations within a population (e.g., a postal district) giving rise to a higher frequency of defaults than predicted by the model. Another outcome is that the severity of default is higher than predicted.

Model error is within the broad scope of operational risk. Although incremental enhancements are made to credit scoring models, it is likely to be a change in economic environment, for example the onset of a recession and/or increasing unemployment that gives rise to results outside expectations. A change in the economic environment may change the frequency and severity of default within a given postal district.

Another source of interaction between credit and operational risk is fraud. Fraud is one of the event types that is categorised as being operational risk. Fraud in lending can take several forms, from deliberate provision of inaccurate financial data such as salaries, to unauthorised trading when somebody approves a loan without the requisite authority, to identity theft.

The outcome of fraud is an increase in the probability of default and/or the loss given default. First-party fraud involves the borrower providing deliberately misleading data to the firm. This data will be used as input to the lending decision, for example as input to a credit scoring model. So the credit scoring model gives an accurate answer given the inputs, but the inputs are inaccurate.

Although the fraud may have been committed at the time that the loan was granted, there is no event until the payments are not made and a default declared: credit risk.

12.3.3   Market Risk or Operational Risk as the Severity Driver

Fraud can also have an impact on market risk. The most discussed fraud variant, in relation to market risk, is "rogue trading" or unauthorised trading. The initial question is whether this is market risk driven by operational risk, or an operational risk where the severity is driven by market risk. Other forms of fraud influencing market risk include insider trading. Other interactions between these two sources of risk include model errors.

"Rogue trading", in the trading book context, seems to involve deliberately hiding positions from control functions. The assumption is that when the positions are profitable they will be revealed to the control functions.[2]

The hiding of positions has a number of impacts. As the positions are not recorded it means that the inputs to the VaR model are incomplete. This results in a VaR value that does not reflect the complete range of market risks being faced by the organisation. In turn this has implications for the economic capital estimate of market risk and probably the amount of regulatory capital required. Rogue trading effectively results in operational risk causing a degree of uncertainty around the market risk figures used in the organisation and the amount of available capital due to size of losses involved.

It should be noted that the same effect, of mis-stating the VaR and thus the economic capital, can also be achieved by executing a transaction correctly, but recording it incorrectly, for example a purchase as opposed to a sale. To get the VaR back within the risk appetite, the trader may initiate trades to reduce the apparent risk, but actually increasing the risk.

---

[2] Court cases show that the psychology around rogue trading can be complex, for example the desire to save the team's bonus. Added to this can be unclear communications down the chain of command.

Other sorts of fraud may involve insider trading. The traditional view of insider trading is that it relates to knowledge about a company's activities before they are publicised. Other forms of insider trading, not necessarily linked to corporate activity, involve the deliberate manipulation of market or model prices by one or more individuals. These individuals may be members of staff or completely independent of the firm.

With derivatives, including options, the firm does not need to hold a position in the infected security to be affected. The pricing of a future, forward, option or swap is usually based on a particular benchmark, for example LIBOR or a security. If the distorted price is 99.5, but the true price is 100.5, then the impact on the derivative price is unlikely to be 1:1. This difference in sensitivity can be particularly pronounced for options. At certain points in the life a small variation in the price of the underlying benchmark will have minimal impact on the value of the option. However, close to maturity and exercise price a small variation can mean the difference between having value and having no value. For a call option with a strike price at 100 that is about to expire, the distorted price of 99.5 means that it has 0 value, whereas the true price means that it has 0.5 value. Although the price distortion in the security is close to 1%, the impact on the option price is more than 100%.

Whether insider trading or price manipulation, these actions can lead to distorted prices being treated as accurate. When these distorted prices are input to the VaR model the outcome is not a true reflection of the risk being taken. In turn, this affects the economic capital estimates and the regulatory capital requirements.

12.3.4   Funding Liquidity Risk with an Operational Risk Severity Driver

Funding liquidity risk differs from the other major sources of risk in that it is defined as a consequence and not measured using economic capital. Funding liquidity risk is the potential that the firm will not be able to meet efficiently both expected and unexpected current and future cash flow and collateral needs without affecting either daily operations or the financial condition of the firm.

With this definition, a funding liquidity situation could arise from many different actions, for example credit losses or market liquidity risk when selling reserve assets. However, as these two sources of risk each generate their own economic capital requirements, it means that the firm should have enough resources to cover related losses.

One of the issues for funding liquidity risk is the quality of internal information. The relevant dimensions of data quality include completeness, timeliness and accuracy. Without assurance that the information is high quality, the managers are trying to make decisions on inaccurate and/or incomplete information. The source data is held in various internal systems, of varying ages, data architecture and software languages. As a result, there is always the possibility of failure in a system-to-system link. From an operational risk perspective the issue is the occurrence of a technology or infrastructure failure event. It is unlikely that the data can be obtained from the accounting system due to their focus on the end-of-day time horizon. As a result, this produces a dependency on multiple middle-office systems to provide the data.

The dependency of funding liquidity risk management on a myriad of middle-office systems may be amplified by the ownership of these systems. These systems, and the tasks that they perform, will be owned by the businesses to some extent. As a result, if a system is amended to address a business issue it may generate a knock-on effect that has consequences for providing data to the funding liquidity risk management information system. Again this is an operational risk event. In comparison, the accounting system will be owned by the finance and control function and there will be very few different computer programmes that need to be integrated. While these system issues can affect data quality, they are largely under the control of the firm.

The interaction with credit has been briefly mentioned above. There is one variation of credit risk that may cause concern for funding liquidity risk, namely when the counterparty is a centralised counterparty or central bank. The push to use centralised counterparties has increased over recent years. However, if the centralised counterparty has an operational risk event, such as a technology or infrastructure failure, then it may be unable to make or receive payments. As the firm waiting to receive a payment, the failure to receive an expected payment will be classified as a credit risk event even if not default. In other words, the operational risk of the centralised counterparty becomes the credit risk of the firms waiting to receive payments.

If the central counterparty is unable to make the payments then the firm would be expected to resort to another source of funds for the short term. One of these sources of funds might be the wholesale interbank deposit market. However, if the issue at the centralised counterparty is significant then it might affect all payments, in which case several firms may be trying to access the same source of short-term funds at the same time. Owing to the possibility of these knock-on effects, some organisations view the centralised counterparties as a source of systemic risk.

The movements of funds to and from centralised counterparties will normally be a percentage of the value of the underlying instrument traded. However, securities deliveries are usually for the full amount of the transaction value not a percentage. As a result, if a securities settlement fails then it can have a larger impact on funding than missing a receipt of funds from a centralised counterparty at a derivatives exchange.

Over the years, several infrastructure processes have developed to manage the flow of funds and securities between firms. The initial step was to reduce the elapsed time between execution and settlement of the transaction. The next step was to establish delivery versus payment, so there is no movement of assets or funds unless the counterparty is ready. Finally, for different time zones, such as the USA versus Australia, there are continuously linked settlements.[3]

The operational risk experienced, internally, by counterparties is converted into the receiving firm's credit risk and affects the receiving firm's funding liquidity risk management.

12.4   IMPLICATIONS FOR RISK MANAGEMENT AND MEASUREMENT

One of the implications from the interactions between the various risk sources is that each specialist function will need some of the knowledge of the other specialist functions. Each risk specialist function needs tools, in addition to hammers in their tool box. The scope of knowledge of the risk management teams influences their ability to act as a second line of defence in providing effective oversight and challenge to the business.

Figure 12.1 shows the interactions between the various frequency and severity drivers. Funding liquidity risk is in a rectangular box as it is not assessed using economic capital. The white credit risk box shows that the credit risk rating of the firm can influence the ability of the firm to obtain the volume of funds or the price of funds, for example from the wholesale deposit market. Operational risk, due to its inclusion of

---

[3] For more on continuously linked settlements and the 17 currencies involved in the process, see http://www.cls-group.com/Pages/default.aspx

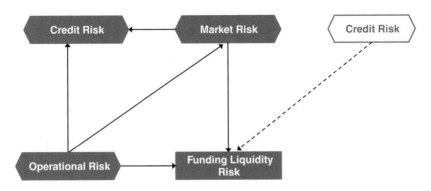

Figure 12.1   Interactions of frequency and severity drivers

models and other elements, can drive the severity of credit and market risk events. The lines in the figure show the interactions between the risk sources and therefore the specialist knowledge about the various risk sources that may be required when making risk management decisions and optimising the result for the firm as a whole.

Each of these risk source specialists has the same customer, the business which owns the risk. The risk source specialist for the frequency of the event will be the one providing the risk management framework. This implies that they will also be getting the budget from the business. However, to obtain the knowledge to support this framework they may need information and data attributable to some of the other risk source specialists. For example, credit risk management teams may need access to some operational risk management expertise. Likewise, market risk management teams may also need access to some operational risk management expertise. Funding liquidity management may need access to credit risk management expertise.

Possible approaches to managing these interactions include:

1. Consult the specialists.
2. Bring the expertise inside a particular risk discipline, such as an operational risk specialist within credit risk management.

These two approaches each have advantages and disadvantages.

Consulting a specialist function has the advantage of consistency in approach and components of the respective risk management framework. For example, the credit risk function may need to use some of the techniques developed and used by the operational risk function. By using the existing techniques the advantages include consistency of approach and not having to reinvent the wheel. The disadvantage is that the risk source specialists involved with the severity driver may need visibility in order to obtain budget to have the resources to support the frequency driver risk source specialists. If the expertise is brought inside the frequency driver risk source team then visibility is not needed, but the wheel may get reinvented slightly differently, giving rise to additional costs for the firm as a whole. These issues may need to be considered explicitly when deciding on the resource allocations for the various risk management specialist teams.

From a risk management perspective it is possible to stay within risk appetite by influencing the frequency of possible events and/or the severity of events. In the credit risk context these are the probability of default (PD) and the loss given default (LGD). If the parameters for the LGD are mainly influenced by historical losses, either directly or indirectly when creating a severity distribution, then they may incorporate some of the severity drivers from other risk sources. For example, the PD and LGD may include historical data on fraud. However, when there is a change in the risk profile, such as the emergence of mis-selling credit products, then (if these losses are included in credit risk appetite and not operational risk appetite), the LGD may be mis-calibrated leading to a difference between the historical data, actual losses, economic capital estimates and comparison against the risk appetite.

Owing to the credit risk economic capital estimate having two main inputs, the PD and LGD, there is a possibility of amending the inputs to take into account the changes in the drivers, for example in a stress test. For market risk there is less flexibility. There is currently no opportunity to separate out data quality issues, such as lost trade tickets (operational risk) from the inputs to the market risk economic capital calculation. Currently, these operational risk events, related to trading book and other positions, need to be captured in the operational risk economic capital estimate. If these issues are not identifiable and separated in the P&L, they can disrupt the performance attribution and back testing to validate the VaR model output. The outcome may be false positives resulting in increases in the capital required to support market risk.

As operational risk is across the firm internally and has several external sources, this may need a different approach. Having operational risk management expertise embedded in the other risk functions may seem the ideal approach. However, as operational risk is a relatively young discipline that is still advancing rapidly, there is the issue of the number of people in the firm with the requisite knowledge. An approach around this issue is to have operational risk training to raise awareness and where to go for expert help.

12.5   ISSUES TO CONSIDER

- Given the complexity of interactions between risk sources, whether as frequency or severity drivers, how are these reflected in the risk appetites and the respective risk estimate calculations – implicitly or explicitly?
- Are incentives built into the risk measurement framework, at the risk taker level, that may lead to distortions in risk management decisions?
- When reviewing changes to the risk profile, or emerging risks, is consideration given to the interactions between the sources of risk?
- Are there sufficient resources for experts in second-order effects to support those with oversight and challenge responsibilities for the first-order effects?
- How often do risk specialists meet for a multi-disciplinary discussion?

FURTHER READING

Bank of England (2011) Systemic Risk Survey.

Coogan-Pushner, D. and Bouteille, S. (2012) *The Handbook of Credit Risk Management: Originating, Assessing and Managing Credit Exposures.* John Wiley & Sons, Chichester.

Financial Stability Board (2009) Report to the G-20 Finance Ministers and Central Bank Governors: Guidance to Assess the Systemic Importance of Financial Institutions, Markets and Instruments: Initial Considerations – Background Paper.

Financial Stability Board (2011) Policy Measures to Address Systemically Important Financial Institutions.

Financial Stability Board (2011) Intensity and Effectiveness of SIFI Supervision.

Randall, A. (2011) *Risk and Precaution.* Cambridge University Press, Cambridge.

Schwarz, S.L. (2008) Systemic risk. *Georgetown Law Journal* **97**, 193.

de Weert, F. (2010) *Bank and Insurance Capital Management.* John Wiley & Sons, Chichester.

Part III

Regulatory Environment

Risk Management at the Top

Ch. 1: Introduction

Part I: Risk Oversight

Ch. 2: Risk – An Overview	Ch. 3: Risk Oversight	Ch. 4: Risk Management	Ch. 5: Risk Appetite	Ch. 6: Risk Culture

Part II: Specific Risks

Ch. 7: Credit Risk	Ch. 8: Market Risk	Ch. 9: Operational Risk	Ch. 10: Liquidity Risk	Ch. 11: Other Risks	Ch. 12: Risk Interactions

Part III: Regulatory Environment

Ch. 13: Regulatory Environment

Part III – Regulatory Environment describes the influence of Banking Regulators. Other segments of the financial industry will have similarities in their relationship with their regulators. For example, following the financial crisis a new category of bank was created, the Systemically Important Financial Institution, and consideration is being given to allocating this category to insurance companies and Central Counterparties.

The Banking Regulators are empowered to look after specific interests on behalf of the wider society. In particular these regulators are focussed upon the smooth functioning of this sector so that payments can be made, funding provided and deposits taken as a minimum. As unpleasant as it may sound, the regulatory goal is not to prevent financial institutions from failing.

Due to its role in the functioning of modern society, the financial sector is subject to these requirements in addition to other laws. The other laws apply to all companies, for example Health & Safety, Employment and statutory governance requirements. These broadly applicable laws and regulations are not extensively covered in this book.

The chapter illustrates some of the initiatives that the regulators have emphasised, such as risk management enhancements as well as the quality and quantity of capital. Some of these initiatives are a reflection that many banks operate across borders so a failure of a subsidiary in one country can affect banking activities in other countries. In addition, there are concerns about competition and the levelness of the playing field between different countries and firms within a country. This can add complexity to the operation of cross-border branches and subsidiaries.

While the regulators operate at a national level there are international co-ordinating bodies. The most well-known is probably the Basel Committee of Banking Supervisors. These co-ordinating bodies enable regulators to share experiences and jointly address issues. In establishing widely accepted standards, the Basel Committee has been a success. Relatively recent developments, such as regulatory colleges to focus upon a single banking group, also look as though they are here to stay.

The regulators are not only interested in the quality and quantity of capital that a bank holds. They are also interested in risk management and the oversight of risk by the Board and Senior Management. This promotion of risk management may start with a particular emphasis from a leading industry participant, which in the view of the regulators should be more widely adopted. The regulators encouraged the development and use of Value-at-Risk models. Many of the preceding chapters recommend regulatory documents as part of Further Reading.

Broadly, on risk management the Board and the regulators are directionally aligned.

13

Regulatory Environment

Risk Management at the Top

Ch. 1: Introduction

Part I: Risk Oversight

Ch. 2: Risk – An Overview	Ch. 3: Risk Oversight	Ch. 4: Risk Management	Ch. 5: Risk Appetite	Ch. 6: Risk Culture

Part II: Specific Risks

Ch. 7: Credit Risk	Ch. 8: Market Risk	Ch. 9: Operational Risk	Ch. 10: Liquidity Risk	Ch. 11: Other Risks	Ch. 12: Risk Interactions

Part III: Regulatory Environment

Ch. 13: Regulatory Environment

Regulation is an influential factor on risk management in the financial sector. It is not clear if regulation is a leader or a follower, but as a minimum it promotes risk management. While there is focus on the capital aspect of regulation there is also considerable attention paid to conduct of business, in particular with counterparties.

Regulation has implications for the amount of capital that needs to be held by firms, the types of instruments that can be considered as eligible for capital and the return on equity. Some of these requirements are established by a single country and some features are common to many jurisdictions.

The regulators, whether prudential and/or financial conduct focused, whether national or international, are amongst the most influential stakeholders with which the Board and senior management will engage, directly or indirectly.

13.1   INTRODUCTION

Owing to their role in economies, agents need to be appointed to look after the way in which the interests of wider society are met by firms in the financial sector. Governments allocate this responsibility to regulators. Often these regulators are required to give account of their activities to the government on a periodic basis. This can give rise to seismic change when the interpretation of what is adequate or appropriate is realigned. The regulators are very influential, but they are not directors of the Board, nor are they executive management. Although they are stakeholders, they are not shareholders.

There is a balancing act to be performed by the regulators and the regulated. On the one hand there is the need to have an efficient financial sector to invest savings, make loans and payments and provide other products and services. On the other hand there is the need to take risk and generate a return for shareholders and reinvest in the business. This reinvestment may be in maintaining existing systems or developing new ones to support the management of risks.

Some financial institutions have such a role in the economy that if they were to fail there would be widespread consequences. Organisations with this role are often referred to as systemic firms. With their role on behalf of society, regulators take a special interest in these firms. Firms need to be allowed to fail, but not in a manner that causes chaos.

For example, in some countries the number of financial institutions has reduced by thousands over a relatively short period, as happened to US savings and loans during the 1970s and 1980s. Without the ability to fail there is the potential moral hazard that firms may focus entirely on the desirable portion of the risk outcomes and not give due emphasis and attention to undesirable risk outcomes. This ability to fail encourages stakeholders, in addition to regulators, to express their views – including shareholders, bond holders, rating agencies and employees.

This chapter focuses on the prudential aspect of regulation as opposed to the financial conduct aspect. Increasingly, the financial conduct aspects are being overseen by institutions separate from those responsible for the prudential aspects. In part, this separation is in response to the financial crisis.

The rest of this chapter looks at the:

13.2 Structure of Prudential Regulatory Process
13.3 Scope of Prudential Regulation
13.4 Regulatory Influence

The next section provides some context and history to the international prudential regulatory arrangements. These international arrangements need to be implemented nationally, which can create tension due to variation in detailed implementation.

Section 13.3 considers the structure of prudential regulation as applied to banks; Pillars 1, 2 and 3. This broad structure appears to be adopted and adapted for parts of the insurance industry.

The last section looks at the non-capital influence of the prudential regulators. The prudential regulators do not imagine that capital can resolve all the issues encountered by firms in the financial sector. As a result, they have an interest in the governance and risk management of firms.

13.2   STRUCTURE OF PRUDENTIAL REGULATORY PROCESS

Regulation of banks has been a feature of their operating environment for many years. This section looks at the background of international prudential activities and how they relate to the national regulators and current activity. Although the focus is on banking, it appears that other sectors – such as insurance – are following the same or a similar path, for example within the European Union and Solvency II Directive.

One of the first developments involving international coordination was the report to the Basel Governors in September 1975 from the Committee on Banking Regulations and Supervisory Practice.[1] The focus of the report was on cooperation between regulators in supervising branches, subsidiaries and joint ventures. The report was replaced, in May 1983, by the Principles for the Supervision of Banks' Foreign Establishments (the Concordat). The focus of the Concordat was on internationally active banks.

The report and the Concordat paved the way for subsequent agreements, such as Basel I, II and III, numerous consultations, guidelines and recommendations prepared by the Basel Committee on Banking Supervision. This committee – sometimes referred to as the Basel Committee – reports to the governors of central banks.

At about the time that the Concordat was being developed, the capital available to support the risks of a bank varied significantly. The Tier 1 capital ratio might be as low as 0.5%, compared with today's common ratios of 7% and higher. The existence of the Basel Committee has helped to promote consistency across national boundaries and reduce regulatory arbitrage. Within the European Union this consistency is enforced by legally binding documents referred to as directives, in particular the Capital Requirements Directives (CRD).

Some of these regulatory arrangements have been tested by events. One particular test related to the Bank of Credit and Commerce International (BCCI).[2] BCCI was registered in Luxembourg in 1972, but had head offices in Karachi and London – which national regulator was in the lead? BCCI was effectively closed by the regulators in 1991, requiring cooperation across a number of jurisdictions. It is assumed that the coordinated regulatory action was in part enabled by the discussion around and the framework established by the Concordat and subsequent documents. Today, some of these cooperation arrangements are included in Memoranda of Understanding (MoU) between two or more national regulators.

---

[1] The governors of many central banks and lenders of last resort meet at the Bank of International Settlements (BIS) on a regular basis.

[2] http://en.wikipedia.org/wiki/Bank_of_Credit_and_Commerce_International

13.2.1   Mapping the Regulators

The Basel Committee currently has 27 countries on the committee.[3] There is also a representative of the EU in addition to many of the EU members.

Reporting to the Basel Committee on Banking Supervision are:[4]

* The Standards Implementation Group
* The Policy Development Group
* The Accounting Task Force
* The Basel Consultative Group.

Each of these groups may have supporting subgroups and task forces.

While the documents issued by the Basel Committee may be in the form of "guidance", partly for sovereignty reasons, they do carry a great deal of weight amongst the national regulators. Basel I has been implemented by over 100 countries. The Basel Committee "guidance" enables a degree of customisation by a national regulator to reflect local market conditions when transmuted into national requirements. The customisation, at national level, is reviewed by other members of the Basel Committee to prevent regulatory arbitrage and reduce the emergence of fault lines of systemic weaknesses. This does not prevent national regulators having additional requirements, for example the USA had leverage requirements long before they were introduced internationally in Basel III.

With nine of the Basel Committee members also being in the EU there is a slightly different path between Basel "guidance" and national

---

[3] Countries on the Basel Committee on Banking Supervision in August 2012 are:

Argentina	India	Saudi Arabia
Australia	Indonesia	Singapore
Belgium	Italy	South Africa
Brazil	Japan	Spain
Canada	Korea	Sweden
China	Luxembourg	Switzerland
France	Mexico	Turkey
Germany	The Netherlands	The United Kingdom
Hong Kong SAR	Russia	The United States of America

http://www.bis.org/bcbs/index.htm

[4] For more information see http://www.bis.org/bcbs/about.htm

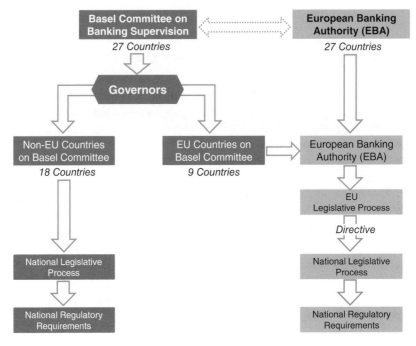

Figure 13.1 Flow from Basel Committee and EBA to national requirements

requirements for these countries. The EU has the European Banking Authority,[5] but no pan-EU banking regulator (yet). The EBA works closely with the Basel Committee and may consult on issues at the same time as the Basel Committee (Figure 13.1). It is in the interests of the Basel Committee and the EBA to work closely together; having different requirements would put nine countries, which belong to both, in a difficult situation.

As mentioned above, the EU generates a directive that establishes legally binding minimum requirements for its member countries. In addition, due to competition and level playing fields, the directive will apply to an entire sector of the financial industry, not just the internationally active banks, for example all banks. This can lead to tensions on various topics, such as the range of instruments eligible

---

[5] Homepage of the European Banking Authority http://www.eba.europa.eu/

to be considered as Tier 1 capital. It is probably also one of the influences behind the need to have regulatory capital calculations that are not dependent on costly complex models.

If firms want to provide input to prudential regulation refinements, then timing is crucial. Most flexibility is available when the Basel Committee is in initial consultation mode. By the time that the "guidance" gets to the governors there is little chance of substantial amendment. The next opportunity is as part of the national legislative process, but even here there may be no opportunity for significant change. This leaves the transposition into the national regulatory requirements, where the flexibility of the national regulator is constrained by earlier decisions. The regulators will give firms time to amend their systems before the compliance date. The period of consultation, finalisation, publication, various legislative processes and compliance means that firms may need to provide their comments 2 to 7 years before the implementation date. With this lead time it can be difficult to apply resources due to higher immediate priorities.

13.2.2   Impact on Firms

An impact of the structure of this prudential regulatory process has already been mentioned: the timing of contributions to the discussion. However, there are other aspects that affect internationally active firms and some of these are addressed below.

The Concordat and subsequent documents have enshrined the concept of home and host prudential regulators. The home regulator is the one that looks after the consolidated group. The host regulator is the one that looks after subsidiaries operating within its jurisdiction. Branches are not locally incorporated and are within the scope of the regulator of the parent entity for prudential purposes. However, for a branch to be permitted to open, as opposed to creating a locally incorporated subsidiary, the regulatory framework applied to the parent entity may have to meet particular requirements. One of these requirements may be the operation of consolidated supervision by the home regulators.

This difference in jurisdiction between branches and subsidiaries can be confusing. For example, to many it was not clear who had authority over the London branch of JP Morgan Chase in 2012 when losses were crystallised in the investment portfolio. Unless there was a separate MoU between the Office of the Comptroller of the Currency (OCC) and

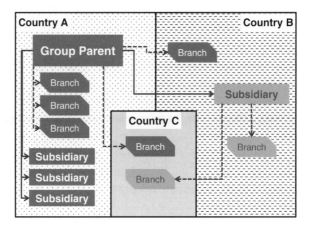

Figure 13.2   Schematic of branches and subsidiaries

the UK Financial Services Authority, the responsibility was probably with the OCC.

Figure 13.2 illustrates some of the organisational complexity and prudential regulatory oversight. The home regulator is in Country A. The parent group has subsidiaries in Country A and B. Depending on the nature of their activities, the subsidiaries in Country A may be overseen by the same prudential regulator who looks after the parent. The subsidiary in Country B will be overseen by the prudential regulator in Country B, the host regulator. The prudential regulator in Country C will have little prudential involvement with the two branches operating in its jurisdiction. Likewise, the prudential regulator in Country B will have little prudential oversight of the branch from the group parent operating in its jurisdiction. Figure 13.2 is highly simplified. Internationally active firms may have hundreds, if not thousands, of subsidiaries, some will be special purpose vehicles and not necessarily operating companies.

One of the practical issues can be internal systems to comply with the prudential requirements. If the national regulatory requirements are all 100% consistent then implementation can be an efficient process for internationally active groups. The reality is that the national regulatory requirements differ. If one national regulator's requirements were simply higher than others then the firm may decide to adopt these higher standards across the group. Much more difficult is where the requirements are different, but not necessarily higher. Under these circumstances the firm has a limited choice and is required to implement the home regulator's requirements across all entities and have additional local capabilities for the host regulator's requirements. This increases the cost of initial implementation and ongoing system maintenance.

The differences between national regulatory regimes may be most evident in reporting requirements. However, the financial crisis emphasised the benefits, to the regulators, of having consistent reporting across borders. This consistency assists in managing financial groups that cross borders in times of crisis.

There are a number of initiatives that are increasing the complexity and cost of prudential supervision. Some of these initiatives are being adopted by individual national regulators, separate from Basel or the EU, and some are being adopted more widely. One of these initiatives relates to trading.

The scope of trading activities for banks with prudential oversight in the USA will be influenced by the requirements in the Dodd–Frank legislation. Depending on the scope of activities that will no longer be carried out, for example trading in non-US government bonds, this has implications for market liquidity. Market liquidity has a cascade effect on the management of collateral and the reserve asset portfolio for funding liquidity.

Meanwhile, in the UK there is the concept of ring fencing retail and related banking activities from investment banking activities. Part of the rationale for this ring fencing is to prevent cross-contagion between these two activities. In turn, this ring fencing has practical implications for governance (including of risk), the distribution of capital and its movement across the fence.

A broad-based prudential regulatory initiative is the Recovery and Resolution Plan, also known as the "Living Will". This initiative is being encouraged by the G20 and the Financial Stability Board (FSB).[6] Part of the impetus for Recovery and Resolution Plans has been the difficulty of liquidating Lehman Bros with its subsidiaries and branches in various countries. Other sources of enthusiasm for the plans include the involvement of taxpayers in the rescue of various firms during the crisis. The aim of the plans is to facilitate the liquidation of a complex firm with cross-border activities.

---

[6] Financial Stability Board (October 2011) Key Attributes of Effective Resolution Regimes for Financial Institutions.

It is natural to subdivide the plans into distinct recovery and resolution components.[7] The purpose of the recovery component is to reduce the need to liquidate the firm in the event of a crisis. The purpose of the resolution component is to support various regulators in the event that a firm needs to be liquidated and reduce the risk that taxpayers will be involved in providing support. At a more fundamental level the plans are an opportunity to prepare for a crisis during a period of relative calm.

Recovery:

- sufficient number of material and credible options to cope with a range of scenarios, including both firm-specific and market-wide stresses;
- options which address capital shortfalls, liquidity pressures and profitability issues and should aim to return the firm to a stable and sustainable position;
- options that the firm would consider in more severe circumstances, such as disposals of the whole business, parts of the business or group entities, raising equity capital which has not been planned for in the firm's business plan, complete elimination of dividends and variable remuneration, debt exchanges and other liability management actions.

Resolution:

- ensure that resolution can be carried out without public solvency support exposing taxpayers to the risk of loss;
- seek to minimise the impact on financial stability;
- seek to minimise the effect on UK depositors and consumers;
- allow decisions and actions to be taken and executed in a short space of time (or the "resolution weekend");
- identify those economic functions which will need to be continued because the availability of those functions is critical to the UK economy or financial system, or would need to be wound up in an orderly fashion so as to avoid financial instability (critical economic functions);
- identify and consider ways of removing barriers which may prevent critical economic functions being resolved successfully;

---

[7] Financial Services Authority (August 2011) Recovery & Resolution Plans, CP11/16.

- isolate and identify critical economic functions from non-critical activities which could be allowed to fail;
- enhance cooperation and crisis management planning for global systemically important financial institutions (G-SIFIs) with international regulators.

A factor behind the complexity involved is the varying treatment of claims in a liquidation of an internationally active company. For example, these claims may be treated differently between Germany, the UK and the USA due to their legal codes. These codes not only affect individual transactions, but portfolios of transactions when netting arrangements for credit risks have been established between two counterparties. The scope of differences also includes the treatment of client monies held for investment, assets held in custody on behalf of clients and collateral.

One of the consequences of these plans may be on the distribution of capital within a group and amongst its legal entities. Following a stressful event, individual legal entities may have shortages of capital. However, addressing these shortages, by moving capital from entities with apparent surplus, may be limited by the prudential regulators overseeing the legal entity with the surplus, possibly in a different jurisdiction.

Some of the initiatives outlined above are having an impact on the assessment of the amount of capital required and its distribution across the group. In terms of minimising the amount of capital issued, and influencing the return on equity, the most efficient approach is full consolidation. Under full consolidation the positions, for example credit and market risks, would be combined to determine the required regulatory capital. This has the advantage of making full use of diversification benefits across the group and netting any offsetting positions.

However, full consolidation does not take into account the capital required to be held in the individual subsidiaries, which will be determined by the host prudential regulators. The sum of the capital requirements for the individual subsidiaries will usually be higher than the capital requirements calculated by full consolidation. This situation holds even assuming that all of the host prudential regulators have absolute consistency. The reason for the sum of the parts being greater than the consolidated approach is the reduced benefits from diversification and offsetting positions in the individual capital calculations. One outcome may be to have a single trading book in a single subsidiary in a region, rather than have trading books in each country in a region.

When assessing the capital adequacy of the group parent, the home prudential regulator needs to take into account the capital invested in the subsidiaries. This approach is known as deduction-plus. The capital in the group parent is reduced by the amount required to be held in the individual subsidiaries as determined by the host prudential regulators. This assumes that in the event of a crisis capital will not easily be transferred from locations of surplus to locations of deficit, as anticipated by the Recovery and Resolution Plan.

13.3   SCOPE OF PRUDENTIAL REGULATION

Prudential regulation of banks has been in existence for many years. Prudential regulatory requirements are primarily related to capital held by a firm. However, capital is not a substitute for risk management. In the event that there is a stressful event, it is often risk management that prevents it from being catastrophic. As a result, the regulators can incentivise improvements in risk management frameworks through the use of capital increments for an individual firm.

The last 35 years have seen a significant increase in the technicality of prudential regulation. This technicality started with Basel I, and Basel III is evidence that the trend continues.

Basel I was published in July 1988. Basel II was published in June 2004. The timing of the financial crisis meant that not all members of the Basel Committee had implemented Basel II before the crisis reached a crescendo. Basel III, published in December 2010 and revised in June 2011, was partly a reaction to the financial crisis and partly ahead of scheduled review and revision of Basel II.

Between these major revisions the Basel Committee publishes various papers. The papers range from responses to frequently asked questions to significant revisions to prudential capital calculations to principles for the sound management of a bank's activities. The market risk amendment to Basel I, published in 1996, is an example of a significant revision to the framework, as is a further amendment in 2009, sometimes described as Basel II.5. Sometimes the guidance is aimed directly at the banks and sometimes it is described as guidance for supervisors, which means that, in time, it will be applied to banks.

Basel II introduced the concept of the three pillars in the prudential regulatory framework and they continue in Basel III:

• Pillar 1 relates to minimum capital requirements;

- Pillar 2 refers to the supervisory review process;
- Pillar 3 is concerned with market discipline, achieved by disclosure and transparency.

Funding liquidity risk issues do not fit into Pillar 1, as there is no related capital requirement, so instead they fit into Pillar 2. The guidance provided in relation to management practices is part of the Pillar 2 regulatory environment.

Figure 13.3 presents a simplified view of the regulatory framework, including the role of the regulators acting on behalf of wider society.

The expectations and requirements published by the Basel Committee are intended for internationally active banks. When transposed into legislation, additional issues become important. For example, with the competition framework in the EU there needs to be a level playing field. As a result, the EU Directives adopt minimum standards from the Basel Committee. In other countries there is explicit recognition of the difference between internationally active firms and those that are predominantly domestic. As discussed below, these national implementation considerations result in the Basel Committee providing a number of acceptable capital calculation methodologies.

Overall, the regulators are looking for a proportionate risk framework that suits an individual firm. Aspects that the regulators will take into account include the range of activities, the geographic scope, the complexity of products and services, the complexity of the organisational

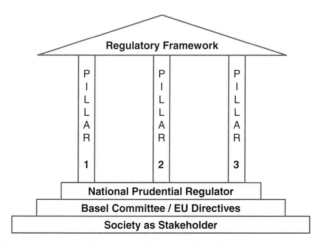

Figure 13.3   Prudential regulatory framework

structure and overall sophistication. As a result, the regulators do not adopt a "one size fits all" approach.

13.3.1 Pillar 1 – Minimum Capital Requirements

Pillar 1, determining the minimum capital requirements, is possibly the easiest place to start exploring the three pillars. This section is in three parts:

(a) Capital Requirements
(b) Capital
(c) Meeting the Capital Requirements.

13.3.1.1   Capital Requirements

The capital requirements are determined using various capital calculations covering specific risks and whose output corresponds to regulatory specified criteria. The regulatory specified criteria are focused on a time horizon into the future and a confidence interval. The time horizon is usually the next 12 months on a rolling basis. The confidence interval is commonly 99.9% of a one-tailed distribution of losses.

There is a "chicken and egg" situation between economic capital models and regulatory capital models. There are benefits for both firm and regulator if the economic and regulatory models are closely aligned. For the firm it means greater efficiency, for example using the same inputs and generating broadly similar outputs. For the regulator, if the firm is using the same data then the data quality oversight will be equally good for both calculations. This is preferable to a firm having to create a distinctly separate data set only for regulatory purposes.

Under Pillar 1 banks need to calculate capital for

- credit risk
- market risk
- operational risk.

The regulators permit two approaches to determining the capital requirement, a simplified or standardised approach and a model. (In reality, both approaches are models of sorts.) The standardised approaches are prescribed by the regulators, for example defining gross income and how it is averaged for the operational risk standardised approach. The regulatory guidance on the model approaches are less detailed on the "how" but tend to be specific on the "what". The "what" may include specific data types that need to be included in the model, for example probability of default, non-linear components of market risk and scenarios for each of credit, market and operational risk.

In some regimes the choice between standardised and model approaches is made by the firm, possibly with some encouragement from the national regulator. The existence of choice means that relatively straightforward firms do not have to go to the expense of designing, building and implementing a complex model.

For credit and market risk it is possible to buy models from vendors. While the purchase of a model can reduce the time to production, some degree of customisation is inevitable. One of the more time-consuming and expensive tasks is collecting the data to feed the model. Then there is the issue of how the model fits into the risk framework, for example its role in producing numbers for comparing against the risk appetite. This can result in changes from the Board down to the risk taker.

The regulators have responded to the ability of banks to develop models to estimate their economic and regulatory capital through the creation of specialist review teams. These teams of specialists will perform on-site reviews of the models in their operating environment. These reviews will consider the structure of the model, including the assumptions, and how and why certain decisions were made during construction. It also gives the regulators the opportunity to talk to users of the inputs and outputs of the economic and regulatory models. For example, are the embedded assumptions appreciated by the users of the model outputs and how do they influence decision making?

These model reviews have advantages for both the firm and the regulator. The firm can construct a model that, provided it meets the regulatory "what", also meets the firm's requirements. The regulators, generally, get to see more than one model for a risk source within their jurisdiction. This oversight provides the opportunity to perform a compare and contrast between the models implemented by various firms. While the compare and contrast may be frustrating for the model designers and builders, it does provide greater confidence over various features and assumptions for both the regulator and the regulated.

The outcome of the review is approval to use the model for regulatory purposes. As part of the approval the regulators may specify certain values, for example minimum values for certain correlations. It is normal for the regulators to require being updated on changes to the model design, for example a change in the number of credit cohorts. The regulators expect such changes to be implemented in the economic capital first on the basis that if there is not a risk management purpose behind the change then why would the firm have made it? This may be followed by a period of parallel runs between the approved regulatory model and its successor, so that the firm and regulator can perform comparisons under a variety of market conditions.

One of the benefits of the models over the standardised approaches is their degree of risk sensitivity. The calculations are sensitive to their inputs, but some of the inputs to the standardised approaches are not related to risk, but instead relate to size. The operational risk standardised approach is a particular example, with its dependence on gross income. In recognition of the assumptions in the standardised approaches there is usually a regulatory capital benefit from moving to a model approach. However, before a regulator is likely to provide approval to use a model, the firm needs to have a risk management framework that can also use the inputs and outputs from the model in decision making. This criterion is often described as the use test and can result in a sophisticated model failing to obtain regulatory approval. The risk sensitivity of models promotes feedback to the Board and down through the organisation to the risk takers and supports its use in decision making.

13.3.1.2 Capital

The regulators specify the type and ratios of financial instruments that can be considered as capital. The regulatory standards differ from the accounting standards for book capital. Some of these differences were identified in Chapter 2 (Section 2.4).

For financial sector prudential regulators capital is to be available to absorb losses. Basel III narrowed the scope of the type of financial instruments eligible to absorb losses in comparison with Basel II. Eligible bank capital is mapped to two categories: Tier 1 (going-concern) and Tier 2 (gone-concern).[8] In the event of liquidation, Tier 1 is written down to zero before Tier 2.

---

[8] Basel Committee on Banking Supervision (originally published December 2010, revised June 2011) Basel III: A global regulatory framework for more resilient banks and banking systems, paragraphs 9, 49–90.

Tier 1 can be viewed as equity-type capital whereas Tier 2 is often in the form of subordinated debt. In addition to specifying the possible composition of these two categories, the regulators specify the ratio between them. For example, Common Equity Tier 1 capital must be a minimum of 4.5% risk-weighted assets (see next section), whilst Tier 1 capital must be a minimum 6.0% risk-weighted assets. Tier 1 + Tier 2 capital must be a minimum of 8.0% risk-weighted assets. These ratios apply at all times. So if the firm has a major loss, for example due to rogue trading, there may be a reduction in Common Equity Tier 1. If there is a reduction in common equity then there will be implications for the amount of Tier 2 due to the ratio between them and other ratios involving common equity.

Part of the rationale for specifying the ratio between Tier 1 and Tier 2 is that debt is generally cheaper to issue than equity. Firms may have return on equity targets of 20% (not the same as the cost of equity), however the cost of debt seldom gets this high. Theoretically, optimising the economic value of the firm would involve having the majority of the capital in the form of debt, if fully taxed and with no bankruptcy costs. However, this emphasis on debt has an impact on the ability of the capital to absorb losses.

Financial instruments eligible for Tier 1 include the following.

Common Equity Tier 1[9]

- Common shares issued by the bank that meet the criteria for classification as common shares for regulatory purposes (or the equivalent for non-joint stock companies).
- Stock surplus (share premium) resulting from the issue of instruments included in Common Equity Tier 1.
- Retained earnings.
- Accumulated other comprehensive income and other disclosed reserves.
- Common shares issued by consolidated subsidiaries of the bank and held by third parties (i.e., minority interest) that meet the criteria for inclusion in Common Equity Tier 1 capital.
- Regulatory adjustments applied in the calculation of Common Equity Tier 1.

---

[9] Basel Committee on Banking Supervision (originally published December 2010, revised June 2011), paragraph 52.

Additional Tier 1[10]
- Instruments issued by the bank that meet the criteria for inclusion in Additional Tier 1 capital (and are not included in Common Equity Tier 1).
- Stock surplus (share premium) resulting from the issue of instruments included in Additional Tier 1 capital.
- Instruments issued by consolidated subsidiaries of the bank and held by third parties that meet the criteria for inclusion in Additional Tier 1 capital and are not included in Common Equity Tier 1.
- Regulatory adjustments applied in the calculation of Additional Tier 1 capital.

Financial instruments eligible for Tier 2[11]
- Instruments issued by the bank that meet the criteria for inclusion in Tier 2 capital (and are not included in Tier 1 capital).
- Stock surplus (share premium) resulting from the issue of instruments included in Tier 2 capital.
- Instruments issued by consolidated subsidiaries of the bank and held by third parties that meet the criteria for inclusion in Tier 2 capital and are not included in Tier 1 capital.
- Certain loan loss provisions.
- Regulatory adjustments applied in the calculation of Tier 2 capital.

The regulatory adjustments can include the deduction of goodwill and other intangibles from the value of Common Equity Tier 1. Deferred tax assets whose value is dependent on future profits are also deducted, as are expected losses in excess of provisions. Other deductions relate to pension fund assets and liabilities; holdings in own shares and investments in other banking, financial and insurance entities over a threshold are also deducted.[12]

For debt instruments to be eligible as Tier 2 capital they must be subordinated to claims from depositors and general creditors, have a minimum initial maturity of 5 years and no incentives to redeem before

---

[10] Basel Committee on Banking Supervision (originally published December 2010, revised June 2011), paragraph 54.

[11] Ibid., paragraph 57.

[12] Ibid., paragraphs 66–89.

maturity. From a capital perspective, once the bond has less than 5 years to maturity its contribution to Tier 2 will be amortised, on a straight line, over the remaining life.

If the bank breaches, or in some environments even looks as though it will breach its capital ratios, the regulators can prevent capital distributions. For example, following the financial crisis some US banks were not allowed to pay dividends for several years or buy back shares. Likewise, the regulators may prevent payment of the principal or even the coupon on a bond until the capital has returned to a satisfactory position.

Managing the regulatory capital of a financial institution is complicated.

13.3.1.3 Meeting the Capital Ratios

The calculation to determine whether the firm meets the regulatory capital ratios is derived from a comparison of net regulatory capital and total risk-weighted assets (RWA) – see Figure 13.4. The RWA is used as an intermediary step. The RWA is composed of the risks calculated using the various regulatory approved methodologies, standardised approaches or models or a combination across credit, market and operational risks. Some of these calculations directly produce a RWA value while others require the results to be converted into RWA equivalents.

Where the output of a model produces an estimated capital requirement, this needs to be converted into RWA units. An example is the output from an operational risk AMA calculation. The conversion is achieved by dividing the capital requirement by the capital ratio specified by the regulators for that firm. If the regulatory capital ratio is 8% and the capital requirement from the model is €100 million, then the equivalent RWA is €1250 million.

The aim of using RWA units is to get the outputs from the three Pillar 1 calculations into the same units. The three RWA values are then added together and compared against the Tier 1 and Tier 2 regulatory eligible capital to estimate the capital ratios. This summation and comparison means that either the firm meets the capital ratios or it does not. It is not possible to say that credit and market risk meet the capital ratio, but operational risk does not.

As a generalisation, many banks have their capital ratios set higher than 8% by their national regulators. In some situations the minimum

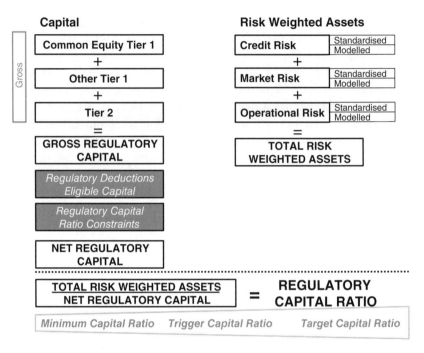

Figure 13.4   Satisfying the capital ratio

capital ratio (for example 8.0%) has a buffer applied to reach a trigger, which then has another buffer to reach a target ratio (for example 9.2%).

Some jurisdictions may use terms other than "trigger" and "target ratios". These ratios, with target being the highest, are to assist the Board and regulators in determining when actions are needed to manage the balance sheet in terms of raising capital or reducing the amount of risk on the balance sheet. The increments of trigger and target above the minimum may be influenced by regulatory determined shortcomings in models, the risk management framework, Pillar 2 and whether the firm is systemic or not.

To reiterate, the firms must meet their regulatory capital ratios at all times. In practice, some of the individual capital calculations will be performed daily (e.g., market risk), others may be performed monthly (e.g., credit risk) and some may be calculated quarterly (e.g., operational risk). The length of time taken to estimate the capital requirement is longer for model-based approaches, such as an internal ratings-based approach, as opposed to standardised methods. This additional time results from the complexity of the methodology and the time taken to gather and quality assure the input data. As a result of the frequency of capital calculations, the firm needs to have a buffer above its minimum Common Equity Tier 1 capital to be able to absorb losses that cannot be met from income between calculations of the regulatory capital ratio.

While the regulatory capital ratio is one of the main influences on the amount of capital required, other influences are the rating agencies and equity analysts. The rating agencies and equity analysts are not necessarily considering the same things as the regulators. In addition to the success of the firm's business models, the rating agencies will also consider the amount of capital that a firm holds when providing a rating on bonds that are issued by the firm. There is a dynamic linkage between the rating of the firm and the cost of issuing debt, for example in the form of Tier 2 eligible bonds.

13.3.2   Pillar 2 – Supervisory Review Process

The process steps for Pillar 1 have stayed much the same since Basel I was published in 1988. The changes in the individual steps have been refinements and increased complexity in response to experience and the market environment. In contrast, Pillar 2 was a new formal requirement that came as part of Basel II and remains unchanged in Basel III.

Pillar 2 focuses on the risk management of the firm, especially at the top of the organisation. In summary, it is a review by the supervisors/regulators of how the firm self-assesses all its risks and their magnitude and the capital required to support them. This process is known as the Internal Capital Adequacy Review Process (ICAAP).

The scope of the ICAAP relates to all the risks faced by the firm. This broad scope means that the Board needs to consider risks beyond the Pillar 1 categories of credit, market and operational risks. Arguably, funding liquidity risk is part of Pillar 2. Also included are issues such as reputational risk and other elements not reflected in Pillar 1. Pillar 2 is also the opportunity to recognise that there may be some emerging risks that are not fully captured in the Pillar 1 models.

Regulatory principles on the supervisory review process are provided below.[13]

---

[13] Basel Committee on Banking Supervision (June 2004) International Convergence of Capital and Measurement and Capital Standards – revised (Basel II), paragraphs 725–760. Reproduced by permission of Bank for International Settlements (BIS).

Principle 1: Banks should have a process for assessing their overall capital adequacy in relation to their risk profile and a strategy for maintaining their capital levels.

Principle 2: Supervisors should review and evaluate banks' internal capital adequacy assessments and strategies, as well as their ability to monitor and ensure compliance with regulatory capital ratios. Supervisors should take appropriate supervisory action if they are not satisfied with the result of this process.

Principle 3: Supervisors should expect banks to operate above the minimum regulatory capital ratios and should have the ability to require banks to hold capital in excess of the minimum.

Principle 4: Supervisors should seek to intervene at an early stage to prevent capital from falling below the minimum levels required to support the risk characteristics of a particular bank and should require rapid remedial action if capital is not maintained or restored.

The Board is expected to take an active role in ICAAP. This expectation is based on the role of the Board in relation to setting the risk appetite of the firm and also the strategic view of the firm's business.

The strategic view, beyond 12 months, means that some of the Pillar 1 capital calculation results need to be augmented. The additional steps often include stress tests. A stress test might include the capital implications of an economic downturn, on a national or global level, and its impact on the credit portfolio. These stress tests may also identify particular concentrations. The results of a stress test may have implications for capital, but also risk management actions, as described in the rescue and resolution processes.

For the non-Pillar 1 risks, the Board should take into account issues such as the interest rate risk in the non-trading book/banking book. For funding liquidity risk, this may include a review of the transformation of behavioural deposits to support loans with a fixed maturity and the impact on internal transfer pricing.

ICAAP is also the opportunity to consider some of the risks mentioned in Chapter 10. Not all of these risks can be addressed via capital, some need risk management in terms of risk prevention, detection and mitigation. While business risk can be measured, effects on the firm's reputation are much harder to model and estimate.

One of the outcomes of the supervisory review and ICAAP process can be an amendment to the minimum overall capital ratio to create trigger and target increments. There may also be additional requirements on the proportion of Common Equity Tier 1 that needs to be held. For example, although the minimum ratio of Common Equity Tier 1 to RWA is 4.5%, the Board decision may be to manage to a ratio of 7% or higher.

The ICAAP is also the process to consider some of the benefits. The total RWA is the result of a summation of the individual components. However, looking at the range of risks as a portfolio, the summation makes the assumption that the risks have a correlation of 1. That is when credit risk has maximum losses so market and operational risks also have their maximum losses. In addition, the firm has insurance policies that may offset some of the operational risks. In some jurisdictions certain insurance policies are mandatory and ICAAP is an opportunity to recognise the benefit of insurance if not already reflected in the operational risk capital estimate.

One of the conclusions of this brief review of ICAAP is that the process involves qualitative as much as quantitative aspects of risk management.

13.3.3   Pillar 3 – Market Discipline

Like the supervisory review process (Pillar 2), market discipline was introduced as part of Basel II. Pillar 3 involves the disclosure of information, additional to the financial condition of the firm. Publication of this additional information began before Basel II was published and continues to evolve.

The provision of the additional information tends to be risk related and is a deliberate effort to support the dialogue between the firm and various stakeholders. Banks now provide statements, as part of their quarterly and annual disclosures, on the risk management framework and the various risk silos; annual reports contain a significant volume of risk information. The material on credit risk may discuss not only the risk estimation methodology but also include comments about the composition of the portfolio and trends. The market risk section may mention trends in the VaR figures for the past 12 months.

An issue for firms and the regulatory community is which stakeholders are the intended audience for this material. For example, the material may be too technical for retail investors and most counterparties. The inference is that the target audience is equity analysts and debt analysts, including rating agencies. This audience is influential, as their material can influence the opinions of retail and institutional equity and bond investors. In turn, this affects the cost of raising capital.

Another influential audience is the credit review functions at counterparties. These reviews will affect the volume of lines of credit available in the wholesale money markets, such as interbank deposits. They may also influence the terms for the provision of collateral on long-term transactions, such as derivatives, between firms.

Once the intended audience has been identified, the discussion settles on the amount and type of material to publish. What to publish is influenced by the assumed knowledge of the target audience. Given that there is limited opportunity for dialogue with the intended audience over the published material, the tendency is to be less quantitative than internal reports on the same risks. The published material represents a balance between providing transparency and avoiding the creation of confusion. This also leads to an incremental approach, so the detail of the disclosure can increase over time and in line with the disclosure by peers and knowledge of the intended audience.

Part of the disclosure on the main sources of risk may include the proportion of capital allocated to each. For example, does the firm have less capital devoted to credit risk even though the volumes of credit exposure have increased? The assumption here being that the firm is lending to higher-quality counterparties, with the possibility for a reduced provision and income stream. Other information may include how the risk performed during an industry-level stress test exercise conducted by the regulators. These reports may be published by the regulators and can result in individual firms raising capital in response to the stress test results.

Often the material is published alongside various accounting reports. For example, the annual report is expected to have the majority of the material. However, the risk-related material published does not have to be audited by the external auditors; nevertheless, it should be subject to independent review.

The accounting reports are produced annually, semi-annually and, in some jurisdictions, quarterly. These provide an opportunity for formal publication of this risk-related material. With websites there is more flexibility in timing and format of the material to be published. For example, websites enable the results of an industry stress test to be published a short time after completion, rather than waiting 3 or 6 months until the next formal publication of accounts. Some of these statements, which may be over a hundred pages, are entirely unsuitable for disclosure with accounts. The timing and extent of disclosure may be an element of reputational risk management.

13.4 REGULATORY INFLUENCE

The earlier parts of this chapter have described some of the more explicit ways in which prudential regulators are influential, primarily focused on capital. This section describes some of the other influences and benefits from interaction between the firm and the prudential regulatory community.

Prudential regulatory interest is in risk management. Even aspects of regulatory focus on financial conduct can be seen as risk management. Their interest in risk management is not limited to capital. For example, even if the model is leading practice it is unlikely to receive regulatory approval for use if the model is not aligned with the risk management framework and activities.

The regulatory perspective covers multiple firms within a jurisdiction. There are also mechanisms by which regulators can gain insight into what is happening in other jurisdictions. This may be achieved by supervising subsidiaries whose parent is in another jurisdiction. Looking at the techniques and approaches adopted in the subsidiary will provide insight into how risk management functions across the group.

A more formal approach to gaining cross-border insight is via "supervisory colleges". These colleges are established for each of the major international banking groups. The college is managed by the home regulator or supervisor who supervises the consolidated group. The home regulator will formally engage with the host regulators of subsidiaries and possibly branches in various jurisdictions. The college gives the regulators, who combined have a complete view of the group, the opportunity to exchange views on risks and capital. It should also be expected that the colleges are considering or will consider the rescue and resolution plans for the consolidated group.

From these mechanisms the regulators have a background on which to make judgements on whether the risk management is proportional to a firm.[14] Comments by regulators that a firm's risk management is proportionate also assist in offsetting groupthink within a firm. Groupthink can result in an over-optimistic view of the risk management environment within a firm. On occasions this can be the result of not having, or being able to make, a comparison with a comparable firm.

---

[14] It is this proportional aspect that results in "leading practices" as opposed to "best practices", since what may be proportionate leading practice for one firm may be inadequate for another.

This interest in risk management extends to producing guidance. The prudential regulators are often the only group that can provide this guidance as others are concerned with the broader universe of corporate entities, for example COSO and the OECD. The guidance documents may be published on a national or international basis (e.g., by the Basel Committee and EBA).

Following the financial crisis the banking regulatory community reviewed their guidance on governance and issued a revised document. The first document was published in 1999 and a revised version issued in 2006. The most recent document (2010) has 14 principles and supporting commentary.[15] The 14 principles are:

1. The Board has overall responsibility for the bank, including approving and overseeing the implementation of the bank's strategic objectives, risk strategy, corporate governance and corporate values. The Board is also responsible for providing oversight of senior management.
2. Board members should be and remain qualified, including through training, for their positions. They should have a clear understanding of their role in corporate governance and be able to exercise sound and objective judgement about the affairs of the bank.
3. The Board should define appropriate governance practices for its own work and have in place the means to ensure that such practices are followed and periodically reviewed for ongoing improvement.
4. In a group structure, the Board of the parent company has the overall responsibility for adequate corporate governance across the group and ensuring that there are governance policies and mechanisms appropriate to the structure, business and risks of the group and its entities.
5. Under the direction of the Board, senior management should ensure that the bank's activities are consistent with the business strategy, risk tolerance/appetite and policies approved by the Board.
6. Banks should have an effective internal controls system and a risk management function (including a CRO or equivalent) with sufficient authority, stature, independence, resources and access to the Board.

---

[15] Basel Committee on Banking Supervision (October 2010) Principles for Enhancing Corporate Governance. Reproduced by permission of Bank for International Settlements (BIS).

7. Risks should be identified and monitored on an ongoing firm-wide and individual entity basis, and the sophistication of the bank's risk management and internal control infrastructures should keep pace with any changes to the bank's risk profile (including its growth), and to the external risk landscape.

8. Effective risk management requires robust internal communication within the bank about risk, both across the organisation and through reporting to the Board and senior management.

9. The Board and senior management should effectively utilise the work conducted by internal audit functions, external auditors and internal control functions.

10. The Board should actively oversee the compensation system's design and operation, and should monitor and review the compensation system to ensure that it operates as intended.

11. An employee's compensation should be effectively aligned with prudent risk taking: compensation should be adjusted for all types of risk; compensation outcomes should be symmetric with risk outcomes; compensation payout schedules should be sensitive to the time horizon of risks; and the mix of cash, equity and other forms of compensation should be consistent with risk alignment.

12. The Board and senior management should know and understand the bank's operational structure and the risks that it poses (i.e., "know your structure").

13. Where a bank operates through special purpose or related structures or in jurisdictions that impede transparency or do not meet international banking standards, its Board and senior management should understand the purpose, structure and unique risks of these operations. They should also seek to mitigate the risks identified (i.e., "understand your structure").

14. The governance of the bank should be adequately transparent to its shareholders, depositors, other relevant stakeholders and market participants.

These guidance documents, combined with the regular onsite visits from regulators and feedback, encourage firms to continually invest in their risk management. For example, if there was a need for cost cutting then the regulators, and probably other stakeholders, would take a dim view if the entire burden fell on the risk management function. The regulators may even go as far as saying that none of the cost-cutting burden should fall on risk management.

This broad-based explicit and implicit dialogue between the firm and the regulators means that the firm needs to commit resources. While this may seem a cost burden on the P&L, there may also be benefits from keeping the trigger and target capital ratios closer to the regulatory minimum than might otherwise be the case. In addition, this team can coordinate the material for visits by regulators in different locations. If the same framework has been rolled out globally by the firm then the regulatory relationship team can recommend reuse of certain documents and raise the efficiency of the dialogue.

Additionally, a number of national regulators have the authority to engage in discussions with individuals who potentially or currently fill key influencing functions. These discussions and conversations may happen while the appointment is being considered and on a regular basis thereafter. The discussion for a Chairman, Chair of the Board's Audit, Compensation and Risk Committees would be expected to be more rigorous than for another Non-Executive Director role. Likewise, members of the Executive may also have initial and regular bilateral dialogue. Additionally, the regulators may have discussion with the auditors. The purpose of these discussions can be traced back to the principles reproduced above.

From these discussions the regulators can construct a more detailed picture of the firm's capabilities than provided in the regular regulatory returns. Building these relationships helps during times of stress, whether at the level of the firm or the industry. Under stressful conditions, which can evolve day by day if not hour by hour, regulatory returns may lag the action by weeks. While management information is expected to be available on a daily basis, it may be difficult for regulators to interpret if they get copies.[16]

This regulatory interest in the way in which a particular firm operates effectively recognises that capital may be part of the answer towards having a robust banking system, but that it is not the complete answer.

---

[16] Regulators may ask for copies of management information reports, possibly as evidence that the risk management material is being used in decision making. However, expecting regulators to react to the content of a particular report begins to blur the line between regulator, executive management and NEDs.

FURTHER READING

Barfield, R. (2011) *A Practitioners Guide to Basel III and Beyond.* Sweet & Maxwell, London.

Basel Committee on Banking Supervision (July 1988) International Convergence of Capital and Measurement and Capital Standards (Basel I). http://www.bis.org/publ/bcbs04a.pdf

Basel Committee on Banking Supervision (June 2004) International Convergence of Capital and Measurement and Capital Standards – revised (Basel II). http://www.bis.org/publ/bcbs107.pdf

Basel Committee on Banking Supervision (October 2010) Principles for Enhancing Corporate Governance. http://www.bis.org/publ/bcbs176.pdf

Basel Committee on Banking Supervision (originally published December 2010, revised June 2011) A Global Regulatory Framework for More Resilient Banks and Banking Systems (Basel III). http://www.bis.org/publ/bcbs189.pdf

Basel Committee on Banking Supervision (June 2011) Principles for the Sound Management of Operational Risk. http://www.bis.org/publ/bcbs195.pdf

European Banking Authority (September 2011) EBA Guidelines on Internal Governance; GL44 Basel Committee on Banking Supervision (October 2010) Principles for Enhancing Corporate Governance. http://www.eba.europa.eu/cebs/media/Publications/Standards%20and%20Guidelines/2011/EBA-BS-2011-116-final-(EBA-Guidelines-on-Internal-Governance)-(2)_1.pdf

Financial Services Authority (August 2011) Recovery & Resolution Plans, CP11/16. http://www.fsa.gov.uk/static/pubs/cp/cp11_16.pdf

Financial Stability Board (October 2011) Key Attributes of Effective Resolution Regimes for Financial Institutions. http://www.financialstabilityboard.org/publications/r_111104cc.pdf

Disclaimer Regarding Excerpts from S&P Materials

Standard & Poor's Financial Services LLC (S&P) does not guarantee the accuracy, completeness, timeliness or availability of any information, including ratings, and is not responsible for any errors or omissions (negligent or otherwise), regardless of the cause, or for the results obtained from the use of ratings. S&P GIVES NO EXPRESS OR IMPLIED WARRANTIES, INCLUDING, BUT NOT LIMITED TO, ANY WARRANTIES OF MERCHANTABILITY OR FITNESS FOR A PARTICULAR PURPOSE OR USE. S&P SHALL NOT BE LIABLE FOR ANY DIRECT, INDIRECT, INCIDENTAL, EXEMPLARY, COMPENSATORY, PUNITIVE, SPECIAL OR CONSEQUENTIAL DAMAGES, COSTS, EXPENSES, LEGAL FEES, or LOSSES (INCLUDING LOST INCOME OR PROFITS AND OPPORTUNITY COSTS) IN CONNECTION WITH ANY USE OF RATINGS. S&P's ratings are statements of opinions and are not statements of fact or recommendations to purchase, hold or sell securities. They do not address the market value of securities or the suitability of securities for investment purposes, and should not be relied on as investment advice.

Please see material reference in Tables 7.2 and 7.3.

Index

Index compiled by Terry Halliday